THE
COMPLETE
GREAT
BRITISH
RAILWAY
JOURNEYS

FOREWORD

By
Michael
Portillo

Like most people, I thought travel an adventure when I was a child, and most of those adventures were by train. There were still some steam trains around for me. There was a tank engine-hauled service from Belmont to Harrow and Wealdstone, close to where I grew up. My eldest brother, Charles, would take me on the 'Belmont Rattler', and I remember the panting engine, the smoke and my excitement.

For summer holidays we would go to the Isle of Wight by electric train from Waterloo, but from Ryde we would pick up the steam service along the island's east coast. The tunnel beneath the Boniface Downs would fill with the pungent stench of steam locomotive just before we pulled into Ventnor.

Then there was the annual excursion to my mother's hometown of Kirkcaldy. My parents were not well off, so we took the overnight train without sleeper reservations, travelling second class, sitting upright, sustained by Lucozade and peanut butter sandwiches. On at least one occasion it took 13 hours, and the service was known, to our sardonic amusement even then, as the Starlight Special.

After childhood, trains became mere tools for me. As a politician I visited most places to campaign, cut a ribbon or make a speech. The train got me there, or got me there late. The glamour was gone, and I was all too ready to criticise the lateness, the absence of the refreshment trolley or the failure of the air conditioning.

Now I find myself drawn to the railways once again. Making the two series of Great British Railway Journeys has meant spending almost 100 days travelling the length and breadth of the country and has brought back for me the idea of railway journey as adventure. Catching the train has been a key part of the experience, not merely a chore.

I was always travelling to see. I journeyed with curiosity and optimism, and I was rarely disappointed.

My guide was a Victorian called George Bradshaw. In 1839 he started producing railway timetables and then a handbook to journeying through Britain by train. Even though I have travelled most of the routes before, this book shone an endlessly fascinating light on everywhere I visited. I have studied the Victorian period at school and university, but no document that I have read before is quite as revealing of the Victorian outlook as this travel guide.

FORMER MINISTER MICHAEL PORTILLO REVISITS HIS LOVE OF RAILWAYS.

Bradshaw's generation was highly excited by its central role in a world that was moving forward at an exhilarating pace. His wonder and pride spill from every page. Enthusiastic, patriotic, opinionated, he writes in an era unrestrained by egalitarianism, let alone political correctness. His age values reason, experimentation and excellence. It is serious and largely unsentimental. For Bradshaw there was no shame in imperialism, no consideration of taste to restrain his bombast. Manchester manufacturers, he records with pride, could import the cotton crop from India, spin it and export textiles that would then undercut local production in India. London, he says, is the greatest city that exists, or has ever existed. He is right that London stood at the heart of an empire that exceeded that of the Pharaohs or Caesars, and considering Britain's mastery of technology there was no serious competition to be found anywhere in the world's history.

Bradshaw's first enthusiasm was for canals, a prodigious achievement in themselves with a great impact on business. But the railways were faster and more versatile. Above all they were for the masses. Without large numbers of passengers they were uneconomic. They altered the geography of Britain by making places accessible, and they transformed the social landscape because people of modest means could travel.

The speed of the change is difficult even for us to grasp, because although the mobile phone and computer have led to a revolution over the last 20 years, modern-day Britain doesn't undergo physical change as fast as Victorian Britain did. The world's first intercity line opened between Liverpool and Manchester in 1830. Twenty years later over 6,000 miles of track had been laid, reaching all but the remotest parts of the country. Railways sprang up everywhere. Some important lines were built in their entirety in just two years. Although steam engines were used in construction, most of the work was done by hand. Thousands of navvies occupied camps along the route, and dug the cuttings and raised up the stones for the viaducts. We would have to visit modern Shanghai, perhaps, to gain any understanding of the speed of change and the scale of the undertaking.

The handbook's itineraries follow the tracks. Towns are listed not alphabetically but in their order along the main lines and branch lines. I have been asked a lot whether I didn't find that many of Bradshaw's routes have gone. Some have, of course. But I think I was more struck but the degree of continuity between then and now. Britain today, despite its post-war motorways, depends upon an infrastructure laid down by the Victorians. They built to last, and often grandly. As the refurbishment of St Pancras has shown, the best thing to be done with a Victorian building is simply to undo the damage of decades caused by smoke and rain and, particularly, cheapskate makeovers. Stand on Waterloo Bridge with Bradshaw's book and you may find that the finest buildings today are still the ones that he picked out: Saint Paul's cathedral, Somerset House and Parliament.

That gives a clue as to why travelling with Bradshaw is still useful today. Not to despise the work of later generations, but to appreciate the magnificent and formative legacy of that era. It led me to explore places that are no longer in fashion, like Scarborough and Weston-super-Mare, and to hunt for trades that were big in his day, like Walsall saddlers, Bristol glass blowers and Denton hatters.

I never intended my journeys to be purely nostalgic, and they have not been. British cities are rejuvenating themselves and British resorts cling on or fight back. There is vibrancy and enthusiasm wherever I have been. The Britain of today would be ethnically, culturally and socially unrecognisable to George Bradshaw. I hope that in my journeys I portray Britain as it is.

Michael Portillo
2010

INTRODUCTION

By
Charlie
Bunce

There are some ideas for television programmes that, when you hear about them, you just know in your bones are destined for success. That was certainly the case when I was asked to produce a new series being developed for the BBC which was then called *Adventures with Bradshaw*.

The idea emerged from a brainstorming session with Liam Keelan, BBC Controller of Daytime and Camilla Lewis, Head of Factual Features at talkbackTHAMES. Liam was keen to find a programme that would work at 6.30 p.m. on BBC2. He wanted a travelogue by train, which had an historical angle. Liam knew the railways were rolling out across Britain during one of the most exciting and rapidly advancing periods of history when ordinary lives were being irrevocably changed.

Camilla had long been obsessed with finding a new way of investigating our social history. Her brother-in-law, an antiquarian bookseller slotted the last piece of the puzzle in place when he told her that George Bradshaw, the man who famously started producing monthly railway timetables in the mid-nineteenth century had also published a guide-book on travelling across the country by train.

After a £500 investment, a battered and broken copy of Bradshaw's guide arrived at the office. A drab brown cover was misleading as its contents were anything but dull and dreary. Its well-thumbed pages offered a remarkable insight into the life and times of Victorian Britain.

The more I read Bradshaw's guide, the more I could hear his voice. As I understood him better I began to see the age in which he lived and worked, and to see what excited him and why. His minute observations and comments gave me a sense of Victorian Britain different from anything I'd read before.

His rich words conveyed to us another age. A section about Sandwich in Kent is an ideal example. 'The traveller, on entering this place, beholds himself in a sort of Kentish Herculaneum, a town of the martial dead. He gazes around him and looks upon the streets and edifices of a bygone age. He stares up at the beetling stories of the old pent-up buildings as he walks and peers curiously through latticed windows into the vast low-roofed, heavy-beamed, oak-panelled rooms of days he has read of in old plays.'

How could you not want to visit Sandwich and find what he had seen. Beyond lyrical descriptions, Bradshaw deposited on his pages a wealth of information about where his readers should stay, how to get money, what day the market took place, local sights of interest and on occasion where

GEORGE BRADSHAW COMBINED HIS ENTHUSIASM FOR CARTOGRAPHY WITH A PASSION FOR TRAINS.

to sit to get the best view from the train. He revelled in detail, giving the span and height of bridges to the foot, or the length of station platforms. He loudly and proudly celebrated every British success.

Bradshaw described how the railways were a great leveller, literally and metaphorically. While the land was planed so the trains could run on as few inclines as possible, the barriers that divided a class-ridden society were at the same time pared down.

For the enterprising, railways represented a golden opportunity. Although they were initially seen as a way of transporting freight, it wasn't long before moving people by rail was just as important, sometimes even more so. Commerce spread across neighbourhoods and regions. Trades that were once restricted to narrow localities could now take advantage of markets worldwide. The notion of commuting was born. Holidays, once the province of the rich, came within grasp of ordinary people.

It is difficult to imagine now just how fundamentally life changed and the speed at which those transformations came about. Where railway stations were made, hamlets mushroomed into towns while those settlements that were leapfrogged by railway lines were left in the doldrums.

BRADSHAW WAS AN EXPERT ARTIST, AND HIS LINE DRAWINGS OF SOME OF THE COUNTRY'S FINEST BUILDINGS WERE INCLUDED IN HIS POPULAR GUIDEBOOKS.

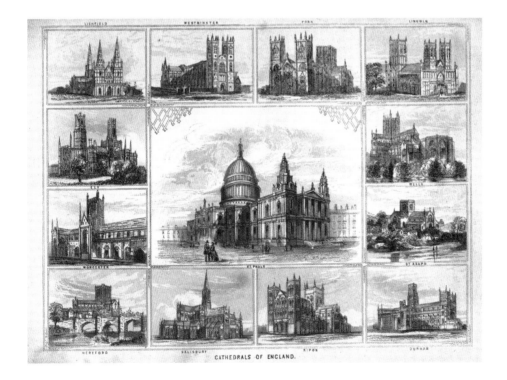

CATHEDRALS OF ENGLAND.

It wasn't all good news, though. Amid the euphoria that accompanied the age of steam there were many who fell victim to railway mania, including those who died laying tracks in hostile terrain and the unwary who invested heavily in lines or companies that failed to flourish.

As far as the programme was concerned, the idea was beguilingly simple. We would travel Britain by train with Bradshaw as our guide. Through it, we'd explore the impact of the railways on our cities, countryside and coast. Thanks to Bradshaw, we could celebrate triumphs of yesteryear and match fortunes past and present. We would see how the country had been transformed in a matter of a few short years and understand why, at the time, the British Empire was so successful at home and overseas. But, as importantly, we would search out what of Bradshaw's Britain still remains today.

The next question was who should present it. In television, getting this agreed is often a monumental feat. On this occasion it wasn't. Michael was suggested, and within 30 seconds of meeting him I knew he was the perfect candidate. The son of a Spanish refugee and a Scottish mother, Michael not only had a lifelong fascination for history but was also a

BELOW: LONDON LANDMARKS WERE ALSO ILLUSTRATED BY BRADSHAW FOR VISITORS TO THE CAPITAL.

OVERLEAF: MICHAEL PORTILLO SPOKE WITH FELLOW RAILWAY ENTHUSIASTS UP AND DOWN THE COUNTRY – HERE WITH IAN GLEDHILL, CHAIRMAN OF VOLK'S ELECTRIC RAILWAY ASSOCIATION.

VOLKS

Brighton & Hove
City Council

Railway Fares

		£1.80
	To	£2.80
	the	90p
	Marina	£1.40
		£1.10
	To	£1.80
	the	£3.80
	Marina	£6.40
...ngs		
		£2.10
		£1.10
Bookings 01273 292718		
		£1.00
	Halfway	£1.80
	Paston	50p
	Place	80p

Danger

Middle rail is electrified
⚠ 110 VOLTS ⚠

NO ENTRY

883

Last Train Tonight

5pm

Health & Safety

Pushchairs...

must be folded
stowed correctly
re the train depart

a safe day.

former Minister of Transport. Years spent in both government and opposition did nothing to diminish his abiding passion for railway journeys. Forty-five episodes later I have never once regretted the decision to have him present the show. The energy and intelligence he brings to every situation make the series stand out.

Strangely, the most taxing bit of the whole process was coming up with the right title. List after list was emailed to everyone concerned with the project, only to be knocked back, judged not quite right. We must have gone through hundreds of suggestions before ending up with *Great British Railway Journeys*. In the end, it seemed to say very succinctly what the series is all about.

The last question was where those journeys should take us. We could not mimic Bradshaw minutely on our travels. His extraordinary thoroughness meant that was a task too far, and many of the stations he visited are now obsolete, thanks to the policies of the Sixties which saw thousands of miles of branch lines closed in a futile bid to save cash.

Nonetheless, I wanted the trips we recorded to reveal a country that many of us hardly know, or at least seem to have forgotten. With our copy of Bradshaw's guide in hand we've now made nine big journeys exploring the country and discovering new sides to places I thought I knew well. Through making the programmes and writing the book, I have had the chance to tease out dusty nuggets of information to satisfy the most curious of minds. I wanted the chance to trumpet what had been great about Britain, and celebrate the enormous amount that still is. I hope the series and this book do just that.

Charlie Bunce
September 2010

AS HE TRAVELLED THROUGH BRITAIN MICHAEL PORTILLO KEPT HIS WELL-WORN COPY OF BRADSHAW'S RAILWAY GUIDE CLOSE AT HAND.

JOURNEY

1

COTTONOPOLIS AND THE RAILWAYS

From Liverpool to Scarborough

The obvious place to start our journeys seemed to be the birthplace of the modern passenger railway. Lots of places lay claim to that title, but for us, once we'd looked into it, the Liverpool & Manchester Railway was the clear winner. It is true that fare-paying passengers had been carried by rail before its inception, but the Liverpool & Manchester was different. Unlike the other railways that predated this one, carriages were not horse-drawn, nor were they pulled along wires fixed to a stationary locomotive. It wasn't a tiny pleasure railway with limited use. This was a proper twin-track line, the first in the world where steam locomotives hauled paying passengers, and it changed the face of travelling in Britain.

There are certainly longer, older and more beautiful routes, but the line between Liverpool and Manchester seemed to us to be the perfect launch pad into the past.

The original purpose of the line wasn't to service passengers at all, but to move freight between two booming cities. At the beginning of the nineteenth century, most goods were transported on a thriving and extensive canal system, but it was both expensive and slow, and this trip took 36 hours. So in 1822 Joseph Sandars, a local corn merchant and something of a forward thinker, decided to invest £300 of his own money in surveying a route for a railway between Liverpool and Manchester.

The project suffered numerous setbacks as aristocratic local landowners campaigned to prevent the proposed line from passing through their lands, while the canal owners, fearful of competition, tried to stop it altogether. It looked for a while as though it would never get off the ground until another blow turned out to be the line's saving grace. When the project's original surveyor landed himself in jail, George Stephenson (1781–1858) was appointed in his place.

Stephenson was one of those great Victorians for whom nothing seemed impossible. Born to parents who could neither read nor write, he went on to become an inventor, a civil engineer and a mechanical engineer. He designed steam engines, bridges, tunnels and rail tracks. Whilst there's disagreement over whether his skills lay in invention or in harnessing other people's creations, he is rightly known as the father of the railway. Without a doubt, the modern railway developed more quickly than it would have done without Stephenson's involvement.

On the line for the Liverpool & Manchester Railway, one of the first things Stephenson was tasked with was re-examining the route. What

ENGINEER GEORGE STEPHENSON IS CONSIDERED THE FATHER OF THE RAILWAYS.

he came up with was a new plan which as much as possible skirted contested land. In this instance it wasn't an easy option. It would require building no fewer than 64 bridges and viaducts along its 35-mile course and needed Parliamentary permission before it could begin.

It took four years of haggling before the Parliamentary Bill was passed in May 1826, enabling the compulsory purchase of land for the railway. Getting to this point had cost many compromises, however, one of which was that the line couldn't go into Liverpool itself and instead had to halt outside the city centre. After the opening of the line in 1830 it was a further decade before it could be extended into the city and Lime Street station, one of Britain's first railway stations, was opened.

In the middle of the nineteenth century Manchester was the centre of the cotton industry and Liverpool was a bustling dockyard. In fact, Bradshaw's *Descriptive Railway Hand-Book*, the Victorian railway bible that we used throughout our travels around Britain, hails Manchester as 'sending its goods to every corner of the world'. Liverpool had the port to facilitate doing just that. Bradshaw calls the docks 'the grand lions of the town which extend in one magnificent range of five miles along the river from Toxteth Park to Kirkdale'. By 1850 – just 20 years after the Liverpool & Manchester line opened – Liverpool docks were the second most important port in Britain, handling 2 million tons of raw cotton every year destined for the Lancashire mills.

For Liverpool, it wasn't all about freight. Moving people was also big business. Liverpool was one of the points on the notorious transatlantic slave trade triangle. Ships left the port with goods and headed for Africa, where the cargo was traded for slaves. The same ships then embarked on an often treacherous journey known as 'the middle passage' to America. Men, women and children who survived the crossing were consequently sold to work in plantations.

The slave trade – although not slavery itself – was finally abolished in Britain by an 1807 Act of Parliament, despite vociferous efforts by some Liverpool merchants keen to maintain it for financial reasons. Fortunately, there were more people waiting in the wings to fill Liverpool's idle ships, this time willing passengers with an altogether brighter future in mind. It was the age of emigration to destinations such as America, Canada and Australia. Families looking for a new start came from across Britain, Ireland and Europe to Liverpool to take advantage of the numerous available passages and the relatively swift transatlantic journey. Consequently waves of people from many nations arriving or leaving Britain passed through the port. Apart from the wealth generated by ticket prices, there were associated benefits for the city in catering for this transient population. Accordingly businesses such as bars and boarding houses prospered, and as time went on so too did the railway system. In 1852 alone, almost 300,000 people left the Liverpool docks to start new lives in the Americas.

These peoples had an enormous impact on the city and its culture. Peter Grant, a local journalist, historian and specialist in all things Liverpudlian, was enlightening on the issue. 'Scouse,' he explained, 'is an accent, a people and a dish.'

The first two are familiar, but the third is something of an unknown. Originally called Labskause, it turns out to be a mixed casserole dish of mutton and vegetables which had been brought to the city by Norwegian

BY 1872 LIVERPOOL WAS THE NATIONAL FOCUS FOR EMIGRATION.

sailors. 'The dish,' said Peter, 'is a perfect metaphor for Liverpool. You add a bit of this and a bit of that, then put in your spoon and mix. Much like the Scouse accent, which is made up of Scottish, Irish, Welsh, Lancashire and Cheshire accents, and according to where you are in the city it has its own distinct twang.'

From Liverpool we headed east to Rainhill, just 20 minutes down the tracks. Steam trains expert Christian Wolmar waited on the station platform. Although noisy and not that pretty, Rainhill station seemed the most appropriate place for him to talk about what is perhaps the most significant stretch of railway line in the world. As trains thundered past, Christian explained that the first competition between steam locomotives had taken place here in 1829, before train and track were inextricably linked. Indeed, rails had been in existence for years, usually extending between mines or quarries and nearby industrial centres. Loaded wagons were usually pulled by horses. At the time of the contest the notion of an independently powered engine doing the donkey work was still new.

It seems extraordinary now, but the 1829 Rainhill trials were organised to enable the directors of the Liverpool & Manchester Line to decide whether the trains should be powered by locomotives or by stationary steam engines. Five locomotives took part, one of which was powered by a horse walking on a drive belt, and were timed over the same course, with and without carriages. There was a £500 prize for the victor, whether or not a locomotive was eventually chosen. George Stephenson's *Rocket* won hands down, having achieved a top speed of 30 m.p.h., and set a steam locomotive agenda for the Liverpool & Manchester Line, and ultimately the rest of the country. The display was enough to convince any remaining doubters that locomotives were the way forward as far as rail travel was concerned.

A year later the line was opened by the Prime Minister, the Duke of Wellington. But Stephenson's day of triumph was marred by the death, not far from where we stood, of Merseyside MP William Huskisson, who became one of the first victims of the modern railway.

Huskisson accidentally opened a carriage door in front of the oncoming *Rocket*, was knocked off balance and fell beneath its wheels. Although the Conservative MP was rushed by train to the town of Eccles by Stephenson himself, he died there within a few hours. His untimely death gave ammunition to a stalwart band of nay-sayers who opposed the railway on the grounds that it was new, that it threatened

GEORGE STEPHENSON'S ROCKET WON HANDS DOWN, HAVING ACHIEVED A TOP SPEED OF 30 M.P.H.

STEPHENSON'S ROCKET WAS THE WINNER OF A STEAM LOCOMOTIVE COMPETITION HELD IN RAINHILL IN 1829 THAT DETERMINED A BRIGHT FUTURE FOR THIS NEW TECHNOLOGY.

long-established ways of life and that there were unknown dangers associated with it that had yet to become apparent. Iron roads were not welcome everywhere they went. But despite Huskisson's demise it was apparent that the age of rail, indeed rail mania, was here to stay.

Eccles was the next destination for us too. Heading out towards Manchester through the sprawling housing estates, we wondered what Eccles had to offer the Victorian traveller and turned to Bradshaw to find: 'The little village is prettily situated on the northern banks of the Irwell and environed by some of the most picturesque rambles.'

The railway changed all that. Within 30 years, Eccles had been swallowed up into the suburbs of Manchester. Even in Bradshaw's day, though, Eccles's claim to fame wasn't so much about being a pretty village. It was about the cakes produced there.

BELOW: **ECCLES CAKE MAKING WAS BIG BUSINESS.**

OVERLEAF: **MILL STACKS LOOMED LARGE BY THE RIVER IRWELL IN MANCHESTER BY 1859.**

Nobody knows for certain when Eccles cakes were created, but they definitely predate the railway. In the seventeenth century Cromwell and his Puritans even banned them, on the grounds that they were too rich and sumptuous. Fortunately for Eccles and the rest of the Puritan-weary population, the ban was lifted during the Restoration. James Birch opened the first shop in the town to sell Eccles cakes on a commercial basis in 1796. There followed some rather ill-natured rivalry – and even today the townsfolk hold that a cake made outside of Eccles cannot truly be called an Eccles cake.

What the railways did was to make it quick and easy to ship the cakes all around the country. It has also been claimed that they were responsible for a change in ingredients. At the time the cakes were sold from station platforms and laced with brandy to help preserve them. But, the story goes, one driver enjoyed a generously laced Eccles cake too many and fell off his footplate, almost causing a crash. From then on, brandy was banned for the railway's Eccles cakes, though it was still used to preserve cakes made for export to America and the West Indies.

Today the cake is as popular as ever. Ian Edmonds is the fourth generation of his family to produce Lancashire Eccles cakes. The secret of their success, he explained, lies in the ingredients. Ian uses only the very best currants money can buy. Called Vostizza A, they come from a Greek farmers' co-op in a town near Corinth – from which we get the word currant. Ian's team carefully wash 10 tonnes each week to quality-control the fruit. The plumped-up currants are then encased by hand in buttery pastry in a factory that produces 150,000 Eccles cakes a day for the domestic and export markets.

From Eccles the train brought us swiftly into Manchester, to discover more about cotton and the railway. It was clear from reading Bradshaw that the fortunes of the two were intertwined. By the 1830s Manchester was well established at the heart of the cotton industry, but the creation of the line to Liverpool and the subsequent lines that followed transformed its fortunes. At its peak in 1853, there were 108 mills in Manchester and it became known as Cottonopolis.

That history is still evident in the city's buildings and streets. Local journalist-cum-tour guide Jonathan Schofield believes the only way to see the city so as to take it all in is to walk. From the Royal Exchange, where the cotton lords met each Tuesday almost 200 years ago, through the Godlee Observatory on Sackvillle Street, named after local mill

ECCLES'S CLAIM TO FAME WASN'T SO MUCH ABOUT BEING A PRETTY VILLAGE. IT WAS ABOUT THE CAKES

owner Francis Godlee, to the iron street kerbs found around the city built to protect the pavements from the overloaded carts, cotton resonates on almost every route around Manchester. It was cotton that turned Manchester into the fastest-growing city of the nineteenth century.

The terrible congestion, squalid living conditions and harsh working conditions led to unrest, with strikes and food riots culminating in the Peterloo massacre, in which 11 people were killed and hundreds injured. Manchester was at the forefront of the movement towards reform that led to the Factory Acts.

Another of Manchester's many claims to fame is that in 1801 George Bradshaw, author of our guide to Victorian Britain, was born here, in fact just outside the city in Pendleton, near Salford. Bradshaw was an engraver and cartographer who completed a detailed record of the canals of Lancashire and Yorkshire in 1830, known as *Bradshaw's Maps of Inland Navigation*.

When the railways arrived he spotted a lucrative gap in the market and in 1839 started publishing one-off, then monthly timetables in a yellow wrapper which later graduated into a round-England and then a Continental guide. Within four years an eight-page pamphlet had grown to 32 pages, drawing together the times and services run by numerous rail companies. Without Bradshaw passengers were dependent on locally produced timetables that rarely extended beyond the often narrow boundaries of the rail company itself.

His name swiftly became a byword for timetables and featured in several Sherlock Holmes stories and in Bram Stoker's *Dracula*, reflecting its hallowed place in society. Phineas Fogg began his adventure in Jules Verne's *Around the World in Eighty Days* with a copy of Bradshaw under his arm.

An active Quaker, Bradshaw was also notable, if less well known, for his charitable works among the poor of Britain's industrial heartlands. Bradshaw died of cholera in August 1853 during a visit to Norway, where he is buried. But his products continued to flourish, their popularity unabated despite their somewhat complex content. It wasn't until the eve of the Second World War that Bradshaw stopped appearing in print. By this time rail companies were keen to publish timetables of their own.

Whilst much of what Bradshaw marvelled at still exists, today's Manchester is a very different place. The decline of the cotton industry

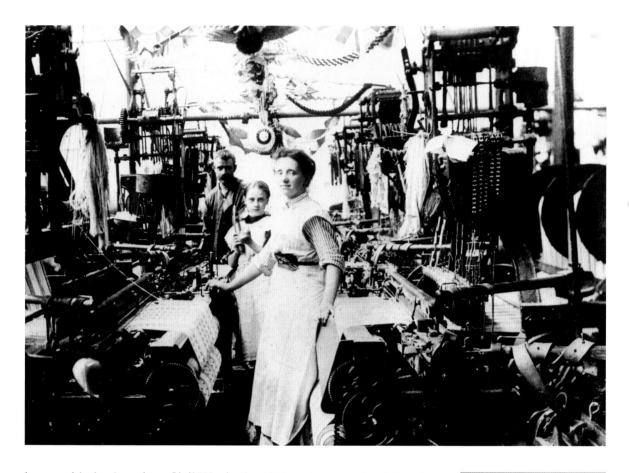

began with the American Civil War in the 1860s, when supplies faltered. The perils of an industry reliant on raw materials grown a vast distance away became starkly apparent. It was only a matter of time before other producers working with reduced costs, including America, Japan and India, began to challenge Manchester's dominance. The mill owners were also slow to update their antiquated machinery, making them less competitive than ever. No amount of import tariffs could halt the inevitable. The Manchester mills were doomed.

Some mills made way for modern developments. Others have been transformed into flats and hotels. The cause of another great change to the city skyscape was the IRA bombing of the Arndale Centre in 1996, which injured more than 200 people and caused £1 billion of damage. Today the surviving mill buildings are surrounded by steel and glass in a city that looks firmly forward whilst still acknowledging the past.

WHOLE FAMILIES RELIED ON MILLS FOR EMPLOYMENT.

There is no more eloquent memorial to that past than the former terminus of the Liverpool & Manchester Railway, which now houses the Manchester Museum of Science and Industry. It is the oldest passenger railway station in the world.

The next leg of our journey took us on a short detour south-east to Denton to visit what was left of another Victorian success story, again driven by the railways – the hat industry. In Bradshaw's Britain there were 90 hat factories around Denton, and at one point almost 40 per cent of the local population was employed in them. It's claimed that the trilby, perhaps one of its finest creations, was born here.

In Denton we found a tale mirrored up and down the country – one of expansion during the second half of the nineteenth century followed by rapid contraction, leaving a few very specialist high-end producers. The period of growth was often tied in with the arrival of the railways, which allowed companies to move their goods further, faster and more cheaply. The contraction usually came as it became cheaper to produce the goods in alternative markets. In Denton, there was a twist.

Denton's felt hat industry had already had a tough time at the hands of the whims of fashion, but its eventual demise was the result of another major invention in transportation – the motor car. After all, who needs a hat when all you have to do is jump in your car? The result is that the only factory remaining is Failsworth Hats.

At Failsworth's, hats have been produced in much the same way since the company was established in 1903, using virtually original machinery. However, manager Karen Turner highlighted one significant change. Up until the twentieth century, mercury was used to separate rabbit hair from the hide used to make felt hats. Not surprisingly, many of workers in daily contact with rabbit hides suffered from poisoning. Symptoms included erratic behaviour and dementia, and it's this, they say, that gave rise to the phrase 'mad as a hatter'.

From Denton we headed north past Ilkley Moor, and back in time, to catch a steam train on the Embsay & Bolton Abbey Steam Railway just on the edge of the Yorkshire Dales. One of my great discoveries making the series was how many steam trains there are still in existence around the country carrying holidaymakers and even commuters. This railway, part of a branch line that was closed by the Beeching cuts in the 1960s, was reopened in stages as a heritage line from 1981 to 1998, when Bolton Abbey station was reopened.

THE PERILS OF AN INDUSTRY RELIANT ON RAW MATERIALS GROWN A VAST DISTANCE AWAY BECAME STARKLY APPARENT

Stephen Middleton, who met us at the station, is unusual even among those passionate about the railway. He doesn't record their numbers or photograph them. He doesn't even drive them. What he does is buy and restore old carriages which are then used, for example, on the Embsay & Bolton Abbey Steam Railway. His aim is to recreate the magic he felt as a boy, riding on a privileged ticket, thanks to his father's job on the railway, in a first-class carriage. It was a boyhood sensation enjoyed by many and rarely bettered. And it was certainly the best way to travel in the age of steam.

Undoubtedly it sounds romantic today, but steam locomotive travel was dirty and smelly, particularly for third-class passengers in the early days who travelled in coaches that were little more than open-topped wagons lined with benches. As if being open to the elements wasn't enough, there was also the hazard of burning sparks and soot spewing from the locomotive. But the idea that everyone could afford at least one trip a week on the railway was enshrined in law in the 1840s, after which all railway companies had to offer at least one 'open to all' ticket. Quick and cheap, a new phenomenon of day-tripping was created by the railway. Almost overnight, Bolton Abbey became a day-trip sensation.

The Abbey is on the 30,000-acre estate owned by the Dukes of Devonshire since 1755. In 1888 the then Duke realised the potential of turning it into a tourist destination and built a station to accommodate day-trippers who came there to marvel at the unspoilt views. Even Bradshaw was wowed by the Abbey and its stunning location, in his stiff sort of way: 'The Abbey is … most charmingly situated on the banks of the river Wharfe. Indeed the picturesque character of this and surrounding districts in peculiarly striking and impressive.'

The Abbey has retained its magic and the journey by steam makes getting there a fantastic adventure, visitors experiencing it today in much the same way as Bradshaw did all those years ago.

For the next part of our eastward journey to York, we were lucky enough to take to the air, something that George Bradshaw would have loved. In his day the railways were kept safe by railway staff called policemen – although they were not part of any constabulary – who had positions at key points along the lines. There were no signals and the policemen's job was to ensure that there was a 10-minute gap between the trains, holding them up if not. They also walked the lines to check for debris. Now, though, the Network Rail helicopter full of gadgets and

RIGHT: **HERITAGE LINES LIKE THE EMBSAY AND BOLTON ABBEY STEAM RAILWAY HAVE LONG BEEN POPULAR WITH YOUNG AND OLD.**

OVERLEAF: **PICTURESQUE BOLTON ABBEY REMAINS EASILY ACCESSIBLE BY TRAIN.**

EMBSAY STEAM RAILWAY

SKIPTON

Visit YORKSHIRE'S FRIENDLY LINE

Telephone: General Enquiries, Skipton (0756) 4727
Talking Timetable, Skipton (0756) 5189
Yorkshire Dales Railway Museum Trust
Registered Charity No. 517804

Grant Aided by
Craven District Council
and S.C.O.S.P.A.

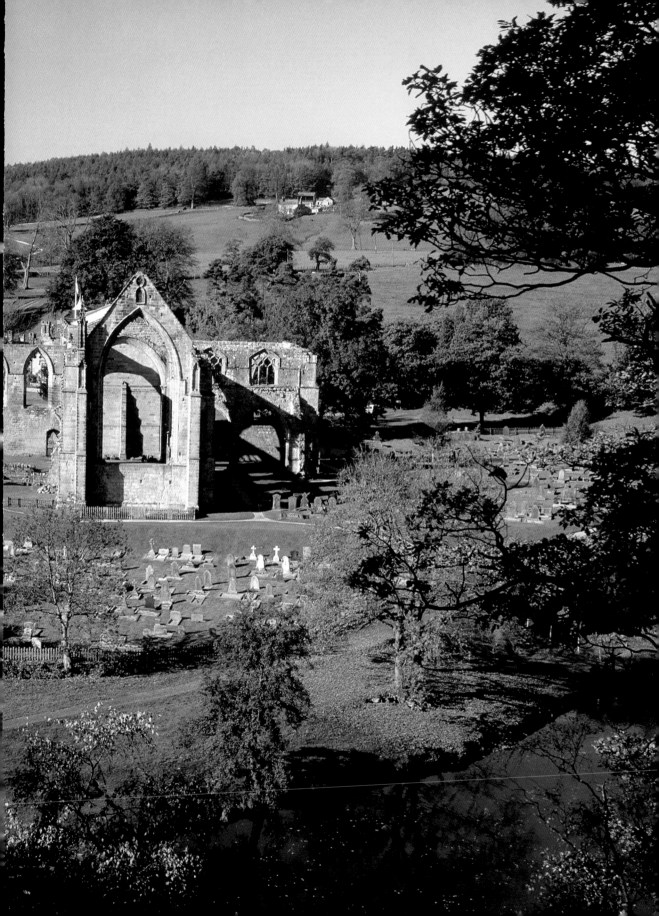

gizmos does much of that work, including using infrared cameras that show whether the heating system on the points is working properly. The helicopter regularly surveys the 20,000 miles of Network Rail track, a feat that would have kept thousands of Victorian policemen busy.

However you approach York, it is a beautiful city. Entering it by rail, though, there is the added beauty of the station itself. Designed by architects Thomas Prosser and William Peachey, it was built in 1877 and was the largest station in the world. It's now one of the busiest, with 400 trains passing though it every day, bringing many of the 4 million visitors who come to York each year.

There's plenty to see. Although best known as a medieval city, York started out in AD71 as a settlement beside a huge 50-acre Roman fortress which housed 6,000 soldiers. It was more than just an important military base: for a short time when the Emperor Severus lived there in 209 the entire Roman Empire was ruled from York.

The most enduring legacy of the Romans is the magnificent city walls, including the Multangular Tower. Although many of the walls were there for Bradshaw to see, since then the city has continued to yield up its Roman secrets, and excavations go on today.

From York our route took us towards Hull via Pontefract. We were in search of liquorice, because in Bradshaw's day Pontefract was famous for the black sweet, with plants being farmed in the fields surrounding the town. It's thought that monks had started to grow liquorice there some 600 years ago when they discovered that the area's deep, loamy soil was perfect for the plant's long roots. They used the roots for medicinal purposes, extracting the sap and using it to ease coughs and stomach complaints.

After the Dissolution of the Monasteries in the sixteenth century, local farmers continued to cultivate liquorice and a thriving cottage industry was established. Then, in 1760, Pontefract apothecary George Dunhill made a breakthrough. He added sugar to the recipe and created the liquorice cake sweet.

Before the railways, almost all the liquorice grown was used locally, but the arrival of the trains saw it transported nationwide. More of the surrounding land was turned over to growing it. There's scant trace of it now, though.

Tom Dixon's family grew liquorice for over 200 years, and in their heyday they supplied Boots – it was a chief ingredient for their throat

sweets. Tom told us that his great-grandfather had even sent liquorice down to Queen Victoria, who was said to adore it. He did so without realising that liquorice brought on high blood pressure, which is what led to her demise.

The death of Pontefract liquorice came much later. It was grown in the fields around Tom's house until the late 1960s, when the last harvests took place. Indeed, Tom is said to have Pontefract's last liquorice bush. Like so many products that boomed for a while with the arrival of the railways, it had become cheaper to import it from elsewhere as travel costs fell across the board. For liquorice, the primary markets became Spain, Italy and Turkey. Curiously, liquorice was known locally as a stick of Spanish – it had originated in Spain.

After the short stop in Pontefract, we were back on the train heading east towards the city and North Sea port of Kingston upon Hull, better

known today as Hull. Bradshaw explains that this was one of the earliest routes used for the popular day-trips which started in 1840 and were known as Monster Excursions.

One of the first Monster Excursions took place in August 1840 when a special Sunday train set off from Leeds to Hull. Organised by the Leeds Institute, it had an incredible 40 carriages transporting 1,250 passengers for the day. Trips like these not only did a huge amount to publicise the idea of railway excursions, but also made Hull a recognised destination. This information might have some locals snorting into their sleeves, but, thanks to Bradshaw, we can glimpse a surprising view of Victorian Hull.

'It presents the eye an interesting spectacle of numerous vessels floating to and from the port of Hull: while that opulent and commercial town in its low situation close to the banks and surrounded by the masts of the shipping in the docks seems to rise like Venice from amidst the sea; the whole comprising a scene which for beauty and grandeur can scarcely be exceeded.'

Believe it or not, Hull was an attractive resort in Victorian times, the sort of place Queen Victoria was happy to visit. In 1854 she stayed in what swiftly changed its name to the Station Hotel, shortly before enhancing it with the prefix 'Royal'. Built in 1851, it was probably the first railway hotel of its kind, literally straddling the platform. It also gets a mention in Bradshaw, along with the zoological gardens, the camera obscura, the music hall, the Crystal Palace and the fireworks held every Monday evening during the season!

Hull's sheltered location on the Humber estuary led to it developing as a prosperous port. Initially the wealth came from whaling, which until the 1840s was subsidised by the government. At much the same time as the subsidy disappeared, the railway line arrived, opening up the opportunity of new markets. The whalers turned to fishing and Hull soon became one of the biggest white fish ports in the world.

The railway was crucial to Hull's growth. There were some 300 miles of railway track transporting fish within the city boundaries, and 20 fish trains left Hull every day for destinations all over the UK, including Manchester's new fish market. Consumption grew from three to 80 tons a week and at a quarter of the price it had been previously.

Hull remained an important white fish port until the 1970s, when the industry collapsed following the Third Cod War. In 1975 Iceland placed a 200-mile exclusion zone around its coastline. Britain refused to recognise the barrier and its trawlers continued to fish in the newly created Icelandic waters. When they were confronted by Icelandic ships the Royal Navy became involved. Although a few shots were fired, it was mostly a war of ramming and stand-offs, peppered with net-cutting incidents.

Almost wholly dependent on fishing, Iceland took its action in the face of diminishing stocks. Britain also realised that fish catches were dipping, but resented the strategic action taken by its small, northerly neighbour. A compromise was eventually reached which permitted a small number of British ships to trawl in the disputed waters while limiting their catch.

The writing was on the wall for the East Coast fishing fleets. In 1977 there were 127 trawlers working out of Hull, but within two years that number had gone down to just six. Today, 97 per cent of our cod is imported and, with the temperature of our coastal waters rising, that's unlikely to change.

If there is an upside to the rising temperature of our coastal waters, it is that other fish like sea bass can tolerate the North Sea. In fact, over the last decade the east Yorkshire coastline has seen a steady increase in the number of sea bass, so we decided our next stop would be Bridlington, 25 miles up the coast, to find the antidote to over-fishing.

Bradshaw describes Bridlington thus: 'This attractive resort lies on the Yorkshire coast, but at that point where the line turns westward from Flamborough Head and then sweeping round to the south forms a capacious bay called Bridlington Bay ... the Esplanade is a spacious level green commanding a beautiful view of the Holderness coast which stretches in a curve as far as the eye can trace.'

The arrival of the railway in 1846 had turned the sleepy fishing village into a popular resort for West Yorkshire's industrial workers and, with much of that Victorian esplanade still intact, it still attracts thousands of holidaymakers every summer.

Fisherman Frank Powell pursues his trade in a way that's about as far away from giant trawl nets and factory ships as you can get. He chooses to fish sustainably, so much so that he doesn't even leave land. He fishes for sea bass from the shore, using a system that relies on the tide, and he only takes a few fish each time. What's more, Frank uses a net that only keeps fish of a certain size, making it a method of fishing which should see stock protected for future generations. Who knows, in years to come maybe the fish in our fish and chips is more likely to be red mullet or sea bass than cod or haddock.

97 PER CENT OF OUR COD IS IMPORTED AND, WITH THE TEMPERATURE OF OUR COASTAL WATERS RISING, THAT'S UNLIKELY TO CHANGE

VICTORIAN VISITORS TO BRIDLINGTON RELISHED THE SIGHT OF SQUALLING WAVES AROUND THE CLIFFS AT FLAMBOROUGH HEAD.

GALES REGULARLY
SMASHED FISHING
BOATS ALL ALONG
THIS COAST, BUT
THE FISHERMEN
FROM FILEY WERE
PARTICULARLY
AT RISK

Winding our way up the coast, our next stop was Bempton, just four miles along the track. Bempton was the closest we could get by rail to the magnificent Flamborough Head, which turned out to be every bit as impressive today as it was in Bradshaw's time, with its 'lofty cliffs of nearly five hundred feet elevation, teeming in the spring and summer months with thousands of birds of every hue and species and exhibiting yawning caverns of stupendous size'.

Meeting Ian Kendall from the Royal Society for the Protection of Birds, Michael discovered that the beautiful, unchanging scenery belies a worrying decline in the North Sea bird population. The change in water temperature over the last 25 years has decimated the sand eel population which is a major food for the birds. The tragedy is that many species of bird are simply starving, leaving them unable to breed and threatening their future.

This coastline also boasts two lighthouses that are worth a mention and a visit. The Chalk Tower is an ancient beacon built around 1674 which lays claim to being England's oldest lighthouse. Then there's a far more recent one designed by architect Samuel Wyatt and built by John Matson in 1806 for the princely sum of £8,000. Wyatt's lighthouse used red glass for the first time, giving the characteristic lighthouse flash of two white flashes followed by one red flash. The red flash was easier to see in thick fog and was quickly adopted in other lighthouses.

Another 15-minute hop up the coast lies Filey, which is described by Bradshaw simply as 'modern'. When the railways arrived in 1846, Filey grew as a quieter alternative destination for visitors wanting to avoid its more lively neighbour, Scarborough.

Tourism wasn't the only industry growing in Filey. Fishing was expanding too, and in 1870 there were 100 vessels manned by around 400 men. But it was a tough and dangerous job on the treacherous coast here, and many lost their lives. Bradshaw makes an oblique reference to the tragedy of fishing here, observing that 'owing to a great number of men being drowned in 1851, the population of women is considerably greater than that of the men'.

It's not clear exactly which disaster he's referring to, or whether it was one or several, but it's not difficult to believe. Gales regularly smashed fishing boats all along this coast, but the fishermen from Filey were particularly at risk. They used and still use boats known as cobles, which are flat bottomed with no keel, making them easy to launch and land at the

FLAMBOROUGH LIGHTHOUSE,
BUILT IN 1806 AND AUTOMATED
SINCE 1996, ACTS AS A BEACON
FOR SHIPS TO BRIDLINGTON.

DURING 'WAKES WEEK',
WHEN THE MILLS CLOSED,
SCARBOROUGH WAS
THRONGING WITH FAMILIES.

beach. They also have high bows, which make them better for ploughing directly into the surf. They are very stable for their size, but the men of Filey used them for winter fishing. Whilst boats from neighbouring towns were laid up, the men of Filey were out long-line fishing at a time when gales were most likely.

It was so dangerous that the tradition of knitting jumpers took on a different, darker role. The style and pattern of these not only varied from town to town but also from family to family – to ensure that bodies of people lost at sea could be identified.

In the neighbouring coastal towns fathers and sons worked on different boats to prevent whole families being killed. For the men of Filey, the tradition was for a man to be accompanied by his sons on his boat, this being the best way to pass on the necessary skills. But it meant that the cost to one family following a tragedy was immeasurable. It's claimed by Filey people that, proportionately, no maritime community has lost so many men as their own.

Scarborough, the final stop on our journey, has also had its fair share of fishing boat disasters. But the town's sons had other career options. Scarborough had long been a holiday destination for the rich, who were attracted to the spa and its iron-rich waters. Indeed, their beneficial effects were well known in the seventeenth century, and the town can claim to be England's first seaside resort. Once the railways put the town on the map as a major holiday destination for the masses, the numbers increased dramatically. As Bradshaw writes, 'There are thirty-three miles of coast which may be inspected at low water over a course of the finest sands in England.'

As the cotton mills across the north-west closed for a holiday called 'wakes week', the workers headed to the coast, and especially to Scarborough. Bradshaw describes many attractions in detail: the iron bridge, the twelfth-century castle and hilltop walks complete with panoramic views. But they also flocked to see a skeleton called Gristhorpe Man. On his discovery in July 1834, the remains of this Bronze Age man became a national sensation. It was thought to be the best-preserved example of an oak tree trunk burial – a coffin made from a hollowed-out tree usually reserved for a tribe's elite – and Victorians travelled from far and wide to see him.

Gristhorpe Man is still on display in the town. In 2005 a team of experts arrived to take a closer look and were at first sceptical. He was so

SCARBOROUGH, THE FINAL STOP ON OUR JOURNEY, HAS ALSO HAD ITS FAIR SHARE OF FISHING BOAT DISASTERS

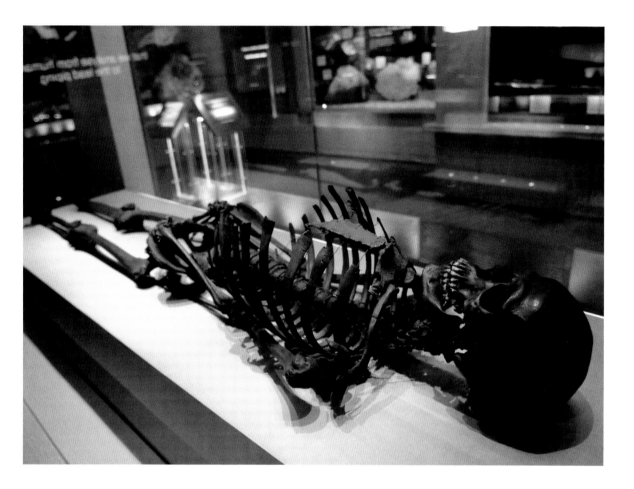

well preserved that they were convinced he was a fake. But after a close examination using the most modern forensic tests they concluded that he was in fact a genuine Bronze Age man who had died in his sixties, possibly from a brain tumour. Tests also revealed that he was likely to have lived locally, on a high-protein diet full of meat, and had kidney stones. Even after 2,000 years, modern methods were able to peel away Gristhorpe Man's secrets.

Before the railways Gristhorpe Man might have recognised some aspects of English life. Afterwards the fundamentals of everyday living changed. In our 10 days' travelling from Liverpool to Scarborough the enormous impact the railways had on almost every aspect of Victorian life became starkly apparent. In a matter of a few years everything changed in a revolution that then proceeded to sweep the world.

GRISTHORPE MAN DATES FROM THE BRONZE AGE AND DIED IN HIS SIXTIES, PROBABLY FROM A BRAIN TUMOUR.

Nursery

COTH

COTHAM

Turnpike

KINGS

Pembroke Ho

Zoological Gardens

Oakfield Ho

County Boundary

THE PARK

Conservative Rooms

Clifton Rd

Park Gate

Walker on Rr

Chapel Pl

Somerset Place

Bristol & Exeter Rooms

Bishops Col

Blind Asy

Suspension Bridge

Royal York Cres

Lower Crescent

Spring Ho

Clifton Ch

Clifton Hill

Consumption Hos

Brandon Hill

Chapel

Foot Path to Ashton

CLIFTON

WELS

Avon Str

Hotwell Road

Pembroke Place

The Dock Act of 1803 extends the boundaries of the City for certain objects, to accompany the Docks & together with the paths & roads on each side to take this below to Wells.

Ship Yard

Sea Bank

Send Rocks

Coronation

Cliff Ho

JOURNEY

2

THE
HOLIDAY
LINE

From
Swindon to
Penzance

Most of us take it for granted that we'll take a holiday at some time. Indeed the number of Britons going abroad each year is now more than 56 million. Before the spread of trains, though, vacations at home or overseas were exclusively the province of the rich. For want of time and money, the majority could not dream of spending a week or even a day away – until the railway system spider-webbed the country and changed every thing. And no line was more instrumental in unshackling swathes of the population from their homes and employment for a short spell than a 300-mile stretch nicknamed the Holiday Line.

Initially the man behind this westward-bound railway was the far-sighted engineer Isambard Kingdom Brunel (1806–59), working for the Great Western Railway. His hallmark designs are still apparent today in the shape of Paddington station, the original Bristol Temple Meads station which stands disused next to the current station, and the Box tunnel, as well as all the bridges, viaducts and other tunnels along the line – engineering feats that doubtless concerned him more than fortnights away. The more westerly sections of the line were in fact not finished until after his death, and it wasn't dubbed the Holiday Line until 1908 by GWR spin doctors.

The Holiday Line still runs between Paddington and Penzance. By the time of its completion, bucket-and-spade holidays had become the norm rather than the exception.

However, it wasn't the spread of railways alone that sparked an explosion in the popularity of British seaside resorts. The Victorian era was the age of philanthropy, and crucially employers began to embrace the idea of holidays for the workers, none more so than those at the Great Western Railway.

The GWR was based in Swindon, our first stop along the holiday line. Its enormous works, constructed there in the early 1840s, were described by Bradshaw as being 'one of the most extraordinary products of the railway enterprise of the present age. A colony of engineers and handicraft men.' Soon Swindon, previously a small market town, was wholly reliant on the railway. Although buildings that once held bustling workshops are now empty shells, they are testament to the thriving industry that was once centred here.

When it first opened the GWR works employed 200 men. A decade later the number had risen to 2,000 men, and by the end of the century

THE GENIUS OF ISAMBARD KINGDOM BRUNEL TRANSFORMED TRANSPORT IN ENGLAND'S SOUTH WEST.

some three quarters of Swindon's working population were employed by the railway company. There was no facet of train or track that could not be built or repaired at the vast complex, a fact that inspired pride among the workforce.

Better still from the workers' point of view were the terms and conditions of the jobs. Not only did GWR build an entire village to house its workers, but with it came a school, a church, a hospital, hairdressers, swimming baths, a theatre and even a funeral director's. Then, from 1848, it started to run free trains for employees and their families heading to the West Country every July, a tradition which continued until the 1970s.

ABOVE: **HOLIDAYMAKERS HAD BRUNEL TO THANK FOR PADDINGTON STATION AT THE START OF THEIR JOURNEY WEST.**

OVERLEAF: **GREAT WESTERN RAILWAYS NOT ONLY BUILT TRAINS AND TRACK BUT ALSO SCHOOLS, HOMES AND SHOPS FOR ITS SIZEABLE WORKFORCE.**

These holidays, known simply as 'Trip', were extraordinary feats of organisation. Tens of thousands of people were transported to resorts all over the south-west, the largest recorded trip being organised on the cusp of the First World War. On 9 July 1914, with tensions rising in Europe, 25,616 people headed west on trains that started to leave at four o'clock in the morning.

Trip veterans Ron Glass and Mary Starley, whose fathers both worked for GWR, recall with fondness later trips and the company's cradle-to-grave umbrella of care. 'Virtually the whole town was coming to a stand-still for a week,' explains Ron, who was himself a GWR employee.

Dressed in their Sunday best for both travelling and the beach, trip-pers were assigned trains that left throughout a Friday so as not to disrupt weekend timetables for the rest of the travelling public. The journey itself had a smell, a taste and a rhythm of its own, as packed carriages towed by GWR steam engines painted in Brunswick green sashayed towards the seaside.

Although the train journey was free, families still had to finance their accommodation, which was a challenge when no one prior to the Second World War received holiday pay. The week after trip became known as the dry week, because workers had received no wages and therefore couldn't afford a drink at the pub. Ron remembers his father giving up smoking for a spell each year to pay for the holiday. For Ron, Mary and the thousands of others, their holidays had started at Swindon station, famous in Bradshaw's day for having had the first refreshment rooms in the country. At the time, there were no buffet cars or tea trolleys on trains, so every GWR train stopped at Swindon for a 10-minute break. According to Bradshaw, the rooms were 'abun-dantly supplied with every article of fare to tempt the best as well as the most delicate appetites and the prices are moderate, considering the extortions to which travellers are occasionally exposed'.

The story Bradshaw didn't know, or at least didn't tell, was that when Brunel was building the Swindon complex he was so short of money that he struck a deal with his contractors. They built the works, houses and the station in return for the rent revenue and a lease on the sta-tion refreshments, 'with the obligation that Great Western stop all trains there for ten minutes for the next hundred years and refrain from offering alternative catering'. It was a deal that stayed in place until 1895, when the company finally bought itself out.

THE JOURNEY ITSELF HAD A SMELL, A TASTE AND A RHYTHM OF ITS OWN, AS PACKED CARRIAGES SASHAYED TOWARDS THE SEASIDE

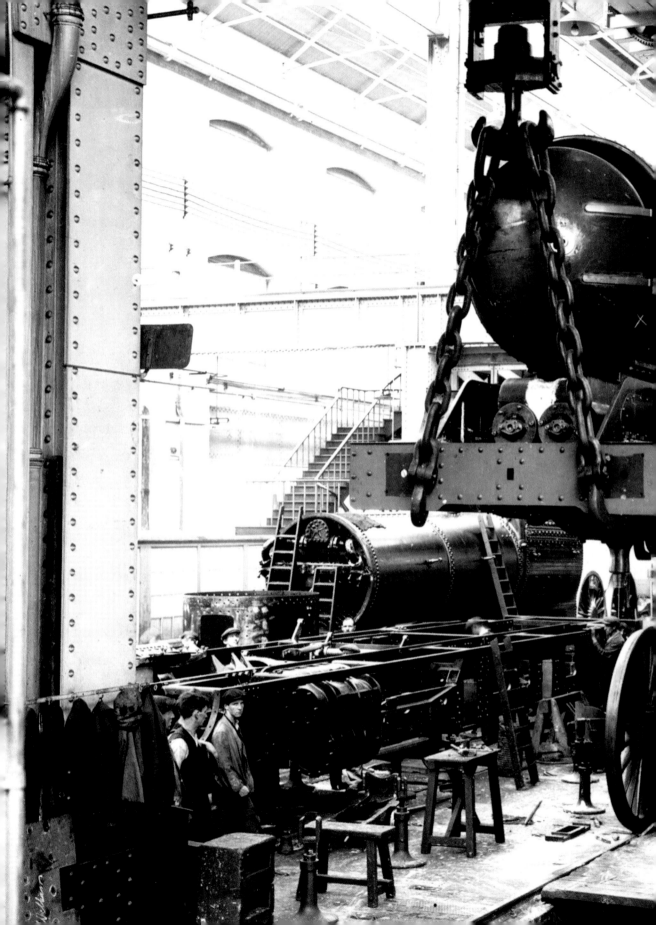

From Swindon, the train heads south-west to Bath, passing through one of Brunel's most spectacular engineering achievements. Brunel knew that the straighter the route, the faster his trains would go, so Box Hill in Wiltshire, five miles east of Bath, posed a particular challenge. Rather than curve round it and lose speed and time, Brunel made the decision to go straight through it. It was to be the longest tunnel in the world.

It took 4,000 men more than four years to carve a path through the limestone rock – also known as Bath stone. Almost 100 men lost their lives as a tunnel length of 1¾ miles was forged by two gangs, one each side of the hill, who successfully met in the middle thanks to Brunel's astonishingly accurate calculations. In building Box Tunnel, Brunel acquired an adversary, one Dr Dionysius Lardner, who claimed that travelling at speed through a tunnel would render breathing impossible. Put simply, everyone using it would die. When the tunnel finally opened, publicity garnered by Dr Lardner meant that many passengers were too frightened to pass through it. Instead, they left the train prior to Box Hill and took a coach for the remaining distance to Bath. Impossible to know what, 170 years on, nervous passengers would have made of the new Gotthard base tunnel currently being built beneath the Alps, which will be more than 35 miles long.

If Swindon is a shadow of the place Bradshaw trumpeted, the Bath he describes is, for the most part, completely recognisable today: 'Spacious streets, groves, and crescents lined with stately stone edifices and intersected by squares and gardens complete a view of the city scarcely surpassed by any other in the kingdom.' Bath's elegant streets, crescents and circuses remain stunning. The most eminent were designed in the eighteenth century by the renowned architect John Wood (1704–54) and his son, also John, whose genius was to create classical, uniform façades in Bath stone that gave terraced town houses the grandeur of stately homes. Intriguingly, behind the facade the houses are very different from one another, as the original owners were able to dictate the individual layout of their home.

The regimentation was a great success and turned Bath into the playground of high society. That was until the arrival of the railways when, for the first time, the middle and lower classes could afford to travel there and sample what the wealthy had been enjoying for centuries – the spas.

People had bathed here since Roman times, believing the waters – absorbed through skin pores – to be a cure for everything from

ALMOST 100 MEN LOST THEIR LIVES AS A TUNNEL LENGTH OF ONE AND THREE-QUARTER MILES WAS FORGED

TWO GANGS FORGING A TUNNEL FROM EACH SIDE OF BOX HILL IN WILTSHIRE MET IN THE MIDDLE THANKS TO BRUNEL'S ACCURATE CALCULATIONS.

FOR YEARS VISITORS TOOK TO
THE SPAS IN BATH, CONVINCED
IT WOULD BENEFIT THEIR
HEALTH AND WELLBEING.

THROUGHOUT
THE LATE
NINETEENTH
CENTURY,
THE RAILWAY
BROUGHT
ORDINARY
PEOPLE TO THE
SPAS IN THEIR
THOUSANDS

infertility to gout. It turns out they were partially right, but for the wrong reasons. The minerals are not absorbed through the skin, but Dr Roger Rolls, a local GP, historian and author of *The Medical Uses of the Spa*, has studied the water's medicinal properties and points out that it did have some benefits.

The Victorians drank an abundance of cider, port and Madeira, all contaminated by high quantities of lead from the fruit presses. As a result, many of Bath's 'fashionable invalids', as Bradshaw terms them, had ailments arising from lead poisoning. Modern research has shown that immersion in hot water up to the neck increases pressure and makes the kidneys work harder, causing people with raised levels of lead to excrete it more quickly. So the spa water does help with poisoning.

Throughout the late nineteenth century, the railway brought ordinary people to the spas in their thousands, but by the mid-twentieth century the baths fell out of fashion and their doors finally closed in 1978. However, in 2006 – albeit behind schedule and over budget – the Thermae Bath Spa opened. It is a stunning piece of architecture, one that the Woods themselves might have approved. Once again people are flocking to Bath to take the waters, wallowing in a rooftop pool whilst gazing out over the majesty of the city.

From Bath the line heads west, along the valley of the meandering River Avon, to Bristol, where some of Brunel's finest work can be seen, including the Clifton Suspension Bridge and his great steamship *Great Britain*, then the largest ship in the world, and the first large iron-hulled steamship powered by a screw-propeller.

In Bradshaw's day Bristol lay in a different time zone from London. Victorian Britain enjoyed an assortment of times, as clocks were set locally according to the setting sun. London was 10 minutes ahead of Bristol, which was fine until, like Brunel, you were trying to create a timetable for a fast-moving steam train. Brunel's solution was to standardise time across his network, using what he called railway time, and George Bradshaw ably assisted him. When he started putting his timetables together in 1840, Bradshaw also stuck to railway time and ultimately convinced all the other railways to follow suit. Within 10 years the whole country was in a single time zone. It was arguably Bradshaw's most significant contribution to modern society.

REJUVENATED POOLS IN BATH, INCLUDING ONE ON A ROOFTOP, HAVE IGNITED A FRESH DEMAND FOR THE TOWN'S NATURAL SPAS.

IN 1934 BRISTOL TEMPLE MEADS
STATION WAS HECTIC WITH
COMMUTERS AND FREIGHT
AFTER A RECENT EXPANSION.

The grand terminus, Bristol Temple Meads, designed by Brunel and opened in 1840, is today a ghost station. Changes made as Bristol became a major rail junction rendered Brunel's great passenger shed obsolete. From 1999 it was the home of the British and Commonwealth Museum, until that was moved to London. It's not about to be pulled down any time soon, however. The historic nature of the building means that it is still highly prized. What is a shame is that it is now closed, so few people are aware of it and no one steps inside to soak up the grand flavour of the architecture.

Our next stop was at Yatton in Somerset, another reminder of how quickly change occurred with the advent of the railway. In our battered copy of Bradshaw's guide, Yatton barely warrants a mention. Later, in 1868, a new branch line was added, feeding Cheddar into the national network, which put Yatton at the centre of a booming strawberry industry.

The London markets were already catered for by Kent's strawberry growers. But this new branch line, nicknamed the Strawberry Line, meant that for the first time huge quantities of fresh Cheddar Valley strawberries could be whisked around the country, especially to the north. In its heyday, there were 250 growers here producing strawberries which, for those few weeks each year, were picked and transported to market every Friday. Today there are just four growers left, while the Strawberry Line itself fell victim to the Beeching axe in 1964.

LEFT: BRUNEL'S CAVERNOUS PASSENGER SHED WAS BUILT TO ACCOMMODATE THE ORIGINAL LINE FROM PADDINGTON.

RIGHT: BRISTOL'S CLIFTON SUSPENSION BRIDGE WAS ANOTHER OF BRUNEL'S GRAND DESIGNS.

OVERLEAF: TOURISM THRIVED AT CHEDDAR GORGE AFTER THE RAILWAY BROUGHT VISITORS BY THE THOUSAND TO THE NEIGHBOURHOOD.

CLIFTON SUSPENSION BRIDGE

BRISTOL

 Illustrated Booklets from
Development Board, BRISTOL

Sir Richard Beeching, then known as Dr Beeching, was the chairman of the railways at a time when they were considered too costly. The railways had been losing money since the 1950s, and a decade later the government, whose transport minister Ernest Marples was the director of a road construction company, decided enough was enough. Beeching came up with a plan that he believed would save the railways from financial meltdown. It resulted in the loss of 2,128 stations, 5,000 miles of track and 67,000 jobs, with rural Britain the hardest hit. As the expected savings failed to appear on the balance sheet, Dr Beeching's name became a by-word for ill-considered and ineffective cuts. Perhaps the move towards reducing our food miles may yet herald the rebirth of the Somerset strawberry industry.

One local industry that's not in decline is tourism. Before the railway, Cheddar Gorge on the edge of the Mendip Hills was a destination for rich, independent travellers who came to marvel at the deepest gorge in Britain. The trains gave thousands of day-trippers the chance to enjoy it too. They flocked to see what Bradshaw describes as 'a place of some notoriety from the discovery of two caverns in its vicinity, one called the Stalactite and the other the Bone Cave, which now attract a great number of visitors'.

Today half a million people visit each year, but few are as fortunate as my team, who got a personal tour from archaeologist and director of Cheddar Caves and Gorge, Hugh Cornwell. Hugh wanted to reveal a set of caves discovered by an eccentric sea captain and showman called Richard Gough. Gough had turned them into a tourist attraction, the first caves in Britain to be lit with electric light.

As more of the caves were opened to cater for the growing number of visitors, they revealed secrets Bradshaw would have relished. The most important of these was the 1903 discovery of Cheddar Man, the oldest complete skeleton ever found in Britain, dating back some 9,000 years. Examination suggested that as a teenager Cheddar Man had been hit on the head with an axe, but had gone on to live into his twenties. It was odd that he had been buried on his own away from the rest of his tribe. Hugh's theory is that Cheddar Man suffered a brain injury which resulted in antisocial behaviour that doubtless ruffled feathers among fellow tribesmen. When he died, his tribe didn't deal with him in the usual way but buried him instead in the cave, believing it to be a sort of twilight zone that would prevent Cheddar Man's spirit from joining his ancestors in the next world.

From Yatton, the line continues west, past the resorts of Weston-super-Mare, birthplace of John Cleese, and Burnham-on-Sea, before turning inland and heading south. After Bridgwater and Taunton it swings westwards into Devon and then south again towards Exeter and the coast.

The section of route to our next destination, Torquay, is one of the most picturesque rail journeys in existence. Hugging the western side of the Exe estuary and then sliding its way along the coast through Dawlish and Teignmouth, it's a route that's barely changed in the last 170 years. In the words of Bradshaw: 'There is scarcely a mile traversed which does not unfold some peculiar picturesque charm or new feature of its own to make the eye dazzled and drunk with its beauty.'

And the line is not only generous with exceptional vistas but remains an extraordinary feat of engineering. This was one of the most challenging sections of the GWR to construct. In fact, the Exeter Corporation wanted it to stay inland but the redoubtable Brunel insisted it follow the coastal wall, which meant boring five tunnels through the cliffs and building four miles of sea wall to protect the tracks. The result is a magnificent, memorable journey, beneath towering red cliffs, with repeated plunges into darkness as the train goes through one tunnel after another, and all within a few feet of the sea. One signal box was built so close to the waves that the signalmen used to be issued with the oilskins worn by sailors.

The line reached Torquay with its warm microclimate in 1848, and immediately the Great Western Railway started promoting the town as a perfect holiday spot. They even coined the phrase 'The English Riviera' to describe the resort. A few years later, Bradshaw is again comparing Torquay with the south of France, suggesting that 'those English invalids who, in search of a more congenial temperature, hastily enter on a long journey to some foreign county and wilfully encounter all the inconveniences attending a residence there' would do better to 'make themselves acquainted with the bland and beautiful climates which lie within an easy jaunt'.

The English invalids seem to have listened. It wasn't long before they were arriving by the coach-load to relax and enjoy the 19 beaches and coves spread over 22 miles of coastline. On one particular Bank

IN THE WORDS OF BRADSHAW: 'THERE IS SCARCELY A MILE TRAVERSED WHICH DOES NOT UNFOLD SOME PECULIAR PICTURESQUE CHARM'

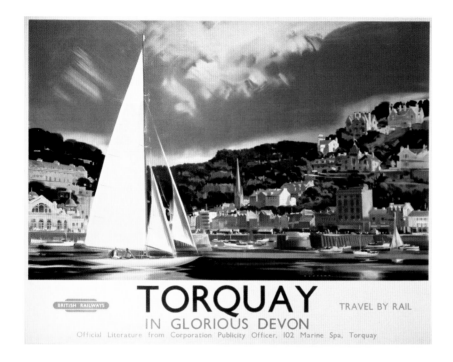

TORQUAY

IN GLORIOUS DEVON

BRITISH RAILWAYS · TRAVEL BY RAIL

Official Literature from Corporation Publicity Officer, 102 Marine Spa, Torquay

Holiday, 20,000 people arrived there by train in a single day. Thanks to the railway, Torquay had become a major resort.

From nearby Paignton it's possible to recreate the train journeys that Bradshaw and Brunel would have recognised. A steam train travels south to Kingswear, first alongside charming beaches among abundant wildlife, then through some of the most idyllic countryside of South Devon by the tranquil River Dart, and all at a sedate 25 miles per hour.

But the railway of Bradshaw's day wasn't only concerned with getting from A to B. It was also about what you did when you got there. Salmon fishing on the Dart became a popular sport for Victorian tourists, and recreational fishermen arriving by train could even buy their fishing permit at the station. In the early 1900s a train laden with salmon and trout from Loch Leven in Scotland would stop at several points along the river to release the exported fish. The railway also encouraged an explosion of commercial salmon fishing, allowing the catch to be swiftly transported inland.

Today salmon stocks have declined in the Dart and there are strict regulations controlling the catch. There are now only three families still licensed to fish for salmon, and all of them have to use the traditional

ABOVE: **SUNNY TORQUAY QUICKLY EARNED ITSELF THE SOUBRIQUET OF 'THE ENGLISH RIVIERA'.**

OVERLEAF: **WITH STUNNING SEA VIEWS AND LUSH COUNTRYSIDE, A TRAIN JOURNEY ALONG THE SOUTH COAST OF DEVON WAS THE STARTING POINT OF A HOLIDAY.**

method called seine-netting. Travelling in an oared seiner, fishermen shoot a weighted net in a semicircle back towards the shore which is then hauled in, often all but empty.

Reading our Bradshaw, it occasionally seemed as though little had changed in 170 years. The book found us hotels, told us what to see, even gave tips for our journey. It was Bradshaw who highlighted that we'd need to take the ferry to cross to Dartmouth because there was no bridge there over the Dart. For nearby Totnes, though, change has certainly come.

Bradshaw was clearly not particularly impressed with Totnes. The book gives the town scant mention. It lists the population as 4,001, suggests one hotel, The Seven Stars, and tells us that, because the town is situated on the River Dart, most people are employed in the fishery. It's a very different place today, with double the population in the Totnes parish alone and a radical outlook.

Totnes is part of a global campaign for sustainability called Transition Towns. It was started there by Rob Hopkins in 2006 as a reaction to climate change and the challenge posed by the age of cheap oil nearing its end. Rob's idea was to treat this as an opportunity rather than a crisis, and in Totnes it seems to be working. One of the key elements is a garden share scheme, which Rob described as being like a dating agency. To reduce the distance food is transported they have a land swap system, putting people who want to grow their own food in touch with people who have spare bits of land they could use.

Totnes also has its own local currency, which can be spent in over 80 shops there. Rob likened Totnes to a leaky bucket, with money coming in and then pouring out again. Of every £1 you spent in a supermarket, 80p was out of Totnes by the next day. But this currency, which you obtain in exchange for cash at one of the local businesses participating in the scheme, can't go anywhere else – it encourages you to spend your money locally and support the town's economy.

Rob's tips for creating your own Transition Town start with finding a few reliable like-minded people to form a steering group. Before your official launch, arrange a few thought-provoking events, so people understand what the issues and aims are. If you can create a groundswell of people fired up on the key issues, you're much more likely to be successful as you move forward. The extraordinary thing is that what started in a small way in Totnes is now being used by thousands of towns, cities and villages around the world.

From Totnes the line skirts the southern edge of Dartmoor and then, after crossing the Tamar at Saltash on Brunel's enormous Royal Albert Bridge (his last great achievement, completed in 1859, the year he died), you are in Cornwall. We carried on west through St Germans, and shortly before St Austell we stopped at a small town called Par, which Bradshaw described as 'a mining town in west Cornwall near the sea with several important mines round it in the granite producing copper, nickel, with clay, and china stone for the Staffordshire potteries'. In fact, Par was an important hub for the huge industry fed by the biggest china clay deposits in the world. For almost 100 years clay used in the Potteries for making porcelain was shipped northwards by sea and canal. In the 1840s the railways took over, and soon it was being ferried on a network of lines that criss-crossed the county.

Most of those lines are long gone now, but one that does still run is used by the clay train that carries 1,140 tons of clay each day to the port of Fowey. Though it rarely takes passengers, we were lucky enough to hitch a ride along a single-track line through stunning Cornish countryside towards to the sea.

Because it's a single track, the trains have a very simple safety system that Bradshaw would have recognised. For the train to go down the track, it has to collect from the signal box a token in the form of a staff, like a heavy relay baton – and there's only one token in circulation for the line, so once you have it you know there's nothing about to come the other way.

The first Cornish clay mines opened in 1746, and by the middle of the eighteenth century 60,000 tons were being extracted each year. Although there are only three mines in operation now, thanks to modern techniques those remaining mines are thriving, extracting 1.5 million tons a year. Today 85 per cent of the total tonnage goes abroad, where it's used for everything from paper whitening to the manufacture of paint, plastics and pharmaceuticals.

Many of the scars left by the closed mines have been disguised with landscaping, but one pit has been radically recycled and is now home to the Eden Project. Its two bio-domes, recreating the rainforest and the Mediterranean, are the largest conservatories in the world. The founders didn't want the project to overwhelm the landscape, so they located them discreetly in the disused pit. Supported by a good train service, it's become one of the country's greenest tourist attractions.

Our next stop was only a few miles further down the line at St Austell, the closest we could get by train to the fishing port of Mevagissey on Cornwall's south coast. Whilst the Mevagissey that Bradshaw visited was on the Holiday Line, it was anything but a popular destination at that time, being 'so filthy that it is a very hot-bed of disease, when the cholera is abroad'.

Mevagissey would certainly have been messy, because it was the centre of the pilchard industry, which in the nineteenth century provided jobs for thousands of locals. It wasn't a glamorous profession.

BELOW: **THE ROYAL ALBERT VIADUCT LINKING DEVON AND CORNWALL WAS COMPLETED BY BRUNEL IN THE YEAR OF HIS DEATH AND CROSSES THE RIVER TAMAR.**

OVERLEAF: **MICHAEL PORTILLO GETS THE FEEL FOR A FISHERMAN'S LIFE.**

Men called huers perched overlooking the sea to spy where the sea-birds were fishing for pilchards. These observers, the origin of the phrase 'hue and cry', then alerted local fishermen, who took off in their boats to bring home as many fish from the vast shoals as they could muster. Often the men would be gone throughout the night, not returning until noon the following day, by which time a crowd would have gathered to meet them. Mevagissey women salted and stored the catch in caskets at processing plants called pilchard palaces. At its peak in 1871, the industry caught, cured and transported 16,000 tons of pilchards. Although the size of the catch diminished, possibly due to over-fishing, there remained sufficient to furnish the market.

In Britain pilchards were mostly sold in tins and were traditionally a cheap, popular food for the masses. However, after the Second World War tinned fish was strongly associated with wartime rationing. As a result, by the 1950s pilchards had become one of the least popular foods in Britain.

In 1997 the industry was in crisis, with fishermen earning as little as 1.5p a kilo. However, the humble Cornish pilchard has since enjoyed something of a renaissance after a local factory owner had a rebranding brainwave. He started marketing his common pilchards as 'Cornish sardines' and, thanks to this new Mediterranean image, sales soared. Fishermen were soon earning around a £1 a kilo, making the enterprise economical once more. There are now 12 boats working out of Mevagissey and neighbouring Newlyn that have pilchards in their sights.

Fortunately, in the interim the narrow alleys and cliff-clinging houses that border the picture-postcard harbour transformed Mevagissey from a down-at-heel fishing village to a hub for tourists. With thousands of visitors passing through its streets and lanes each year, its place on the Holiday Line now seems better deserved.

As a guide Bradshaw's book has its shortcomings. Some places would be easy to bypass thanks to his terse entries. Others are a lot more alluring, especially when his entries hint at something that's mysterious and tantalising. That was certainly the case at Perran Sands, where the very simple description refers to 'the remains of an old church of St Piran, an ancient British edifice which had been covered by the shifting sands for centuries'. The more we delved, the more fascinating the story became.

Perran Sands, on the other side of the peninsula from Megavissey, is an amazing landscape, boasting some of the largest sand-dunes in Britain. As it happens, the sands encase not one but two significant Christian sites. St Piran's Oratory was allegedly built by the saint himself after he landed on Cornish shores. It was here that he apparently healed the sick and even gave life to the dead. And here too he saw molten metal ooze from the Cornish slate that he used as a hearth. He shared this information with local people, and a busy mining industry was founded. The Cornish flag, a white cross on a black background, is said to be inspired by the hearth incident.

In the end the wind-blown sands got the better of the Oratory. It was given up to nature and a new church was built, probably in the tenth century. On the principle that sand would not cross water, a site was chosen with a stream forming a boundary between it and the beach.

This new church became a major draw for pilgrims on their way to Santiago di Compostela in northern Spain, where the bones of the apostle St James are said to be buried. The attraction of the Cornish church was presumably various relics, including the head of St Piran kept in a silver casket. (Apparently it was excavated at the start of the twentieth century, but disappeared almost immediately, into the hands of an unidentified thief.)

Unfortunately, the activities of tin miners underground disrupted the stream and allowed sand to encroach on the church. By the nineteenth century plans to build a third place of worship were well underway. Some but not all the stone from the existing church was taken for the new construction.

Clearly St Piran was an inspiration. But, although he is the patron saint of tin-miners and is generally thought of as one of three national saints closely associated with Cornwall, no one knows for certain who he was. According to legend he came from Ireland, where heathens tied him to a mill-stone before rolling him over a cliff and into a stormy sea. The sea immediately became calm and St Piran floated away, landing on the Cornish coast. He lived in Cornwall, performing miracles, until the age of 206.

The shifting dunes have at times parted to reveal both buildings. However, for their own protection, they have been covered again, the sands only serving to enhance the romance of the site.

FOR A TIME IN THE NINETEENTH CENTURY, CORNWALL'S TIN AND COPPER INDUSTRIES DOMINATED THE WORLD

The railways brought visitors to Cornwall, but they were also incredibly important to local industry. As with the china clay mines, a railway system had developed around the tin and copper mines, with mile after mile of tiny branch lines feeding individual pits. Our next stop, at the town of Redruth, was at its heart

Tin and copper had been extracted here for centuries, but the development of the steam engine put Cornwall on the mining map. Steam-powered pumps enabled miners to dig deeper and faster, producing more ore. The same technology developed the steam locomotive, which meant the metals could be quickly and easily transported around the country. For a time in the nineteenth century, Cornwall's tin and copper industries dominated the world. At the end of the nineteenth and through the twentieth century, however, those mines closed one by one, unable to live with competition from tin mines in Australia and Asia and the copper mines of Chile and America.

The South Crofty mine, near the village of Pool between Redruth and Camborne, had been active for some 400 years. In its heyday it was one of Cornwall's most productive mines, but in 1998, when the value of tin fell to uneconomic levels, Cornwall's last tin mine closed its gates, with little hope for a rebirth in the future.

But it now seems, against all expectations, that there could be a future for South Crofty after all. John Webster, Chief Operations Officer of Western United Mines, is sure that a combination of new technologies and a rise in the price of tin means that we may not have seen the last of Cornish metal mining. Just as the steam technology observed by Bradshaw drove the mining industry forward for the Victorians, new technology is doing the same today. John's team are using modern methods of X-ray analysis to test samples of rock for up to 60 different minerals. It's a hand-held device that can be used

LEFT: **CONDITIONS WERE NOTORIOUSLY GRIM FOR TIN MINERS IN CORNWALL.**

OVERLEAF: **RELICS FROM THE MINING ERA CLING TO THE CORNISH LANDSCAPE.**

in mine shafts as the cores of rock are removed, and it has already revealed South Crofty to be sufficiently rich in metals, including silver, zinc, tin and copper, to make its shafts profitable again. John hopes that within five years they will be extracting 750,000 tonnes of ore annually and, if things go well, the total will ultimately be double that. In South Crofty's heyday annual production was only 10,000 tonnes.

Visiting the mine and seeing the shafts drilled out by hand leaves you in no doubt about how dangerous working there in Bradshaw's day must have been. There were no fans and no ventilation. The average lifespan of a miner was under 40 years, with children working there from as young as eight. While vast fortunes were made for some entrepreneurial Victorians, the flipside of this was that the miners and their families remained desperately poor.

Our journey continued by stunning seascapes and some of Britain's most popular holiday resorts. It was very clear from reading Bradshaw that these had become destinations only since and as a result of the arrival of the railways. St Ives, for example, is synonymous today with its artists' community and holidays, but when the railway came in 1877 it was to a town dependent on fishing.

That industry was so important that an enormous pier and harbour had been built in the eighteenth century to handle the 400 or so fishing boats working out of the port. Whilst St Ives still boasts a working harbour, it's mainly pleasure boats that now head out to sea. Its streets and lanes are packed with tourists who have come here to enjoy the beautiful beaches and turquoise seas. The Great Western Railway was enormously instrumental in that change, even buying Treganna Castle, then the home of the Stephens family, high on the hill overlooking St Ives, and turning it into a luxury hotel to promote tourism and rail travel.

For the last leg of our journey, we headed to Penzance – as far west as it is possible to travel by train – completing a journey from Swindon that would have taken two days by horse and coach. The railway cut that time down to about six hours, and changed the people and the towns and villages along the route for ever. Even the tiny remote village of Penzance, at the very end of the Holiday Line, was soon turning its back on its traditional vegetable-growing businesses as it attracted holidaymakers in droves. Today 5 million tourists spend £1.5 billion in Cornwall to ensure its economic survival, in a success story that began 170 years ago with the birth of the modern railway.

THE AVERAGE LIFESPAN OF A MINER WAS UNDER 40 YEARS, WITH CHILDREN WORKING THERE FROM AS YOUNG AS EIGHT

BY 1930 THE VEGETABLE GROWING BUSINESS IN PENZANCE WAS SECOND STRING TO THE TOURISM INDUSTRY, WHICH BEGAN WITH THE ARRIVAL OF THE TRAIN.

GREAT WESTERN RAILWAY
PENZANCE
THE IDEAL HOLIDAY CENTRE

S.C.ROWLES

WARM IN WINTER   COOL IN SUMMER
GOOD FISHING HUNTING GOLF AND TENNIS
FOR FULL PARTICULARS AND GUIDE BOOK WRITE TOWN CLERK'S OFFICE PENZANCE

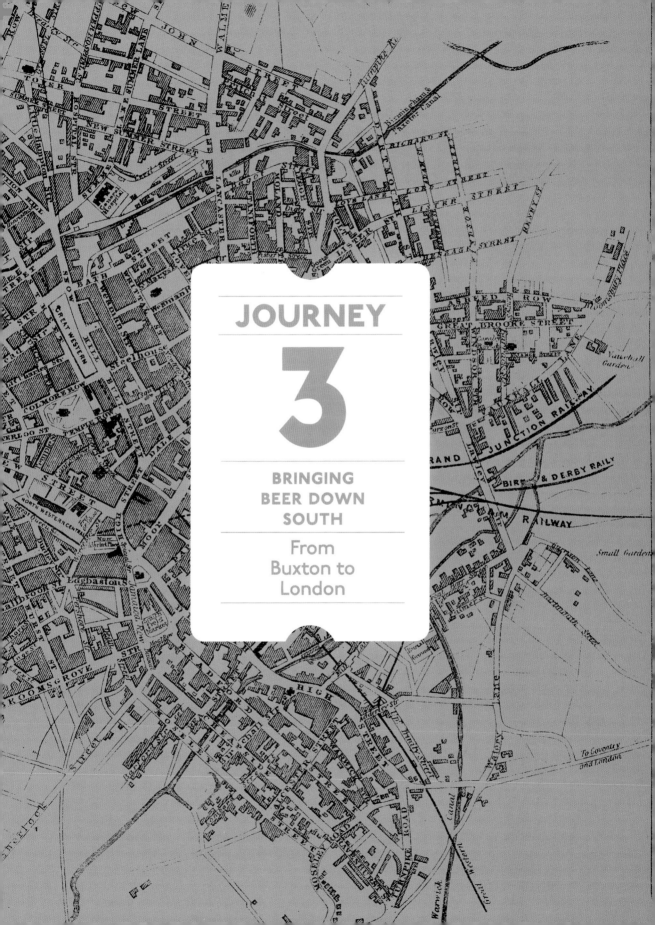

JOURNEY
3

BRINGING
BEER DOWN
SOUTH

From
Buxton to
London

These days, most of our freight is transported around the country by road, but in the nineteenth century it was the new railways that hauled goods most cheaply and swiftly, revolutionising industry in the process. Our next journey started in the open spaces of Derbyshire's Peak District on one of the earliest railway routes in England, built to transport freight from north to south. This gave towns at the heart of the Industrial Revolution an artery through which to whisk their goods into the nation's capital. It created booms in the towns through which it passed, and we wanted to retrace that route to see the impact the railways had on these towns and the people living and working in them.

Our first stop was Buxton. Just like Bath, it was founded by the Romans as a spa settlement and in the eighteenth century was an upmarket resort, to which the rich travelled from all over Britain to sample the waters. Even Buxton's architecture mimics its southern sister, with a crescent that Bradshaw describes as 'the principal building of Buxton … erected by the late Duke of Devonshire and has three storeys and extends for 257 feet'. Built in the 1780s, The Crescent in Buxton was a direct copy of Bath's Royal Crescent, designed by architect John Wood the Younger.

For the next 40 years the Duke of Devonshire led the building of new attractions, including the Opera House, the Pavilion Gardens and the Palace Hotel, all funded by the citizens of Buxton themselves. His vision paid off, never more so than after the arrival of the train in 1863, bringing thousands of paying customers. Buxton flourished as a resort, and the efforts of the incumbent Duke are still reaping rewards. Even though spas have fallen from grace, more than 100 years later these Victorian attractions are still drawing the crowds all year round.

One of Buxton's most magnificent buildings is the Duke of Devonshire's extraordinary stable block which today houses a university campus. According to Bradshaw, it was built at a cost of £120,000, which equates to about £5 million in today's money.

The building, unlike any other stables in the world, is dramatically capped by a huge dome. With a span of 145 feet this dome is larger than those of St Paul's Cathedral and the Pantheon and St Peter's Basilica in Rome. Today, thanks to modern technology, builders can mimic a dome like this or even much larger with little effort, but for its time it was simply breathtaking. It weighs a hefty 560 tonnes and cuts a dramatic

RIGHT: **AN EIGHTEENTH CENTURY OCTAGONAL STABLE BLOCK ROOF WAS REPLACED BY THE WORLD'S LARGEST FREESTANDING DOME AFTER THE BUILDING WAS CONVERTED TO A HOSPITAL IN THE NINETEENTH CENTURY.**

OVERLEAF: **DESIGNERS TOOK HEED OF THE 1879 TAY BRIDGE TRAGEDY, WHICH OCCURRED BECAUSE OF A FLAW WITH THE RIVETS, AND MODIFIED BLUEPRINTS OF THE DOME.**

shape in the Buxton skyline. The dome was finally completed in 1881, over 100 years after the rest of the building, and strangely it probably owes its survival to a distant train crash.

On Sunday, 28 December 1879, the Tay Bridge between Dundee and Wormit was being lashed by a violent storm. The bridge, designed by Sir Thomas Boucher, had opened only the previous summer and was the longest in the world. It also had unusually steep gradients.

No one knows just what happened that night, only that the bridge collapsed as a train crossed at its highest point. The alarm was raised by a signalman, who had waited in vain on the far side of the bridge for the passing of the train. When it failed to appear he went out to investigate, having to crawl on all fours at times to keep his balance in the high winds, and discovered the awful truth. Although there was a search of the Tay that night by steamers, not one of the 72 passengers or three crew was found alive. Indeed, many of the dead were lost to the river waters for ever. Among the victims was Boucher's son-in-law.

When engineers examined the wreckage, they discovered that it was insufficiently braced for high winter winds like those on the night of the disaster. Looking more closely, investigators realised that essential rivets had not been lined up properly with the receiving holes, with the result that rivets sheared off in the high winds and the bridge collapsed.

This shock revelation led to work on similar constructions being halted immediately. These included the Forth Bridge, also designed by Boucher, and the dome on the Duke's stables, designed by architect Robert Rippon Duke. Although the dome was designed to very tight tolerances, prior to the accident a degree of inaccuracy was regarded as acceptable. Where the rivets and holes didn't align, the practice of the time was to force them, which the Victorians called 'drifting' them in. Sometimes the rivets were even heated red hot in order to get them to fit, causing them to lose their shape and strength. Rippon Duke was so worried that he had all the dome's rivets removed and the holes redrilled to align properly, with the result that it stands as strong and proud today as it did when it was finished 130-odd years ago. It was a lesson quickly learnt and one that changed the way the Victorians built, helping them achieve many more incredible feats of engineering that we would pass as our journeys continued.

The lesson was further underlined, as if it were necessary, by the poet William McGonagall (1825–1902), widely regarded as the worst verse-

NO ONE KNOWS JUST WHAT HAPPENED THAT NIGHT, ONLY THAT THE BRIDGE COLLAPSED AS A TRAIN CROSSED AT ITS HIGHEST POINT

writer in British history. His poem about the Tay Bridge catastrophe became his most famous, and it ends like this:

I must now conclude my lay
By telling the world fearlessly without the least dismay,
That your central girders would not have given way,
At least many sensible men do say,
Had they been supported on each side with buttresses,
At least many sensible men confesses,
For the stronger we our houses do build,
The less chance we have of being killed.

Our next destination was Dark Peat in the heart of the Peak District National Park. In Bradshaw's day we would have been able to enjoy the natural beauty through the window of our train. 'The tourists will seldom see such glorious landscape from the window of a railway carriage,' the guidebook says. 'Whilst at one moment the bold hills rise up before us, behind us and on either side, the next a winding valley shows us a charming picture stretching away for miles.'

Although many of the lines that brought Victorian visitors into the National Park have long since gone, more than 10 million people still visit it each year. Britain's first National Park, created in 1951, is a major tourist attraction, reaching into five counties: Derbyshire, Cheshire, Staffordshire, Yorkshire and Greater Manchester.

Park Ranger Chris Dean has become something of an expert on the unforeseen cost of the railways which still haunts some of its most beautiful stretches today. Acid rain from coal-fired industries, including the railways, has caused immense damage to the soil. So much so that the vegetation can't grow back. Where the soil lies bare, the peat – which is a natural store for carbon dioxide from decaying leaf matter – is exposed to the elements and is gradually eroded. As this happens, CO_2 is released into the atmosphere, adding to global warming.

Chris is heading up a team of people dealing with this unfortunate legacy from the Industrial Revolution. They are trying to save the bog and reduce the CO_2 emissions by replanting 35 square kilometres of impaired landscape with vegetation that probably grew there in the first place. It is an enormous job. After treating the soil to reduce its acidity, they plan to plant half a million plants. The first phase, due to

BATHING POOL, NEW BATH HOTEL, MATLOCK BATH.   No.6463.

be completed by 2015, should protect the peat from erosion and even encourage more to be produced.

From the peaks we headed to Matlock Bath. Like Buxton, Matlock Bath had long attracted visitors to its thermal springs, and indeed our hotel, which is mentioned in Bradshaw, once boasted its own spa in the basement. When the railways arrived at nearby Ambergate Station in 1840, the town chose a very different route to ensure its survival. No opera house or extensive stables here. Despite being 90 miles from the coast, Matlock Bath decided to model itself along the lines of the big seaside resorts like Blackpool. Funfairs and fish and chip shops opened, along with the town's own annual illuminations, and they're still there today, alongside a more genteel café culture, attracting hundreds of thousands of visitors each year.

For Bradshaw, Matlock Bath conjured up something seemingly rather more international than Blackpool. Our guide calls it 'unquestionably the sweetest and most charming of the Derbyshire spas. It is at the bottom

ABOVE: **THE NEW BATH HOTEL IN MATLOCK BATH BOASTS A HEATED SWIMMING POOL FED BY NATURAL THERMAL SPRINGS, AND HAS BEEN A POPULAR STOP WITH TOURISTS SINCE THE START OF THE NINETEENTH CENTURY.**

OVERLEAF: **SMEDLEY SALESMEN STAND BY TO SELL KNITWEAR ACROSS THE BRITISH ISLES ON BEHALF OF A FIRM THAT CONTINUES TO ENDURE.**

of Matlock dale, a narrow defile, the rocky limestone sides of which are piled up in the manner of the undercliff in the Isle of Wight but covered with a profusion of pine, fir, yew, box and other hardy trees. The scenes through Matlock Bath are exquisitely beautiful and may be compared to a Switzerland in a nut shell.' Although the Swiss nut shell reference now seems odd, it was a well-used travel term in Victorian times, designed to attract tourists.

Our next stop was just nearby, at the sleepy station of Cromford. Today the two trains an hour which stop there belie its past, because in Bradshaw's day Cromford was at the heart of the Industrial Revolution. Bradshaw says simply, 'Here Arkwright built his first mill in 1771.' As Michael put it, 'Never was so much important history crammed into such a small half sentence as that.'

The cotton industry revolved around a network of cottage industries, with people spinning and weaving in their own houses. Entrepreneurial inventor Richard Arkwright (1732–92) brought them all together under one roof in a factory, where they used a mechanical water frame powered by the River Derwent. It was a brand new system, soon to be copied across Britain, and then the world.

Arkwright was born into a poor family but was taught to read and write by a cousin. He didn't turn his attention to the cotton industry until his once thriving wig-making business suffered when hairpieces went out of fashion. Although he is credited with the design of the water frame it was in reality a joint enterprise. In fact, many of his attempts to patent his 'inventions' were turned down in the courts following opposition from jealous rivals and aggrieved fellow inventors. His one undisputed skill was in organising industry, and his enterprises spread across the Midlands, northern England and Scotland. When he died he was a rich man. Arkwright's factory is now a museum, but nearby is another factory, opened 13 years later, which is now the oldest factory still working in the world. It was set up in 1784 by Peter Nightingale, a relative of Crimean nurse Florence Nightingale. He had helped finance Arkwright but decided on a new venture. His business partner was a man called John Smedley, whose family has been producing knitwear here ever since.

Today Smedley knitwear is exported to over 30 countries across the world. Smedley's claim to fame is that the long underpants called long johns were invented here, named after the man who started this factory more than 200 years ago.

FOR BRADSHAW, MATLOCK BATH CONJURED UP SOMETHING SEEMINGLY RATHER MORE INTERNATIONAL THAN BLACKPOOL

At the time the only transport available to take produce from the factories to buyers was horse and cart. The Cromford Canal was completed at extraordinary expense in 1794, but its limitations frustrated burgeoning trade. As early as 1825 Parliament agreed the construction of a wagon way entirely for freight between Cromford and Whalley Bridge – four years before Stephenson's Rocket was up and running. The rail track was completed in 1831, but it was a decade before locomotives were used, and it was another 14 years before passengers could travel on the line, which ultimately closed in 1967.

Fifteen miles further down the line we arrived in Derby, to stay in a hotel recommended by Bradshaw. In fact he didn't just recommend it, he raved about it. Normally, he does little more than list where to stay, but Derby's Midland Hotel gets a whole paragraph. 'It's gratifying to be able to refer to an establishment like this which deservedly enjoys the highest reputation. It possesses all the comforts of a home and there is no lack of spirit necessary to provide to the fullest extent everything which can recommend it to its patron. It is conducted in the most able manner by Mrs Chatfield and may claim to rank amongst the first Hotels in England. If further commendation were needed, we may add that the utmost politeness and economy may be anticipated.'

Opened in 1841, the Midland Hotel was the second railway hotel in England, and the first outside London. It was reserved exclusively for first-class passengers, and there was a tunnel linking it to the station so that luggage could be transferred directly to a traveller's room. Unfortunately you now have to carry your own bags, but today its doors are open no matter which class you travelled in.

Derby, like many places across Britain, was transformed into an industrial centre by the railways. They brought huge wealth and investment to the town. It was a time when great fortunes were made and accordingly beckoned in a golden age of philanthropy. In Derby, one notable act of benevolence was performed by the Strutt family, who gave the town a park. The Strutts had made their fortune in the cotton and silk trade and, in Bradshaw's words, created 'the new Arboretum of 16 acres laid out in 1840 by Loudon, given to the town by Joseph Strutt Esq., – a noble gift estimated at £10,000'.

As Arboricultural Consultant Jonathan Oakes explained to us, this arboretum lays claim to being the first purpose-built public park in England. Up until then, parks had been privately owned by the nobility,

but this was gifted to the council and run for the public. At first entry was free two days a week, and from 1882 this was extended so that there were no charges on any day. For the first time the working classes could enjoy these spaces, previously the province of the rich, and it became the model for public parks around the country.

As our journey continued through England's industrial heartland, we headed south towards the home of brewing, Burton-on-Trent. Its entry in Bradshaw states, 'Bass, Allsopp and Worthington are the chief ale kings here and acres covered with barrels and casks may be seen. Vast quantities of pale ale are exported to tropical climates and drunk by thirsty souls at home as a tonic.'

Before the railways arrived there were only 10 breweries in Burton, but that number quickly tripled. That's when 25 ale trains left Burton every day for destinations all over Britain. The railways were seen as so

BELOW: MILES OF TRACK WAS LAID INSIDE BREWERY YARDS TO BRING BARRELS FROM THE FACTORY TO THE NEAREST TRAIN STATION.

important to the industry that brewers started building their own tracks to connect with the main lines run by the railway companies.

Arriving in the town today, the first thing you see is that the barrels and casks have been replaced by enormous silver steel vats stretching into the horizon. It is still clearly a town dedicated to producing beer. Geoff Mumford and Bruce Wilkinson, who co-own the largest independent brewery in town, revealed to us why Burton became synonymous with great beer.

In Bradshaw's day Burton produced one in every four pints of beer drunk in England. This was just the start, though. By 1890 there were over 30 breweries exploiting the local climate, which was perfect for winter fermentation. According to Bradshaw, the other reason the area was so successful at brewing beer was the local water. Bruce concurred, explaining that the hardness of the water is essential to giving Burton beer its taste and its colour. Hard water makes it crisper, cleaner and clearer, making the perfect ale.

The purity of the water also meant that Burton beer could be transported all over the world, starting its journey from the breweries on what, according to Geoff and Bruce, was the biggest private rail network in the country.

There has, not surprisingly, been an environmental cost associated with Burton's beer production: centuries of intense brewing have scarred the landscape. Action to remedy this is in hand with the creation of the new National Forest, a colossal project spreading forestry into parts of Derbyshire, Leicestershire and Staffordshire. Not only are the scars of Buxton being masked, but also those of some defunct coal mines. Millions of trees are being planted which will eventually cover 200 square miles, with tree coverage already three times bigger than it was in 1991. As on Dark Peat, the damage done by our massive industrial expansion is slowly being put right.

Our journey took us next through Walsall and Birmingham, and down to Bournville, a place synonymous with chocolate. When the railway opened in 1874 the station was called Stirchley Street, and five years later the Cadbury family opened their factory there. They needed the railway to transport cocoa and sugar to the factory from the ports of London and Southampton, and to transport manufactured chocolate bars out. They also needed the canals to bring the milk in. Stirchley Street offered both. Before long three trains a day were leaving the factory, each pulling

BEFORE THE RAILWAYS ARRIVED THERE WERE ONLY 10 BREWERIES IN BURTON, BUT THAT NUMBER QUICKLY TRIPLED

60 cars full of chocolate. The Cadburys built six miles of their own internal railway and even ran company engines to take the chocolate to the main line.

As the business grew, brothers George and Richard Cadbury ploughed their profits back into the newly named village of Bournville. Like the best philanthropists of the time, they built new houses for their workers and designed a model community spread over about 1,000 acres. As Quakers, the brothers saw alcohol as the cause of the working class's social problems, so the amenities they laid on did not include pubs. Their argument was that if they provided good living conditions, job security and green spaces to exercise, the workers and their families would build a happy, healthy community. With Bourneville now acknowledged as one of the best places to live in Britain, that idea seems to be as valid today as it did over 100 years ago.

PREVIOUS PAGE: BROTHERS GEORGE AND RICHARD CADBURY CAME TO BOURNVILLE IN 1879 AND BUILT NOT ONLY A FACTORY BUT A RICH COMMUNITY TOO, IN KEEPING WITH THEIR QUAKER PRINCIPLES.

BELOW: LOCOMOTIVES LIKE THIS ONE HAULED CHOCOLATE BARS AFTER THEY WERE MADE AT THE END OF THE NINETEENTH CENTURY.

Our next stop was Coventry, which is now a very different city from the one Bradshaw visited. Its entry in his book runs to a highly respectable 74 lines, all extolling the city's virtues. 'The fine steeples of St Michael and the Trinity are the first to strike one in this old city which is the seat of the ribbon trade … many old-fashioned gable houses are to be found in the back streets … handsome buildings with noble halls.' Bradshaw's Coventry was essentially a rich medieval city. Built in the fourteenth century, it was once the fourth wealthiest city in England. But one night in 1940, when the Luftwaffe seemed poised to win the battle of the skies in the Second World War, it was all but wiped off the map.

Resident Judith Durant remembers that night well. Judith was 10 years old at the time and explained that, although it began as a normal night, the air-raid siren started just as they were getting ready for bed. She and her family hid in the air-raid shelter in their garden at the start of what turned out to be one of the worst bombing raids on Britain of the war. The operation called Moonlight Sonata saw 600 planes carpet-bomb Coventry for six hours. Five hundred people died as the city was blown to smithereens – targeted because of its great number of munitions and aircraft parts factories. Judith remembers being able to pick out the sounds of the German planes and the whistling of the bombs as they fell; the acrid taste of the dust, so thick you could chew it; enormous explosion after explosion. Judith's memories of that horrendous night will be with her for the rest of her life.

Coventry today is very different from the medieval city that was obliterated that night but, to Judith, every bit as beautiful. One building that encapsulates that rebirth is St Michael's Cathedral. Built to incorporate the ruins of the fourteenth-century cathedral, which apart from its spire was destroyed in the Blitz, it's a very clever piece of sixties architecture by Sir Basil Spence which gives reference and reverence to what was there before but looks forward as well as back.

The surprise about Coventry, though, is that despite the pummelling it received during the Blitz, parts of the medieval city survived. As you wander the streets, there are numerous hints of the Coventry Bradshaw must have seen, and it is certainly somewhere that should still be on the visitors' trail.

We now headed 60 miles south to overnight in Aylesbury, in Buckinghamshire, at the beautiful Hartwell House. It was here that Louis XVIII lived for six years with his family and 100 courtiers during

THE OPERATION CALLED MOONLIGHT SONATA SAW 600 PLANES CARPET-BOMB COVENTRY FOR SIX HOURS. FIVE HUNDRED PEOPLE DIED

his exile from France after the Revolution. Like many stately homes, Hartwell House is mentioned in Bradshaw, which provided the necessary information for Victorian travellers to arrange their own visit with the owners. These days the arrangements are rather easier to make. Like many other stately homes, it's now a hotel.

It's impossible to visit Aylesbury without seeking out its duck. In the eighteenth century Aylesbury duck was a delicacy for the rich. But the arrival of the railways in the 1860s changed that. According to the town's entry in Bradshaw it wasn't long before 'as many as three quarters of a million ducks [were being] sent to London from this part'.

A century ago 'duckers', the area's distinctive white ducks with flesh-coloured beaks, could be found all over the Vale of Aylesbury, but today there is only one farm in the county producing them. Richard Waller's family have been farming Aylesbury ducks since 1775, but it's altogether a much tougher business today.

Until recently, the majority of his ducks were sold directly into London's market at Smithfield – and were transported there by train. Now, owing to new EU regulations, Richard's ducks have again become a speciality exclusive to the area, and around 3,000 of them are sold each year to a local pub, The King's Head, in the village of Ivinghoe. Co-owner George De Maison cooks duck to a recipe perfected over a period of 50 years. For George, the key is using a range of fresh herbs and fruit from their garden, like bay leaves, sage and apples, to lock in and complement the duck's delicate taste.

Twenty-five miles further south, Watford gets a simple mention as 'a busy thriving and populous town consisting of only one street with minor ones diverging from it'. The reason we wanted to stop there wasn't to investigate how much it had grown and changed, which of course it has, but to highlight its role at a particular point in British history.

As early as 1938 the British government had formulated an evacuation plan that would swing into action in the event of war. In fact, the majority of children and mothers with babies from inner-city areas began the evacuation procedure before the declaration of hostilities. In September 1939, in just one week, 3,000 trains were used to evacuate 1.5 million children as part of Operation Pied Piper. By the end of the war, more than 3.5 million children had been relocated.

To reduce the pressure on overburdened stations in London, towns such as Watford were used as departure points. School-aged children

IN SEPTEMBER 1939, IN JUST ONE WEEK, 3,000 TRAINS WERE USED TO EVACUATE 1.5 MILLION CHILDREN AS PART OF OPERATION PIED PIPER

were unaccompanied, except for siblings, and had no idea where they were going to live. For some of the younger children it was an exciting day, as they were herded aboard the packed trains heading out to the country, though none of them had any idea of just how long they'd be away. Some managed only a few weeks, others stayed away from their home for years.

The success of the evacuation often depended on the kindness of the host families. Some of the pairings were disastrous. Country families sometimes complained of lice-ridden, ill-mannered children being foisted on them. Meanwhile some city children felt they were treated like slaves. But for others there was kindness and empathy – and a carefree childhood that would otherwise not have been available to them.

CHILDREN WEARING NAME TAGS AROUND THEIR NECKS ARRIVE IN WALES FROM BIRMINGHAM ON ONE OF MANY TRAINS USED IN OPERATION PIED PIPER, DESIGNED TO SAFEGUARD INNER CITY CHILDREN AND MOTHERS WITH BABIES BY MOVING THEM TO THE COUNTRYSIDE BEFORE THE OUTBREAK OF THE SECOND WORLD WAR.

As Britain became a safer place, children went back to their homes, often meeting a father they didn't remember and a mother they might have seen occasionally but whose wartime experience was completely different from their own. It's impossible to say how many lives were saved by the railways transporting children to safety, but it must have been thousands.

The last stage of the journey took us into London's St Pancras station, gateway to what in Bradshaw's time was the most powerful city in the world, at the heart of an ever-expanding empire. St Pancras is described by Bradshaw as 'the vast and magnificent terminus of the Midland Company eclipsing every other, having a roof 240 feet in span and 150 feet high and faced by a splendid hotel'.

Such was the rivalry between the different railway companies that when St Pancras was built in 1868, with its spires and mock-Gothic style, it was designed entirely to overshadow its neighbour King's Cross, the terminus for the Great Northern Railway, which had been built 16 years earlier. This southern terminus for the Midland main line was not only bigger and bolder than King's Cross, it was the largest enclosed space in the world. Like many London termini, it was also designed around what the railway was transporting, which was beer from Burton. The station was built on 800 columns, each spaced so that barrels could be stored underneath.

Looking at St Pancras today in all its restored glory and with its shiny glass extension stretching the quarter-mile length of a Eurostar train, it is difficult to believe that once, back in the 1960s, this magnificent station was scheduled for demolition. Thanks to a campaign led by the poet John Betjeman it was saved – just ten days before the wrecking balls were due to begin their work – and the station and hotel were both made listed buildings.

The redevelopment of the station cost £800 million, and now, after 75 years of neglect, the hotel is undergoing its own £170 million facelift. Royden Stock, responsible for looking after the hotel before work started, became something of an expert on the building.

Royden revealed to us how the drawings for the hotel had been produced by renowned architect George Gilbert Scott in just three weeks. His design won a competition that attracted 11 distinguished entrants – although his was by far the most expensive. Like all railway companies, the Midland Railway wanted to show off by building the most

impressive railway hotel in the country, to be called the Midland Grand. Scott's extravagant Gothic style seemed perfect.

Today, as the restoration work continues, more of the original building is uncovered from behind false walls and ceilings. The most impressive feature of all, though, is a stunning cantilevered staircase that seems to float in mid-air as it leads up towards a ceiling painted with stars.

When it opened in 1873, the hotel catered for the wealthiest travellers. Its rooms were amongst the most expensive in London, costing 14 shillings a night. Time caught up, though, and the lack of en suite bathrooms eventually drove guests to other, newer hotels. Hopefully, when its 245 rooms open again for business in 2011, the guests will return.

People often wonder why St Pancras, King's Cross and Euston were all built so close to one another. The reason is that in 1846 Parliament had decreed that all new stations in London had to be built on the edge of the city. A box was drawn around the city's heart, protecting it from railway development. It reflected the views of a powerful lobby that wanted to protect the capital's historic buildings from 'railway vandalism'. It was time, that lobby decided, to stop the railway marching forward at the expense of everything in its path. The result gave the railway companies the perfect opportunity to build ever grander stations. It also led to a revolutionary new transport system to fill in the gaps, called the London Underground.

The world's first underground line, the Metropolitan, was built in 1863 and ran between Paddington and Farringdon, bringing passengers from the railway termini and commuters into the city. Two special trains were run each day for the poorest workers, on which tickets cost only a third of the normal fare. When the line was built, the carriages were pulled by steam trains, so the tunnels had to have openings allowing steam to escape.

For the final part of our journey, we left the trains behind and followed in Bradshaw's footsteps, taking his walking tour of the capital that starts with St Paul's Cathedral, one of London's most impressive buildings and considered by many to be Sir Christopher Wren's masterpiece.

The original cathedral was destroyed in the Great Fire of London in 1666. It fell to Christopher Wren, Commissioner for Rebuilding the City of London, to design and build a replacement, one of 52 churches he was charged with creating. It took Wren 10 years and a number of attempts to come up with the successful design, based on

WREN STARTED WORKING ON ST PAUL'S WHEN HE WAS IN HIS THIRTIES AND WAS 78 BY THE TIME IT WAS FINISHED

the Latin cross and incorporating a large dome. Wren started working on St Paul's when he was in his thirties and was 78 by the time it was finished, but there is no denying it was certainly well worth the wait. As Bradshaw states, 'It's extreme beauty and colossal proportions are worthy of the highest admiration.' Even today, St Paul's Cathedral has a dramatic and romantic impact on the city skyline.

'The most conspicuous object is the river,' says Bradshaw, 'winding its way like a huge artery, beautiful and picturesque bridges spanning the stream.' He recommends standing in the middle of Waterloo Bridge, from where, today as then, you can see St Paul's Cathedral, Somerset House and the Houses of Parliament. Despite 150 years of development, those three buildings still rate amongst the finest the city has to offer.

IN 1862 SELECTED DIGNITARIES TRIALLED THE METROPOLITAN LINE, TRAVELLING AT CLOSE QUARTERS ABOARD SMITH & KNIGHT WAGONS INTO TUNNELS THAT WOULD QUICKLY FILL WITH STEAM AND SOOT.

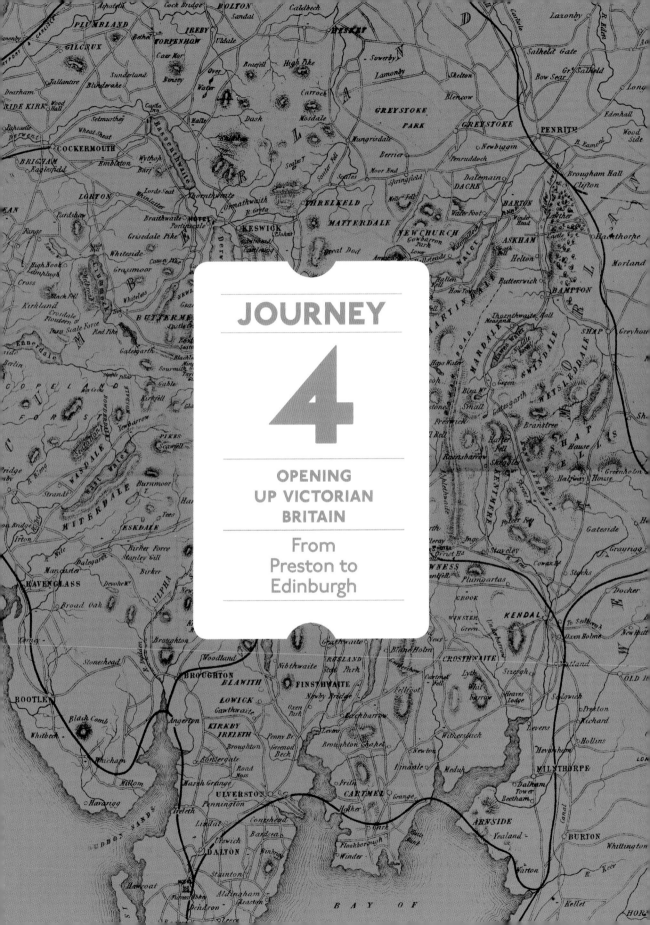

JOURNEY

4

OPENING
UP VICTORIAN
BRITAIN

From
Preston to
Edinburgh

Our next journey took us north on the first rail link between England and Scotland. Until the railways came, the communities of north-west England were almost impenetrable, as the hilly terrain kept road building to a minimum. For better or worse, this route helped open up remote areas of Britain, notably the Lake District and the Yorkshire Dales.

Our first stop was Preston, which is described by Bradshaw as 'One of the principal manufacturing towns of the country. There are upwards of 50 cotton mills in this town.' He goes on to say: 'The commercial annals of this town are memorable for two long continued disputes between the employers and employed.'

Presumably he is alluding to the 1842 riot by cotton workers protesting about the conditions in the mills that ended in four deaths after armed troops opened fire. Twelve years later there was a strike by cotton workers that lasted for more than 25 weeks. Clearly Preston was notorious for its poor industrial relations record.

In Bradshaw's day, Preston's residents also had a reputation for hard drinking, which may explain why it became the home of the British Temperance Movement in 1832, founded by former weaver and cheese entrepreneur Joseph Livesey (1794–1884). The Liverpool-born Livesey believed that alcohol was the root of all social ills, seeing it as a cause rather than a symptom of the abject poverty suffered throughout industrial heartlands.

Cheap travel helped the teetotal movement to mushroom, as trains transported hundreds and eventually tens of thousands of people to Temperance rallies to hear the charismatic Livesey speak. Although Britain stopped short of outright prohibition of alcohol, as was introduced throughout the United States in the early twentieth century, it was estimated that during Livesey's day one in 10 people chose to abstain from drink, a figure that peaked during the First World War when new licensing laws reduced pub opening times.

The next part of our journey took us 20 miles west from Temperance Preston to the coast, and we travelled on the *Blackpool Belle*, better known to countless young lovers as the passion wagon. Blackpool and its bright lights was such a popular destination with young people that the railways ran special services every weekend from other northern towns, operating late into the night.

Norman and Norma Watkins began their romance on the *Blackpool Belle* in the 1950s. Norman remembers how, at the end of a night as the trains slipped out of Blackpool station, the light bulbs would be unscrewed to cast the carriages into a romantic blackout. There was darkness until the train approached their home town of Chorley, when all the light fitments would be returned to their rightful places.

The Blackpool of today is not so different from the one Norman and Norma remember. In Bradshaw's day, however, it was just starting life as a seaside resort and looked nothing like the Las Vegas of Lancashire that it is now. The guidebook describes it as a 'pretty bathing place on the Irish Sea … much frequented by visitors … in 1863 a new pier was opened which forms a most pleasant promenade'.

Bradshaw's Blackpool had a permanent population of about 3,500, but that was soon to change. With the railways that reached Blackpool in 1846 came thousands of holidaymakers, and within a matter of a few years, theatres, the winter gardens and three piers had been built. In 1879 almost 80,000 people came to see the first illuminations. They were marketed as 'artificial sunlight' and have been attracting visitors ever since.

In 1894 another great Blackpool attraction opened, at a cost of £42,000. Early visitors to Blackpool Tower, a half-sized replica of the Eiffel Tower in Paris, were charged sixpence to travel more than 500 feet to the top. Terrifyingly, the last stretches had to be done on ladders. Today the maintenance team, known as stick men, still use ladders daily. From the top it is possible on a clear day to see a panorama that encompasses swathes of Lancashire, the Isle of Man, North Wales and the lower ground of Cumbria. Even at today's peak summer prices it's still well worth the entry fee.

From Blackpool we headed north on another branch line towards Morecambe Bay and a station with the most splendid view out across the sands. In the nineteenth century Morecambe Bay was an isolated area comprising small shellfishing villages. As the trains made it more accessible, the fresh cockles, prawns, shrimps and lobsters were soon being whisked to Manchester fish market.

Bradshaw is very clear about the dangers of the bay: 'Morecambe is a fine sheet of water, eight or 10 miles wide, when the tide is up: but at low tide its quick sands are extremely treacherous and must on no account be crossed without the guide who is paid by Government and carries you over in a cart.'

Incredibly, 160 years on, there is still an official guide, paid by the state, who lives near the remote station of Kent's Bank watching over the enormous mudflats. Cedric Robinson is the current incumbent of a job that dates back to the sixteenth century and is held for life. It became a royal appointment after scores of lives were lost at a time when local people had no choice but to brave the ever-changing sands on foot or by cart. For the annual salary of £15 and the cottage he lives in, every fortnight or so Cedric conducts tours across the treacherous sands for walkers, sometimes taking more than 100 people, and marking the route with laurel branches.

Morecambe Bay hit the news in 2004 when at least 21 Chinese cockle pickers tragically drowned in a racing tide. Cedric knows well that the 200 square miles of sands are perpetually shifting and are licked by a tide that comes in so quickly that you can't outrun it. The tide never tires, Cedric warns. There's also the threat of quicksand, which he has seen swallow tractors and horses. The trick, he says, is not to stop moving and, if you get into trouble, to lie on the sands and roll rather than walk.

The next leg of our journey took us on a detour inland to Settle, starting point of the famous line to Carlisle via Ribblehead, Dent and Garsdale. This line hadn't even been built when our guidebook was written, but it was supposed to be one of the prettiest rail journeys in Britain, scything through northern Britain's limestone and black marble landscape. It was also a journey that we could only take because in 1989 Michael convinced Prime Minister Margaret Thatcher not to approve its closure. At the time Settle was at the centre of a campaign to save the threatened line. Now Michael was returning for the first time in 20 years.

This spectacular Midland Railway line was opened in 1876. Stretching 72 miles, and passing nine tiny stations and through some of the most rugged countryside in Britain, it is a magnificent piece of railway architecture with stunning viaducts and bridges.

It is a pleasure to travel this way through the Yorkshire Dales but, passing through its tunnels and over its viaducts, one wonders how the Victorians ever came to build it. The reason was that the Midland Railway Company was driven by the desire to have a high-speed line that would compete successfully with its rivals. The company's solution was to build straight across the Dales, with little thought for some of the details, such as the safety of construction workers. It took 6,000 men six years, working in miserable conditions, to complete the job.

RIGHT: **GUIDED TOURS FOR HUNDREDS OF WALKERS ARE CONDUCTED OVER THE HAZARDOUS SANDS OF MORECAMBE BAY.**

OVERLEAF: **THE BUILDING OF THE STRIKING RIBBLEHEAD VIADUCT CAUSED MISERY FOR HUNDREDS OF LABOURERS WHO RISKED DISEASE, STARVATION AND EXPOSURE TO COMPLETE THE JOB.**

A hundred years later, in the early 1980s, the Settle & Carlisle line was carrying just a few trains each day; passenger numbers were low; stations along the way had already closed and the route was losing money. What's more, the line was falling into disrepair and British Rail argued that it would now cost too much to maintain. Crucially, the magnificent Ribblehead Viaduct was in danger of crumbling, and British Rail estimated it would cost between £7 and £9 million to repair. It was a major plank in their argument for closing the line.

Tony Feschini, a former British Rail engineer, was employed to inspect the structure. After carrying out trial repairs, Tony was convinced that the viaduct could be saved for a fraction of the price, estimating it would only cost between £2,750,000 and £3,250,000.

Still British Rail mooted closure, but the idea was met with a storm of protest and a lively six-year campaign got underway to increase the numbers using the line, so making it more profitable.

As the crusade generated publicity, more people became rail travellers and the case for keeping it open strengthened. By the time a decision was needed some 300,000 people were buying tickets annually. As Transport Minister, Michael was able to show Margaret Thatcher that it was not only an important line in terms of history and heritage, but also a viable economic proposition. She agreed and, in April 1989, British Rail's request for closure was turned down. Since then, yet more people have started using the line and it now carries upwards of 750,000 passengers a year. For Michael, keeping the line open remains the achievement that he is most proud of from his time in Government.

Two thousand men, a third of the workforce for the whole line, took four years to complete the enormous structure at Ribblehead, with its 24 arches spanning 440 yards across the valley. The tops of the arches are 104 feet from the valley bottom and, despite some limestone cladding, the viaduct is vulnerable to some of England's worst weather.

For the repairing of the Ribblehead Viaduct modern machinery was used. Back in 1869, when work on the viaduct began, the technology available didn't extend much beyond pickaxes and dynamite. The navvies who built it travelled with their families, and ill-equipped shanty towns appeared along the route.

Many lost their lives to smallpox and starvation. At the tiny church of St Leonard's in the hamlet of Chapel-le-Dale, historian Gerald

FOR MICHAEL, KEEPING THE LINE OPEN REMAINS THE ACHIEVEMENT THAT HE IS MOST PROUD OF FROM HIS TIME IN GOVERNMENT

ABOVE: AS THE HIGHEST STATION
IN ENGLAND, DENT IS SUBJECT
TO CATASTROPHIC SNOWFALL.
AFTER A BLIZZARD IN 1947 ONE
LINE WAS CLEARED SO THE
SERVICE COULD CONTINUE.

OVERLEAF: BOAT TRAVEL IS
THE OBVIOUS OPTION IN THE
LAKE DISTRICT.

Tyler revealed that 201 people were buried there within five years and, of those, 110 were aged below 13. So many people lost their lives that the railway company paid for the graveyard to be extended. Even that wasn't enough and, at the far end of the graveyard, dozens of bodies lie in unmarked graves.

Even when the railway was complete, there was the job of keeping it open in severe weather. At Dent, which has the highest station in England at 1,150 feet above sea level, maintaining the line proved almost as difficult as building it. Fifteen men lived beside Dent station in winter, with the job of trying to keep the line free from snow. Workers came for six weeks at a time, isolated and packed like sardines into the small snow huts built in 1885.

The huts are still there today, but have been converted into luxury accommodation for tourists, reflecting the evolving fortunes linked to the railway. Dent station – some distance from the village – was closed in 1970. However, the campaign to keep the line open re-ignited the

tourist trade. With more frequent trains, Dent and other stations re-opened in 1986 and are thriving today.

After the Settle to Carlisle detour, we rejoined the West Coast Main Line heading into the Lake District. Bradshaw was so enamoured of the area that he suggested a variety of different tours according to how much time one had.

In the early nineteenth century poets including William Wordsworth (1770–1850) and Samuel Coleridge (1772–1834) lived in the Lake District and made it popular amongst the educated elite through their writings. Wordsworth, however, didn't welcome tourists to his paradise, believing the poor and ill-educated would not benefit 'mentally or morally' from a visit. So the arrival of the railways in 1847 was hugely controversial among those like him who wanted to maintain the area's isolation. And there's no doubt the onslaught of visitors was in some ways costly.

For the traveller arriving by train Bradshaw promised an immediate delight: 'From Windermere station the lake appears in view, with its beautiful islands and grassy well wooded fells around its borders.' These days it has become so built up that you struggle to even get a glimpse of the lake. To attract more visitors the railway company had changed the name of the station from Birthwaite to Windermere, and the station is still there – only these days it houses a supermarket.

Bradshaw next suggests a trip out on to the lake, and that at least is one of the original delights still available to trippers. All but gone are the days when you could dip a kettle into crystal-clear lake waters to brew a cuppa. One of the major downsides of mass tourism has been the rising levels of pollution in the lake, caused by sewage overflow. Things are better at the north end, where the lake is fed by freshwater tributaries.

John Pinder, from the Environment Agency, monitors the water quality, particularly the level of phosphates found in sewage and fertilisers that stimulate massive growths of algae. As the algae blooms die, they take oxygen out of the water, reducing its quality. For the last two years John has been working with the whole community on trying to clean up the lakes.

Although it was the trains that brought the huge numbers of people to the lakes, all armed with their Bradshaw, he wasn't the first person to promote the area. Ironically, the reluctant Wordsworth – who was Poet Laureate from 1843 and a vigorous campaigner against the railways –

ALL BUT GONE ARE THE DAYS WHEN YOU COULD DIP A KETTLE INTO CRYSTAL CLEAR LAKE WATERS TO BREW A CUPPA

GRAZING IN THE SHADOW OF A LAKELAND FELL, HERDWICK SHEEP ARE NATIVE TO CUMBRIA WHERE THEY THRIVE ON RICH GRASSLANDS WATERED BY FREQUENT RAIN.

has inadvertently done more to attract visitors than anyone else. Now his grave, in St Oswald's Church at Grasmere, is a tourist attraction in its own right.

There was another, less obvious spin-off from the arrival of the railways. Farms that used to supply only their local markets suddenly became national enterprises as their produce was whisked away by rail. In the nineteenth century railway companies not only transported animals but owned the markets where the cattle and farm produce were sold.

Peter Gott's family has been farming Herdwick sheep, which are native to Cumbria, since the seventeenth century. As demand for fresh food grew, farms became bigger, and by the middle of the twentieth century the land was being farmed on an industrial scale. But farmers like Peter became conscious of having to compromise on quality. Now he is part of the slow food movement, which advocates small-scale, sustainable farming involving fewer food miles and resulting in more flavour on the plate.

THE BORDER BETWEEN ENGLAND AND SCOTLAND DID NOT HOLD FIRM UNTIL AFTER THE BATTLE OF CULLODEN WHEN THE LARGELY SCOTTISH FORCE LED BY BONNIE PRINCE CHARLIE WAS SLAIN.

Nowhere outside the Lake District will you find this type of sheep, with its own distinct flavour, raised on old-fashioned herbage in the fells. It is nonetheless very tough to run a small farm, so Peter has had to diversify to keep afloat, producing pies and 30 varieties of his own speciality sausages.

From the lakes, our journey took us further north via Penrith into the Border country and to Carlisle. When the railways arrived in 1847, passengers had to change trains there, making Carlisle one of the busiest stations in the country. Most, though, were simply passing through and never got to see the town itself. Those who did would have been struck by its degree of fortification.

Perhaps it's not surprising. The English and Scots battled for control of Carlisle and its castle for more than 700 years, until the last Scottish uprising led by Bonnie Prince Charlie came to an end at the Battle of Culloden in 1745. But that still left the marauding moss troopers, or Border reivers as they're known locally, for Carlisle to contend with.

Artist Gordon Young is a descendant of this forgotten people. He explained how, 400 years ago, the frontier between the English and Scots shifted constantly. Marching armies from north and south repeatedly laid waste to the area, making it difficult to govern. And the reivers operated within this no man's land, taking full advantage of its lawless state. They were skilled rustlers but often ended up taking anything they could carry. In 1525, in an attempt to bring the troublesome reivers to heel, the Archbishop of Glasgow laid a 1,069-word curse on them, which was read out by priests in every parish.

In those days men gave their allegiance not to their country but to their clan or family. And it wasn't just a case of the Scots raiding the English and vice versa. Feuding families brought bitter disputes to the same neighbourhood. Gordon explained that emerging from this tough, bloody place were dynasties whose names are now known the world over, including Irvine, Carmichael, Johnston, Dixon and Young. There have even been some famous reiver sons such as Richard Nixon and Neil Armstrong.

From Carlisle, the train crossed the River Eden and then the Esk on its way north-west to the Scottish border and, just beyond it, one of Scotland's most famous towns – Gretna Green. Even in Bradshaw's day Gretna was known for one thing. 'It has for more than 80 years been the place of celebration of marriages of fugitive lovers from England.'

'IT HAS FOR MORE THAN 80 YEARS BEEN THE PLACE OF CELEBRATION OF MARRIAGES OF FUGITIVE LOVERS FROM ENGLAND'

The marriage laws in Scotland have always been more liberal than those in England and, when the railways reached Gretna in 1848, the steady stream of runaway lovers turned into a flood. According to Bradshaw, more than 300 marriages took place annually here and in the neighbouring village of Springfield, and the fees varied from 1 to 40 guineas.

But Bradshaw was convinced the practice was coming to an end. 'An Act of Parliament has since come into operation which requires a residence in Scotland of too long a duration to suit the purpose of fugitive lovers and the blacksmith of Gretna Green, like Othello, will now find his "occupation gone".'

Of course, marriage is still big business for Gretna Green, with more than 5,000 couples a year tying the knot there. That's one in six of all weddings in Scotland, and a quick wander around the town makes it clear that it's something that keeps many people in work.

What's less well known about Gretna is that just a few miles down the track are the remains of a secret factory that played a crucial role in the First World War. No one had ever filmed before at what is still an MoD site. Inside we discovered a strange landscape of bunkers and hills built specifically to handle high explosives that were made and stored here.

Today David Watt manages the munitions factory, which came into existence after the Battle of Loos in 1915, when the army found itself critically low on shells. So low, David said, that Britain might have lost the war. As a result this huge facility covering hundreds of acres was built. Shells were made and packed round the clock by women mixing 'Devil's Porridge' – a paste of nitroglycerine and gun cotton that went inside armaments. At its peak the factory was producing 800 tons of it a week. Good wages were paid to the women workers, many drawn from domestic service, but there were multiple hazards from fire, explosions and the noxious chemicals being used. The women were uniformed and wore some protective clothing. The factory even had its own internal railway to carry the munitions around the vast site and the workers from their army-style barracks.

Our next train was substantially larger than the narrow-gauge MoD railway and whisked us swiftly past Lockerbie, Moffat and Lanark towards Glasgow. Even in Bradshaw's day Glasgow was famous for its rivalry with Edinburgh. 'The ancient city of Glasgow,' he asserts, 'is one of the most splendid in Europe and is not surpassed for beauty of

INSIDE WE DISCOVERED A STRANGE LANDSCAPE OF BUNKERS AND HILLS BUILT SPECIFICALLY TO HANDLE HIGH EXPLOSIVES

architecture in its public and private buildings, the length, breadth and elegance of its streets, squares and crescents, even by Edinburgh itself.'

Today the city centre still attracts the tourists, but Bradshaw used to encourage them to venture further afield. 'Glasgow itself is supposed to offer few attractions to the tourist but this is a mistake. Old Glasgow with all its dirt and discomfort … is well worth a visit.' In a Victorian version of poverty tourism, he directed them to Calton, which was and is one of the city's most deprived areas.

In the nineteenth and early twentieth centuries, Calton – the weavers' quarter – was a wretched place. Cholera was a permanent threat, killing thousands every year. Several families were crammed into each small house. Today living conditions are better, but the area still has troubling social problems, including sectarianism rooted in Irish immigration during past centuries. Despite attempts to improve life here, such as the mass rebuilding of the 1980s, the life expectancy for an adult male is 55, decades below the national average.

DURING THE FIRST WORLD WAR WOMEN MUNITIONS WORKERS PRODUCED SHELLS AND OTHER ARMAMENTS AT GRETNA'S SECRET BASE.

LEFT: **SOLID OAK POLES ARE AN ARCHITECTURAL FEATURE OF THE NEW SCOTTISH PARLIAMENT BUILDING AT HOLYROOD.**

OVERLEAF: **THE FORTH BRIDGE UNDER CONSTRUCTION, WITH ITS DISTINCTIVE DIAMONDS STANDING IN SPLENDID ISOLATION.**

Elsewhere the city is enjoying a renaissance. Sleek contemporary museums line the old dock. Grand Victorian buildings in the West End have been restored. Glasgow is a city that retains its civic pride, and that's reflected in how it has become a top tourist destination, welcoming 4 million people each year.

On the 45-mile journey towards Edinburgh through the Clyde Valley the scenery is less dramatic than that of Highland Scotland, but the farms are more abundant. Bradshaw was enthusiastic: 'A district of country rich in mineral wealth, beautiful scenery, celebrated far and near as the Orchard of Scotland and famous for its fine fruit.'

Scotland's cooler weather meant that fruit ripened there long after the season had finished further south. As the railways extended, there was wide demand for fruit from the lush orchards of the Clyde Valley. Picking was organised around the clock and the fruit would be sent on the early freight trains. Today, many of the orchards are neglected and overgrown, but there is a small group of people trying to revive the area's heritage varieties that might otherwise disappear.

It is difficult to see Clyde Valley orchards ever approaching their Victorian peak again, but they are beginning to rekindle their fortunes, offering fruit and juice which growers sell locally.

Soon we are at Scotland's grand capital, Edinburgh. The railway snakes through a ravine to Waverley station, with Edinburgh Castle looming above on an enormous rock that dominates the city.

Among its other claims to fame, Edinburgh boasts the biggest lost property office in Britain, receiving about 600 items a year. As well as the ordinary bags and umbrellas, people lose some bizarre items. Everything from a suitcase containing an octopus to a bag full of live eels has turned up on the shelves of lost property at Edinburgh station.

Edinburgh's first railway was not the line to Glasgow, surprisingly, but went instead to Dalkeith, about five miles to the south-east. On this line, which passed round the edge of Holyrood Park, the trains were horse-drawn, except for a steep incline inside a tunnel, where a stationary steam engine was used to haul the carriages.

In Bradshaw's description Edinburgh is labelled, not for the first time, a 'modern Athens'. But the book also mentions something altogether more mysterious. Bradshaw insists that, opposite the seventeenth-century Tron Kirk, lies a cellar where the momentous Treaty of the Union was signed. This key event, which in 1707 joined England and Scotland together

under one parliament, seemed to have taken place in what is now the ladies' loo in an Italian restaurant. The restaurant gets a steady flow of visitors asking the same question about the political history of the toilets, though probably not all thanks to a 170-year-old guidebook.

Dr John Young from Strathclyde University explained that Scottish politicians who wanted a union with England were jostled and attacked on a regular basis, so there was a possibility that Unionist politicians sought refuge in the cellars of what was then a house. Rumours soon circulated about the surreptitious signing of the treaty in this cellar, and these were repeated in various publications, including Bradshaw's, over the next 50 years. The truth, unfortunately, is far less compelling. The treaty was in fact ratified in the old Scottish parliament buildings on Parliament Square – and nowhere near the Bella Pasta ladies' loo.

The last part of the journey was a sentimental trip for Michael, following a route he had taken many times with his family that used to take him across the Firth of Forth. This was such an exciting journey for Michael and his brothers as children that they couldn't sleep as they waited in anticipation to cross the magnificent Forth Bridge.

As a boy in the 1880s, Michael's grandfather had rowed out to watch the building of this striking piece of engineering, Britain's first major structure in steel. The bridge took seven years to build and cost 75 lives. A mighty 55,000 tons of steel were used to build the bridge, and 8 million rivets bolted the sections together as it was assembled part by part before its completion in 1890.

It looks every bit as magnificent 120 years on. George Bradshaw didn't live long enough to see it built, but if he had he would have marvelled at the achievement.

Michael has seen the bridge from many angles, but one commanding view he had not enjoyed until now was from its very top. Ian Heigh, the man in charge of repairing and repainting the bridge, took Michael 367 feet above water level to look out from the top of one of the bridge's three great diamonds.

Ian is currently overseeing the massive job of blasting off all the old paint added to the bridge during its lifetime – the first time it's ever been done. The bridge will then be recoated using a modern paint with a much longer life. Afterwards it could be as long as 40 years before a team needs once again to perform the legendary, Herculean task of 'painting the Forth Bridge'.

MICHAEL PORTILLO ASCENDED THE FORTH BRIDGE TO TAKE ON A NEW PERSPECTIVE OF THE FAMOUS STEEL STRUCTURE.

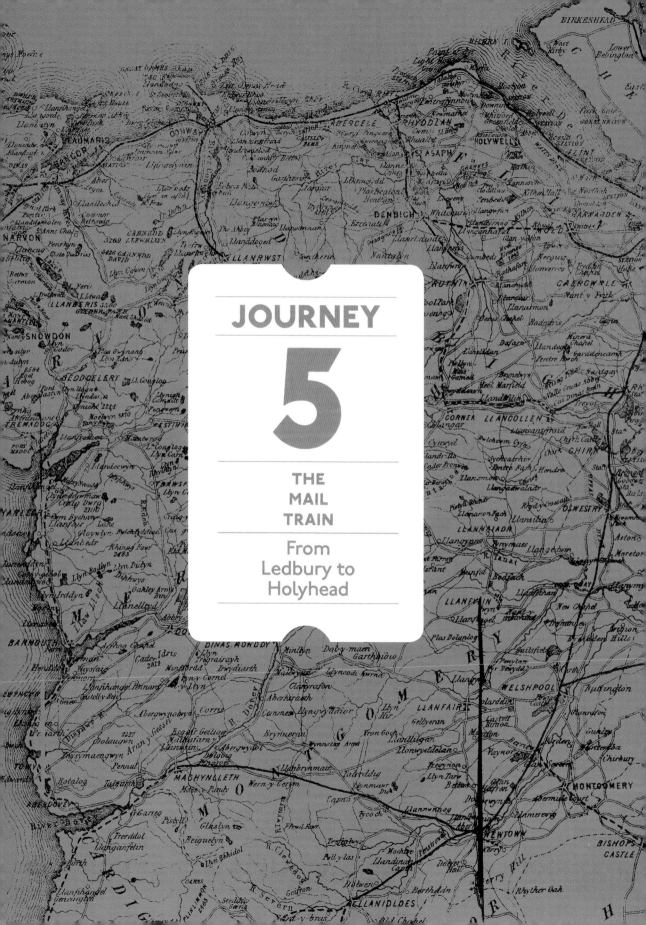

JOURNEY

5

THE
MAIL
TRAIN

From
Ledbury to
Holyhead

Many of the lines we travel on today were built to carry goods around the country, but the one heading out to Holyhead on the northern tip of Wales was created for a special kind of freight. It was to carry the Irish mail. After the Acts of Union in 1800, which created the United Kingdom, it was incumbent on the British government to improve links with Ireland. The shortest sea crossing is between Holyhead, on the island of Anglesey, and Dublin. Clearly, Holyhead would be a pivotal part of any plans. Initially Thomas Telford (1757–1834) came to the rescue with the construction of the post road from London to the port there.

Despite the opening in 1826 of Telford's wrought-iron and stone suspension bridge linking Anglesey with mainland Britain, across the treacherous Menai Strait, the journey remained slow going. There was a golden opportunity here for the railway to prove its worth. The Chester to Holyhead line, built by Robert Stephenson to his father George's coast-hugging design, began construction on 1 March 1845. Chester station opened on 1 August 1848, the same day the first mail train reached Holyhead. The new and lofty Britannia Bridge took trains across the water to Anglesey. A journey that previously would have taken more than a day was cut to a matter of hours.

However, the outlook was not as rosy as the railway operators had hoped. The Chester to Holyhead Railway Company invested heavily in the route in anticipation of also winning the mail shipping contract to Dublin, but ultimately that went instead to the City of Dublin Steam Packet Company. Consequently the company struggled to get on a forward foot and was duly taken over by the London & North Western Railway Company in 1859.

Although the line was built to carry the mail, this historic railway brought change to all kinds of businesses along the route. We would be visiting some of them, but we decided to begin our journey further south, in the undulating countryside of Herefordshire, before joining the historic mail route in Cheshire.

Our starting point was Ledbury, a picturesque market town to the west of the Malvern Hills. Ledbury is best known today for its fine black and white timber-framed buildings, but Bradshaw describes it as a place 'remarkable for its manufacture of rope, twine and also cider and perry'. Perry is an alcoholic drink similar to cider but made from pears. One of the oldest commercial perry producers is still in operation just outside town.

Helen Thomas's family have been making perry for 170 years and now sell a staggering 28 million pints per year. It was originally made for private consumption – like cider, it was traditionally part of labourers' wages in rural areas – though some was sold at the farm gate. Helen's great-grandfather, Henry Weston, began making it on a larger scale at his farm in Much Marcle, having noticed the growing popularity of drinks imported from across the British Empire.

When the railways came, Henry realised the potential for distributing his perry and started to produce it commercially. As the train network expanded through Herefordshire, Henry's business grew and he began processing and bottling other growers' pears. It wasn't long before Weston's perry was being sold all over the country.

Perry pears aren't the same as pears grown for eating. Furthermore each variety of perry pear has a different flavour. At Weston's they are using the same varieties – and often from the same trees – as Helen's great-grandfather in the late nineteenth century.

Another reason for the distinctive taste of Weston's perry is the way it is made. Helen still uses three enormous vats which Henry Weston bought years ago. The largest, known affectionately as Pip, holds around 40,000 gallons. Helen explained that, much like whisky, there are different grades of perry, along with single varieties and blends. The perry of Bradshaw's day was a flat drink, but later bubbles were added, giving it a similar quality to champagne.

Mention perry, and most people haven't heard of it until you mention its branded names like Babycham and Lambrini. But after being out of fashion for decades, it seems as though perry's fortunes are changing. Its beefier brother, pear cider, has become one of the trendiest drinks of the twenty-first century – while some maintain that perry and pear cider are in fact the same thing.

From Ledbury, our next train took us west towards Hereford along what Bradshaw described as one of the most picturesque lines in the country. It still is today, and as you speed through the rich green landscape it seems to encapsulate the very essence of the English countryside.

The reason for our next stop was to search out a local breed of cattle. Familiar for its white face and rich brown coat, and much admired by Bradshaw, Hereford cattle had become one of the country's most popular breeds by the nineteenth century. The Watkins family has been farming Hereford stock for five generations. Standing beside one of the many

MENTION PERRY, AND MOST PEOPLE HAVEN'T HEARD OF IT UNTIL YOU MENTION ITS BRANDED NAMES LIKE BABYCHAM AND LAMBRINI

branch lines closed in the 1960s, David Watkins and son George explained the enormous impact the railways had on farming in Herefordshire. Their arrival meant that George's ancestors' cattle could go straight from market to anywhere in the country in a matter of hours. It wasn't long before three trains a day were leaving Hereford station, all carrying cattle to London. They were also exported across the globe, and today the largest producers of Hereford beef are the United States and Uruguay.

The recent 'mad cow' and foot and mouth disasters decimated beef farming in the UK, but there has been a steady domestic resurgence, David said, during the last 10 years. Known for its succulent meat marbled with fat, the Hereford breed has become the product of choice for discerning customers. At the Watkins' Hereford hotel beef is hung for 25 days in fridges to tenderise the meat. As it gradually loses water, the taste is intensified.

One of the main reasons for the excellence of Hereford beef is the life these cattle lead, grazing in the fields. A diet of grass has now been proved to produce meat with a longer shelf life, a better colour and a delicious flavour, as well as containing an essential fatty acid. We also learnt that Herefords are probably descended from a Roman breed.

While we were in Hereford we wanted to find out more about something to which Bradshaw, in the entry for Hereford Cathedral, gave one short line: 'A curious Saxon map of the world is in the library.' The library is the biggest chained library in the world, and the map, of course, is one of Britain's most important medieval artefacts, the Mappa Mundi.

Drawn on one sheet of calf skin, probably by monks, this map reflects the thinking of the medieval church and thus places Jerusalem at the centre, with the rest of the world spreading out around it. Although it is geographically fanciful it remains an extraordinary work of art and scholarship, containing 500 drawings, including scenes from the Bible as well as classical mythology, and images of various peoples of the world.

Dominic Harbour, the Cathedral's commercial director, explains that the Mappa Mundi should be seen as a virtual map, conceptual rather than geographically accurate. Its purpose was to educate and underline the centrality of the church to everything, while today it has immense value as a thirteenth-century vision of the world.

INTERPRETING THE MAPPI MUNDI TELLS HOW MEDIEVAL SOCIETY SAW THE WORLD.

Leaving the cathedral's great red sandstone tower behind us, we set off towards Shrewsbury, some 50 miles to the north. The line goes through the historic town of Ludlow, with its mighty castle, and threads its way between the hills of Wenlock Edge to the east and the Long Mynd to the west before descending into the Severn valley at Shrewsbury. Here it was industrial rather than medieval history that captivated us. In Bradshaw's day the rural market town was at the centre of the Industrial Revolution, busy with mills and foundries. Among the most important was Ditherington Flax Mill.

John Yates, Inspector of Historic Buildings for Shropshire, explained how this apparently ordinary building was at the very cutting edge of Victorian technology. It was the first iron-framed building, and its construction was, in John's words, 'an astonishing act of virtuosity, bravado and skill'.

All mills were mighty constructions, and Ditherington Flax Mill was no exception. It was 200 feet long, 40 feet wide and five storeys high. But, unlike its neighbours, it could withstand outbreaks of fire. Processing flax produced highly combustible dust, and fire was one of the great dangers for the industry. The cost of a blaze was in the order of £10,000, a small fortune in those days. So architect Charles Bage (1751–1822) was hired to design a mill that wouldn't burn down.

At the time the first cast-iron tracks were rolling off the production line in nearby Coalbrookdale, and Bage used the same technique to build cast-iron columns and beams. The clever design meant internal walls weren't necessary to give it strength. This subsequently allowed the factory owners to create large open-plan floors.

This system also enabled architects to create taller buildings – later using steel rather than cast-iron frames – in a design movement that eventually lead to today's skyscrapers. Without Ditherington Flax Mill the cities of the world would look startlingly different places.

One of the joys of reading Bradshaw's guide is the quirky information it contains. Take this extract from the entry for the Church of St Mary's in Shrewsbury. 'Many years ago a hair-brained fellow undertook to slide down a rope, laid from the top of this spire to the other side of the river. But he was killed in the attempt.'

Keen to discover more, we tracked down Robert Milton from St Mary's. At the top of the tower, looking out across the Severn, Robert told the story of Robert Cadman, a steeplejack who would supplement

DITHERINGTON FLAX MILL,
THE FIRST BUILT TO WITHSTAND
CATACLYSMIC BLAZES, IS
THE ANCESTOR OF TODAY'S
SKY SCRAPERS.

his income by performing high-wire tricks, cashing in on a craze for 'flying' that gripped the imagination of Britain in the 1730s.

Cadman was a master of the art, and it's said that he once slid down a rope from the cupola of St Paul's Cathedral in London blowing a trumpet. As his fame grew, hundreds of people would turn out to watch his performances, and his wife would collect money from awe-struck audiences. At St Mary's he walked up an 800-foot rope anchored in Gaye Meadow and ending at the top of the spire, performing stunts as he went. His finale was to slide down the rope from the spire to the ground, swinging by a wooden breastplate. But on 2 February 1739 the rope snapped where it was attached to the church and he fell to his death. At the church there's a plaque in his memory which reads:

Let this small Monument record the name Of Cadman, and to future time proclaim How by'n attempt to fly from this high spire Across the Sabrine he did acquire His fatal end. 'Twas not for want of skill Or courage to perform the task he fell, No, no, a faulty Cord being drawn too tight Harried his Soul on high to take her flight Which bid the Body here beneath good Night Feb.ry 2nd 1739 aged 28

After Shrewsbury we headed south-east to the village of Coalbrookdale, famous for its role in the development of the iron industry and now the site of a popular working museum of the Industrial Revolution. Bradshaw writes: 'Several important processes in the manufacture ... of iron have originated here ... in 1779 the first iron bridge was made. This still stands in substantial repair, at a point where it crosses the Severn with a single arch.'

Until the eighteenth century, charcoal was used to smelt iron, a process which required an enormous amount of wood to produce a tiny amount of iron. Then Abraham Darby I (1678–1717) developed a new technique, using coke hewn from the surrounding coalfields instead of charcoal. It meant that cast iron could now be made cheaply and in huge quantities. Iron manufacturing swiftly graduated from cooking pots to the first iron wheels and rails, the first iron cylinders for steam engines and, in 1802, the world's first steam locomotive, built by Richard Trevithick.

Eventually other products such as steel superseded this invention. Nonetheless cast iron has a striking monument to its success. Near

Coalbrookdale, where its component parts were made, the first iron
bridge still stands proud today, in the village that grew up around it
and to which it gave it's name. Built by Abraham Darby III (1750–91),
grandson of the smelting genius, it is not only a masterpiece of engineering, but also an elegant addition to the natural landscape of the
gorge it crosses. The bridge carried traffic until 1931, but is now reserved
for pedestrians, who can gaze down at the historic stretch of river where
the first iron boat was launched in 1787.

The technology of cast iron technology spread quickly. Among its
early advocates was Telford, who was one of the most prolific civil engineers of the Industrial Revolution, building roads, canals and bridges all
over the country. Thanks to Telford the aqueduct at Chirk, north-west

ABOVE: **SO INNOVATIVE WAS
THE FIRST IRON BRIDGE, IT
LENT ITS NAME TO THE TOWN
IN SHROPSHIRE WHERE IT WAS
BUILT AND BECAME A SYMBOL OF
THE INDUSTRIAL REVOLUTION.**

OVERLEAF: **CHIRK AQUEDUCT,
OPENED IN 1801, IS MIRRORED
BY A VIADUCT BUILT SOME 50
YEARS LATER.**

of Shrewsbury, where the Ellesmere Canal crosses from Shropshire into Wales, became the first to be lined with cast iron.

For Chirk – already a stopping point on his mail road – Telford and his partner William Jessop designed 10 graceful arches that would carry the canal some 70 feet above the Ceiriog Valley, thus allaying concerns about industrial defacement of a delightful valley. He wavered about the use of cast iron and compromised by using it for the floor of the aqueduct. (Later a cast-iron trough was inserted to solve the problem of water leaks.)

Finished in 1801 at a cost of just over £20,000, it was a vital link between coalfields and granite quarries and the newly developing centres of manufacturing. In 1846 a viaduct was built next to it to accommodate the newly arrived railway. Together the constructions complement the majesty of the secluded valley, home of the kingfisher.

CHESHIRE PASTURES WERE ONCE ENRICHED BY BONE DUST TO PRODUCE VELVETY GRASSLANDS.

As the train continues through peaceful, rolling countryside it's easy to forget that this border was once a battleground between the English and Welsh. The castles along the way are the only reminders. Chirk Castle, just beyond the aqueduct, is described by Bradshaw as a 'noble looking edifice, which has been preserved from ruin and may be regarded as a perfect model of time-honoured castles of the ancient Lords of the soil'. He went on to call it a must for any visitor to the area, and in order to enable the Victorian traveller to make arrangements in advance for a visit he revealed it to be the seat of R. Middleton Biddolf Esq.

R. Middleton Biddolf Esq was no fan of the railways and did not relish the idea of the line coming across his land. But when he realised it was inevitable, he decided to make the best of it and negotiated for Chirk to have its own station.

Tourists flocked to visit the fourteenth-century castle with its tower and dungeon. Subject to numerous alterations since its inception, it remains the only castle built during the reign of Edward I that's been permanently occupied. Today it's the home of Guy Middleton and open for the public to enjoy most of the year.

Our next stop was Wrexham, nine miles to the north, and on our way there we travelled over more viaducts crossing the Welsh valleys. It's extraordinary to see how well they've survived the decades of pounding by the trains.

From Wrexham, we were heading towards the Cheshire pastures, another Victorian success story. According to Bradshaw, 'The famous Cheshire pastures were at one time almost worn out when they were renovated with bone dust and made five times as valuable as before.'

In the nineteenth century chemists began to identify the key ingredients of good fertiliser, and Cheshire became the centre of a huge experiment to use bone dust, or bone meal, to improve the grass. So successful was it that, over the next 100 years, the area became the centre of the dairy trade. Milk could be moved by train to nearby cities, along with associated products like cheese.

A rare farmer who still makes Cheshire cheese in the traditional way is John Bourne. John's family had been making cheese since the 1700s, but the arrival of the railways opened up new markets. By 1845 the farm was producing 12,000 tonnes of cheese every summer. At the end of the century it was making almost 30,000 tonnes. These days,

AS THE TRAIN CONTINUES THROUGH PEACEFUL, ROLLING COUNTRYSIDE IT'S EASY TO FORGET THAT THIS BORDER WAS ONCE A BATTLEGROUND BETWEEN THE ENGLISH AND WELSH

John produces cheese using hands-on rather than industrial methods, in much the same way his grandfather would have done. John's cheese spends up to six months stored in his cellar. As John says, the flavour is all in the maturing.

Now, to the west of Chester, as we join the original mail line to Holyhead, there's an excellent view of the Dee, the banks of which were once a hive of industry.

The railway bridge over the Dee was constructed by Robert Stephenson as part of the Chester to Holyhead railway and opened in September 1846. But a flaw in the design marred an otherwise glowing reputation. It was built using cast-iron girders strengthened by wrought-iron bars, and eight months after its opening it became the first railway bridge to collapse, killing five people as carriages from a local train fell into the river. As a result, bridge builders abandoned brittle cast iron in favour of more flexible wrought iron.

On its way towards the coast of North Wales the line hugs the south bank of the Dee estuary, which in Bradshaw's day was an area of heavy industry. The guide refers to 'extensive collieries, the coals from which are shipped to Liverpool, Ireland and various parts of Wales'. There's no sign of the collieries as you pass through today, but not far from the line there is another landmark mentioned by Bradshaw, Flint Castle, which he describes as 'but a mere shell, there being left only the grey ruined walls'. It's another in the chain built by Edward I to keep the marauding Welsh at bay.

For all its beauty, however, it was not the castle that drew us to Flint. Instead, we were heading to Rhydmwyn, to what was a top-secret chemical weapons factory in the 1940s. According to historian Colin Barber, Churchill had instructed the chemicals firm ICI to set up a factory in 1939, and Flint's remoteness, good rail links and proximity to ICI's chemical works at Runcorn made it the perfect location.

Colin explained that, although the use of chemical weapons such as mustard gas was officially banned by the Geneva Convention, they were made none the less, in case the Germans used them first and as a last-ditch line of defence should they invade our beaches. Tunnels, hundreds of metres long, were burrowed into the hillside to store thousands of tons of gas and chemical weapons.

Initially the work was done by men but, as the war progressed, more women worked on the deadly job of filling the shells. The most haz-

WALKING AROUND LLANDUDNO, YOU CAN'T HELP BUT NOTICE HOW WELL KEPT IT REMAINS

ardous part was adding the explosives and detonators to the shells, a job carried out in a section called the danger area.

Towards the end of the war, work started on an even more hush-hush project. It was here at Rhydmwyn that scientists first extracted Uranium 235, a key stage in the development of the atomic bomb.

A far cry from this dark history is the mood of our next destination, the Queen of the Welsh resorts – Llandudno. Since the arrival of the railways, this stretch of coast, which also includes Prestatyn, Rhyl and Colwyn Bay, has been a popular tourist destination. Llandudno's entry in Bradshaw's guide reads: 'This delightful place has become one of great import as a summer resort ... the air is particularly salubrious.'

Walking around Llandudno, you can't help but notice how well kept it remains. No faded paint and half-dead palms here. One reason could be that it has been controlled by one family for 500 years. Unlike

ABOVE: **FLINT CASTLE IS ONE OF A STRING BUILT BY EDWARD I TO KEEP THE WELSH OUT OF ENGLAND.**

OVERLEAF: **ATTRACTIONS INCLUDING ITS TRAMWAY MADE LLANDUDNO A CUT ABOVE RIVAL RESORTS.**

many landowners, when the railway came the Mostyn family saw the prospect of it running through their land not as a curse but as an opportunity. The Mostyns designed a purpose-built Victorian season resort laid out on a curved grid that matched the sweep of the bay. It has flourished ever since.

One of the most enjoyable things to do here is ride the Great Orme Tramway, one of only three cable-hauled street tramways in the world, whose cars take you high up on to the headland and offer some of the best views in town. It wasn't built until after his death, but Bradshaw would have loved it.

On leaving Llandudno for Conwy, just to the south, the Victorian traveller was advised by Bradshaw to prepare for another wonder of modern engineering skill, Robert Stephenson's tubular bridge, built to the specification of William Fairbairn (1789–1874).

This radical new design was constructed by welding together a series of wrought-iron boxes to make a tube. It was prefabricated on the shore and then hydraulically lifted into place in just nine days in 1848. The innovative system allowed them to create a 400-foot bridge without any extra supports, and at the Conwy end the railway disappears through the town's medieval walls.

It was the first time an engineer and architect had worked side by side on the design of the railway. The intention not to spoil the historic town was largely successful, except for the decision to add medieval-style ramparts at each end of the modern structure in an attempt to blend it in with the castle – and the existing bridge – and proved rather clunky. At Conwy, as elsewhere, Stephenson was following in the footsteps of Thomas Telford, who had completed his suspension bridge there in 1826. Today there's a third bridge, perhaps not as inspirational as its predecessors, to carry cars.

For Stephenson, as for Telford, the building of the bridge at Conwy was effectively a trial run for the greater challenge of crossing the Menai Strait, more of which later.

Opened in 1863, the Conwy Valley line to Blaenau Ffestiniog runs south through breathtaking scenery. Bradshaw describes it like this: 'The vale through which the River Conway flows is remarkable for its beauty and fertility. Its luxuriant pastures, corn fields and groves are finely contrasted with the bleak appearance of the Snowdon mountain, which towers in frowning majesty above it.'

There are 11 stations along the route, all adopted by local people. And it's volunteers from the local communities rather than railway staff who look after them, rewarded simply with free train tickets. To catch a train, you simply flag it down. It's a system that has seen the service flourish.

Just over half-way to Blaenau lies Betws-y-coed, which in the 19th century became the first artists' colony in Britain. It was started by the leading landscape painter David Cox (1783–1859), who came here to paint and encouraged his friends to join him. When the railways arrived, the artists themselves became a tourist attraction, with people coming to watch them at work and visit the scenes like Swallow Falls, made famous by Cox's paintings.

Betws-y-coed was not originally on the line but was linked up with an extension completed in 1868. As a result the population, already boosted by resident artists, was further increased by tourists. Today the visitors are still coming in their droves, but the resident population has nearly returned to where it was when the railway opened.

It is still a beautiful area, but for an abrupt interruption in the view. On the way towards Blaenau Ffestiniog the train passes through a tunnel built in 1879 and emerges among grey mountains of slag. This is because slate was mined rather than quarried. Bradshaw talks about 2,000 hands being employed in hacking and splitting. In its heyday there were six working slate mines in the vicinity, and the railways played a crucial part in their development, transporting slate to Portmadoc to be shipped around the world, particularly to Germany.

Underground it was hot and dangerous work, lit only by candles or sometimes lamps. Men wielding heavy tools worked six days a week from the age of 12. They weren't expected to live into their 60s.

The First World War saw the mines closed. Although there was some resurgence in the industry between the wars, the mines closed again at the outbreak of the Second World War, during which they were used to store treasures from London museums.

Today the industry is a pale shadow of its former self. It has been hit by a flood of cheap imported slate. The slate that is produced now is still prepared by hand and is mainly used in special restoration projects.

In Bradshaw's day the slate left there bound for the port on what is now the oldest serving independent railway in the world. The Ffestiniog Railway, founded in 1832, required a lot of innovation to cope with the loads the trains had to carry through such steep terrain. Finished in

WHEN THE RAILWAYS ARRIVED, THE ARTISTS THEMSELVES BECAME A TOURIST ATTRACTION, WITH PEOPLE COMING TO WATCH THEM AT WORK

1836, the narrow-gauge line was designed to deal with the sharp corners. In those days it was powered by gravity, with wagons coasting downhill to the sea at Portmadoc. Horses were then used to drag the empty wagons back up.

In 1863 steam locomotives finally replaced horses for the uphill leg of the operation. The railway company also pioneered a kind of double engine powerful enough to haul the heavy slate trains through the steep mountains.

The last slate train left in 1946 but, eight years later, the line reopened as a heritage route carrying tourists between Blaenau Ffestiniog and Portmadoc. It is a spectacular railway with stunning views as it takes you down to the sea.

Before heading back to the main line towards Holyhead, we followed Bradshaw's recommendation and made a minor detour to Mount Snowdon, the highest mountain in England and Wales at 3,560 feet. To visit the mountain he suggests that you should hire ponies and guides.

ABOVE: **AN INDUSTRIAL ROUTE HAS TURNED INTO A HERITAGE TRAIL THANKS TO THE FFESTINIOG RAILWAY, ONE OF THE OLDEST IN EXISTENCE.**

OVERLEAF: **A RACK AND PINION TRAIN COPES ADMIRABLY WITH THE SLOPES OF MOUNT SNOWDON, FERRYING LESS ABLE OUTDOOR TYPES UP AND DOWN.**

Today the best option to get you up there is a stout pair of legs. However, for the less sturdy, since 1894 there's been a railway running from Llanberis almost to the top.

The line is so steep that a normal friction railway would run back down the hill, so the trains use a Swiss system called rack and pinion. Between the tracks is a rack of teeth, with which a pinion or cog wheel on the train meshes, thus preventing the train from sliding down the track. It is the only such railway in Britain.

Travelling at a very sedate 6.5 miles per hour, the train gets to the summit in just 50 minutes. At the top you can see the remains of stables and two hotels, a reminder of what a very different experience the ascent would have been before the railways arrived.

The Victorians were great explorers, especially when it came to nature. To help them, Bradshaw's guide lists several types of rare flower to look out for on Snowdon. But as ecologist Dr Barbara Jones pointed out, they didn't just seek and find. They arrived in their droves to pluck and preserve. Some species, like the mountain lily, became even rarer as a result, but thankfully it and many others are now protected by law.

Back on the main line, we headed on towards Bangor and, beyond it, another of those incredible feats of Victorian engineering, Robert Stephenson's famous Britannia Bridge across the Menai Strait. Both the bridge and the station by it on the other side are memorable, although for different reasons.

The station is Llanfairpwllgwyngyllgogerychwyrndrobwllllantysiliogogogoch, which has a whopping 58 letters (51 if you're using the Welsh alphabet). The name only dates from the middle of the nineteenth century, and there's a theory that it was created by villagers in a bid to embarrass the trippers who already inundated the area. The longest place name in Europe, it has in fact turned the station, which had little else to offer, into one of the most popular tourist attractions in Wales. The translation is something like this: 'Saint Mary's Church in the hollow of the white hazel near a rapid whirlpool and the Church of St Tysilio of the red cave'. Busy people tend to use the alternative name of Llanfair PG.

The bridge had Bradshaw almost lost for words. 'This magnificent structure was made to carry the Chester and Holyhead Railway across the Menai Strait. Like the beautiful bridge at Conway, it is on the tubular

BOTH THE BRIDGE AND THE STATION BY IT ON THE OTHER SIDE ARE MEMORABLE, ALTHOUGH FOR DIFFERENT REASONS

principle, but on a much grander scale, and is one of the most ingenious, daring and stupendous monuments of engineering skill which modern times have seen attempted ... we may justly express our admiration of it by calling it Mr Stephenson's chef d'oeuvre, but this would scarcely do justice to the remarkable bridge or its great architect.'

Sadly, much of the original Britannia Bridge, including its train tube, was destroyed in a fire in 1970. The replacement has a road bridge above the rail link. The great limestone lions that used to stand either side of the entrances to Stephenson's old bridge are still on guard, but they have had to suffer the indignity of being set below the level of the road.

The final stop on this journey is at Holyhead. On the mail route from London to Dublin this was the point of departure across the Irish Sea. 'The once small town of Holyhead,' wrote Bradshaw, 'will speedily become an important place.'

It did. When the railways arrived here in 1848 bringing the mail, they brought people too. Irish immigrants, British soldiers and politicians from all sides took advantage of the quick and easy ride to Dublin. Almost 200 years later, Holyhead may have lost some of that importance, but its port is still used by more than two million passengers each year.

EUROPE'S LONGEST STATION NAME IS CARRIED SHOULDER HIGH TO ITS RESTING PLACE.

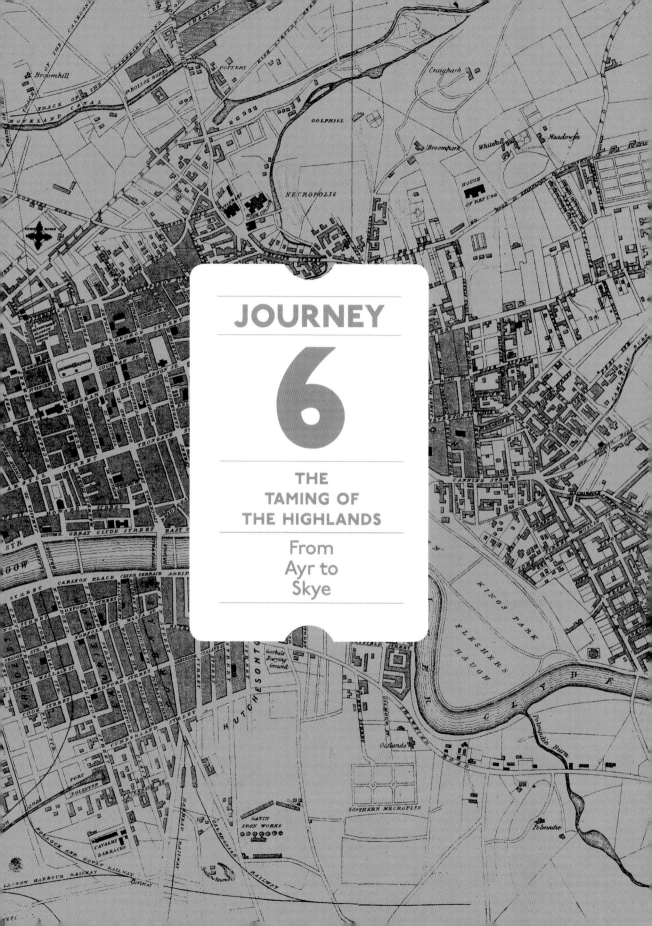

JOURNEY

6

THE TAMING OF THE HIGHLANDS

From
Ayr to
Skye

n the nineteenth century the Scottish west coast was a land of forestry and fishing, heather and haggis, wilderness and whisky. Life in what was frequently hostile terrain was continuing much as it had for centuries – until the arrival of the railway. The iron road was late in reaching its tentacles through the Highlands. Indeed, it was one of the most challenging stretches of line to confront railway builders of the age. Extreme gradients, curves, bogs and scree left engineers scrambling around for ideas. However, all the problems in the path of the ambitious project were finally resolved, and in October 1889 the first earth in the new 101-mile line was shifted with a silver spade. It took another five years and the labours of 5,000 men before the Glasgow to Fort William section of the line carried its first steam locomotive, pulling claret-coloured carriages. By April 1901 the leg to Mallaig – the first subsidised stretch in Britain – completed the route to the sea, and perhaps the most adverse environment in the UK had been tamed.

Was it worth the effort? Today's appreciative travellers seem to think so. In 2009 the West Highland line was voted the most scenic railway journey in the world by the *Wanderlust* travel magazine, above the Trans-Siberian Express and the Cuzco to Machu Picchu line in Peru.

Although the West Highland line starts at Glasgow, we began our journey further south in Ayrshire, to take in more of the joys that west Scotland holds.

The main function of the railways originally built here was to transport freight. As Bradshaw observed, it was a region rich in natural resources: 'It has abundant mines of coal, freestone, limestone, iron, lead and copper, and from the great abundance of sea-weed which is cast ashore, vast quantities of kelp is made.'

By 1840 passenger services were equally valued and there were already five trains each day, in both directions, between Glasgow and Ayr. At the time first-class passengers were paying 2d, while second- and third-class fares cost 1½d and 1d respectively. Initially third-class carriages had seats but, on 15 April 1840, the railway's governing board declared that these should be removed. Later the same year it was decreed that third-class carriages should be hitched directly behind the engine, so the travelling poor would not only be standing but receiving a face full of steam and soot too. At the time 18 passengers travelled in each first-class carriage, situated furthest from the engine, with 30 in second class.

WITH THE DAWN OF THE TWENTIETH CENTURY CAME THE FIRST RAIL LINK TO THE SCOTTISH HIGHLANDS, READY TO SHARE ITS GLORIES WITH TOURISTS FOR THE FIRST TIME.

MONESSIE GORGE, INVERNESS-SHIRE, SCOTLAND

BY RAIL TO
THE HIGHLANDS

BRITISH RAILWAYS

BRADSHAW WAS
SO BOWLED
OVER BY BURNS
THAT HE
DEVOTED THREE
COLUMNS OF HIS
GUIDEBOOK TO
THE GREAT MAN

At least some of those travelling to Ayr were going to pay homage to Robert Burns (1759–96), whose verse had captivated the nation. For the Victorians, famous poems and novels were an immense lure and there was an established Burns 'trail' that involved sites made famous in his works.

Bradshaw was so bowled over by Burns that he devoted three columns of his guidebook to the great man. 'Ayrshire is called the "Land of Burns" who was born near the town of Ayr and every mile we come to is consecrated to that poet's memory. Innumerable pilgrims from all lands visit these scenes, and the place of the poet's residence, to gaze on what has been charmed and sanctified by his genius or merely to have the satisfaction of standing beneath the roof where Burns first saw the light.'

Although he died aged 37, Burns crammed more into his short life than most people manage in their three score years and ten. He was born into a poor family and worked on the family farm as a boy. Unusually, he was also tutored and discovered a love of, and a dexterity with, language.

His first collection of poetry, entitled *Poems, chiefly in the Scottish dialect*, was published in July 1786, with the aim of raising the cash for a passage to the West Indies where he was planning to emigrate. Its immediate success – with 612 copies selling within a month – persuaded him to stay in Scotland, and his body of poems and lyrics in both the Scottish and English tongues grew.

Burns is not only remembered for his verse. He was an incurable womaniser and heavy drinker, who also earned enemies as he poured scorn on national institutions including the Kirk. His politics were, for the era, radical.

His life is marked annually on Burns Night, commemorated on or near 25 January, the Scottish bard's birthday. The menu usually involves 'neeps and tatties' (turnips and potatoes) with haggis, traditionally served to the sound of Burns's poem 'Address to a Haggis', beginning with the lines: 'Fair Fa' your honest, sonsie face, Great chieftain o' the pudding-race!'

Haggis was something of an everyday dish until Burns propelled it to the forefront of the Scottish consciousness. Although it is inextricably linked to Scottish tradition it is likely that the original dish came from France via the Normans or Scandinavia. For any culture it was a way of disguising cheap meat and animal innards.

LEFT: THE LEGACY OF ROBERT BURNS IS A BODY OF VERSE THAT BRINGS THE ROMANCE AND RUGGED NATURE OF SCOTLAND ALIVE.

OVERLEAF: CROWDS AT PRESTWICK GOLF COURSE DURING THE OPEN CHAMPIONSHIP BECAME SO LARGE AND UNWIELDY THAT PLAYERS COULD NO LONGER SEE WHERE THEIR SHOT HAD LANDED.

Butcher Stuart Duguid, who owns one of the oldest butcher's shops in Ayr, still makes hand-tied haggis to a recipe of sheep's heart, liver and lungs minced with onion, oatmeal, suet, spices and stock. It is boiled in the sheep's stomach for an hour before being served. It is perhaps an acquired taste, and Bradshaw was guarded in his response to it. 'Though a heavy mess, some think it by no means disagreeable.'

Like haggis, modern golf is widely accepted as a Scottish invention. Its rapid spread in popularity was undoubtedly helped by the arrival of the railway in this corner of Scotland.

The golf club at Prestwick, just north of Ayr, which opened with 57 founder members in 1851, came hot on the heels of the rail link with Glasgow. One of a limited number of clubs in the country at the time, it hosted the first Open Championship in 1860. Eight competitors played 12 holes in the hope of winning a red morocco belt with silver clasps, worth £25. The victor was the great Willie Park of Musselburgh, who would go on to win the Open three more times.

BELOW: TOM MORRIS WAS INSTRUMENTAL IN LAYING OUT THE COURSE AT PRESTWICK AND STRUCK THE FIRST BALL OF THE FIRST OPEN IN 1860.

OVERLEAF: SHIP BUILDING ON THE CLYDE WAS A WAY OF LIFE FOR GENERATIONS IN GLASGOW.

Players and spectators used the train for easy access to Ayrshire's golf courses. Indeed, by 1925 there were so many people watching the Open Championship at Prestwick that the players had difficulty seeing the fairway. It was never held there again, but by this time golf in general and Scottish courses in particular were firmly established.

The line follows the coast for a while before turning inland towards Glasgow. At Paisley we encountered another Scottish tradition – tartan. In Bradshaw's day Paisley was 'a thriving seat of the cotton trade', famous not only for its distinctive fabric design but also for producing thread. In its heyday there were 800 looms weaving tartan in nearby Kilbarchen. But at Paisley we learnt that, with tartan, not everything is as it seems.

After the Battle of Culloden in 1746, the wearing of tartan was outlawed. When the ban was finally lifted 36 years later, tartan gradually became the thing to wear. Its high point came in 1822 when King George IV visited Edinburgh wearing full tartan Highland dress. A Highland ball was held where Highland dress was compulsory.

Now everyone wanted their own tartan, and in 1842 two brothers claiming to be the grandsons of Bonnie Prince Charlie published a book called *Vestiarium Scoticum*, allegedly drawn from ancient manuscripts, listing lost tartans and their clans.

Thanks to the book, sold at 10 guineas, everyone could track down any relevant tartan. It even contained tartans linked to the lowlands, where none had previously been known. The weavers who benefited from this could not have been happier.

The authority of the book was barely questioned. The fact that tartans had traditionally been linked to clan districts rather than families seems to have been overlooked. And it wasn't until 140 years later that investigations proved the book was a fake.

Even if the fiction had been detected, the truth would probably not have stopped the public love affair with tartan, especially after Queen Victoria and Prince Albert had their new and favourite home, Balmoral, decked in it in 1855.

After arriving in Glasgow, finally it's time to join the West Highland line on one of the world's most beautiful train journeys. Early on the line runs alongside the River Clyde, which was once the home of a thriving ship-building industry. Among the ships forged in this stretch is *Cutty Sark*, now berthed in London and the only surviving example of a tea clipper.

Cutty Sark was launched at Dumbarton in 1869, one of a new type of sailing ship with its iron frame and timber hull and masts that stretched 150 feet into the sky. With this combination she could exceed the speed of rival steamships. She was named after the young witch in Robert Burns's poem 'Tam o'Shanter'.

Builders Scott and Linton were bankrupted by the construction of *Cutty Sark*. She was completed by Denny's of Dumbarton, who later went on to build the world's first passenger turbine steamer and first hovercraft.

Other notable ships – among thousands built on the Clyde – include the Royal Navy battlecruiser HMS *Hood*, sunk in 1941 with the loss of 1,415 lives, the liners *Queen Mary* and *Lusitania*, and the Royal Yacht *Britannia*. It's an area that was once known as Red Clydeside for the colour of the prevailing politics. In the General Election of 1922 several hardline socialists from Clydeside were elected to Parliament.

Leaving industrial Scotland behind, the line heads north-west along the Firth of Clyde and through Helensburgh. Bending to the north, it runs alongside Gare Loch and Loch Long before reaching Tarbet station, where the glorious Loch Lomond comes into view.

In 1263 Tarbet witnessed an extraordinary feat. When King Haakon of Norway sent his invasion fleet to attack Scotland, several ships came up Loch Long. At the end of the loch the Norse crews proceeded to drag them out of the water and across the neck of land between Arrochar and Tarbet, before launching them into Loch Lomond and sailing on into central Scotland. King Haakon was later defeated at Largs on the Ayrshire coast.

This part of Scotland has become a popular tourist destination and another example of Victorian tourism driven by popular poems and novels.

It was Walter Scott (1771–1832), author of the 'Waverley' novels and generally regarded as the father of the historical romance, who put this area on the visitor map. His poem 'Lady of the Lake', set in nearby Loch Katrine, was published in 1810 and sold 25,000 copies in eight months. The novel *Rob Roy*, about a folk hero who roamed the nearby Trossachs, appeared seven years later and sold 10,000 copies.

The first to visit had to do so by coach. But when the railway arrived it disgorged many more people hungry to find out about the backdrop of Scott's masterpieces. A steamer trip completed their exploration of the literary landscape. Although his ponderous

writing style later went out of fashion, Scott did much to bring the Highlands into vogue.

Like vast areas of Scotland, this area was once covered by the Caledonian forest. Only a tiny percentage of the native woodland is left now, and railways played a part in its demise. At the village of Crianlarich, for example, where Glen Falloch meets Strath Fillan and Glen Dochart, the forest was stripped to supply railway sleepers. It suffered again with the advent of the First World War when timber was urgently needed to shore up the trenches of the Western Front. Meanwhile, on top of these sudden needs, wood was in perpetual demand for building and fuel.

A PASSION FOR THE TROSSACHS WAS INSPIRED AMONG TRIPPERS BY THE WORKS OF SIR WALTER SCOTT.

LMS **THE TROSSACHS**
LOCH KATRINE AND BEN VENUE
BY NORMAN WILKINSON, R.I.

In 1919 the Forestry Commission was set up and soon began replacing lost stocks of trees, using spruce seed from Canada. It's why there are numerous neat conifer plantations in evidence across the Highlands. Mature trees from plantations are used to supply timber merchants. For years it was transported to sawmills by train but, to save cash, the service was closed.

As the heavy loads of timber were subsequently transported by lorry, local roads began to suffer. Now there's a move – popular among local people – to reopen the rail service. A proposed terminal at Crianlarich would take 2,500 tonnes of timber off Scottish roads every week with just one train a day.

A more surprising industry is taking shape further up the line at Tyndrum, at the far end of Strath Fillan at the foot of the Grampians. A disused station building is the headquarters of a new company that's hoping to dig for gold. Chris Sangster, an Australian miner who set the company up, intends to bring 20,000 ounces of gold to the surface every year, representing profits of millions of pounds. He believes each tonne of rock mined there is likely to yield up to 10 grams of high-grade gold, worth about £200 and sufficient for a large wedding ring. It would mean jobs for a local economy that's in the doldrums.

Tyndrum owes its existence largely to mining. Lead was mined in the hill above nearby Clifton for 100 years or so from 1741. The nine-teenth century also saw a previous gold rush which brought an influx of people who duly built cottages for accommodation. But the price of gold fell and jobs were then in short supply. Optimists still pan for gold in the local rivers.

Tyndrum has two railway stations, which were built to serve dif-ferent lines. They are only a few hundred yards apart – but 10 miles apart by rail. Shortly before the village the West Highland line splits, with one branch going to Oban and the other to Fort William and on to Mallaig.

In fact it's not an original branch line to Oban but the remnant of a railway that preceded the West Highland line by almost a decade. The Callander and Oban Railway opened fully in 1880. It stopped carrying freight in 1965, the same year the portion of rail from Crianlarich east to Callander was closed.

Oban was still a busy commercial centre, as well as a holiday resort, home port for ships heading to Mull and many of the other Western

ONLY A TINY PERCENTAGE OF THE NATIVE WOODLAND IS LEFT NOW, AND RAILWAYS PLAYED A PART IN ITS DEMISE

Isles. It not only deserved a railway station, it needed one. So the line became a branch, to all intents and purposes, of the West Highland line.

Our battered old copy of Bradshaw was published long before the West Highland line was built, so for this section of our journey we needed to use a later edition. There it tells us that in the 1880s when the railway arrived Oban had a population of just 2,500. Today the number of residents still only numbers around 8,000, although that number triples in the summer with the arrival of tourists.

But it's not only the passenger ferries or indeed the merchant ships upon which the town is centred. It's the home of one of the oldest licensed distilleries in Scotland, and they have been making single malt whisky here for more than 200 years.

ABOVE: **THE SLATE QUARRIES ESTABLISHED BY JOHN AND HUGH STEVENSON IN OBAN HAVE NOT ENDURED IN THE SAME WAY AS THE DISTILLERY THEY STARTED, WHICH IS STILL PRODUCING SINGLE MALT WHISKY TODAY.**

OVERLEAF: **THE ISOLATION AND SOFT GROUND OF RANNOCH MOOR THREW UP NEW CHALLENGES FOR RAILWAY ENGINEERS, WHO ULTIMATELY BUILT THE LINE ON BRUSHWOOD.**

The distillery, dating from 1793, was established in an old brewery by brothers John and Hugh Stevenson, who also set up slate quarries, a tannery and a boat-building yard in Oban. It's changed hands several times since then but it's still a small operation, with two 670,000-litre stills used to produce only high-value single malts.

Back on the West Highland line proper it's time to cross Rannoch Moor, where the line is built on a floating causeway of brushwood. It was the only way engineers could cross the peaty plateau, which is both starkly desolate and stunningly beautiful.

The isolation of Rannoch Moor is difficult to comprehend. Certainly the team of railway surveyors who set off from here in January 1889 found it so. Seven men – among them engineers and a solicitor – set about their task with determination. However, they wore business clothes rather than rugged outdoor gear and carried umbrellas. Their pitiful kit was no match for the weather or the environment. Quickly disorientated, they were soon mired in peat bogs in freezing rain. One man fell and was knocked unconscious for four hours. He got to safety by following a fence which led to a cottage. The rest were saved by a rescue party made up of shepherds. A day later the moor was smothered in snow, and all would have died. Undaunted by their experiences, the party continued with the survey as soon as they were able. It wasn't long before accommodation was built for construction workers. Today it is a hotel and remains, bar the railway line, very secluded, being some 40 miles from the nearest garage and shop.

This section, like most of the line between Loch Lomond and Fort William, is single track. It means there must be special precautions to avoid head-on collisions. When the line was built a single token would be issued for the line section. The train driver in possession of the leather token knew he had right of way. Conversely, a train driver without the token knew something might be coming down the track.

Today it's an electronic token, transmitted by radio signal. It can only be 'released' by the train driver when his journey is completed. It means the line can be operated by few signallers with little infrastructure, so it is safe and cost effective. However, radio electronic token block, as it is properly called, is already obsolete and due to be replaced by European technology.

Corrour, which opened in 1894, is the highest main-line station in the UK. Its purpose was to serve the hunting lodge there. Owners of the estate had invested in the railway so that guests could make their

way towards this remote spot, before a carriage ride and a steamer trip brought them to their accommodation. For the rich it was ideal territory for hunting, shooting, fishing and stalking. While blood sports still play a part, estates like this are now usually more geared to conservation.

Bradshaw's guidebook offered the following description of what it called Inverness-shire but we know better as the Highlands: 'Its surface is in general extremely rugged and uneven, consisting of vast ranges of mountains, separated from each other by narrow and deep valleys. These mountains stretch across the whole country from one end of the island to another and lie parallel to every valley, rising like immense walls on both sides, while the intersected country sinks deep between them with a lake or rapid river or an arm of the sea.'

Among this impressive landscape lie the 'parallel roads', one of the great geological puzzles of the nineteenth century. Travelling through Glen Roy it's impossible to miss what appear to be three parallel roads that stretch as far as the eye can see. The roads form perfect contour lines, snaking in and out of the glen's irregular sides but – like tidemarks on a bath – maintaining precisely the same height throughout. Naturalist Charles Darwin (1809–82) felt sure the marks signified ancient marine shorelines. However, two years after he announced his theory, Swiss scientist Louis Agassiz (1807–73) countered it with another, claiming signs of a bygone ice age. Glaciers had formed plugs in the glen which had then filled with water. In 1861, after in-depth research of the roads was published, Darwin admitted he was wrong.

As Ben Nevis hoves into view it's impossible not to marvel at its dimensions. According to Bradshaw, 'Ben Nevis – the highest peak in Scotland or in the United Kingdom – is 4,406 ft above the sea and 20 miles around the base. The ascent takes three to four hours to the top, from which there is a grand prospect in clear weather.'

For Victorians it was a major draw. A pony track was opened to its top in 1883 and, after the railway reached Fort William in 1894, climbing the mountain became a popular pastime. Two women ran a Temperance hotel at the summit to cater for visitors. The following year a barber from Fort William ran up the mountain in the first timed ascent, giving rise to a series of hill running events. The Ben Nevis race is now a regular sporting fixture every September.

The pony track was created with a more serious venture in mind, however. On 17 October 1883 the Ben Nevis Observatory opened, funded

AMONG THIS IMPRESSIVE LANDSCAPE LIE THE 'PARALLEL ROADS', ONE OF THE GREAT GEOLOGICAL PUZZLES OF THE NINETEENTH CENTURY

by private donations, including one from Queen Victoria. It followed groundwork carried out by Clement Lindley Wragge (1852–1922), who climbed the mountain daily for sustained periods to make observations about the weather. The permanent observatory was a response to this endeavour by the Scottish Meteorological Society, which funded three staff there. Bravely they went out in terrible weather to take readings. Although the building closed in 1904 for lack of cash, the readings taken in the two decades it was open provided fundamental and comprehensive data on mountain weather.

Fort William, the next town on the route, sits on the eastern shore of Loch Linnhe beneath Ben Nevis and was once of major strategic impor- tance. The stone fort held out against attack in both Jacobite rebellions in

BELOW: BEN NEVIS IS A SIGHT OF UNPARALLELED GRANDEUR IN BRITAIN, ATTRACTING WALKERS – AND SOMETIMES RUNNERS – FROM ACROSS THE NATION.

OVERLEAF: GLENFINNAN VIADUCT POSSESSES UNEXPECTEDLY GRACEFUL LINES FOR A STRUCTURE MADE OF CONCRETE.

BEN NEVIS

BRITISH RAILWAYS

Britain's highest mountain · 4406 ft.

BRITISH RAILWAYS

SEE SCOTLAND BY RAIL

the eighteenth century, but when the railway came in 1864 it was in the way and was demolished.

Beyond Fort William is the magnificent Glenfinnan Viaduct, across the River Finnan near the head of Loch Shiel, one of a number of bridges and viaducts that would carry trains onward to Mallaig – and the ferry to Skye.

Sir Robert McAlpine (1847–1934), known as 'Concrete Bob', took charge of the Glenfinnan project. McAlpine was a former coal miner who began his construction company in 1869. When it was announced that he was going to build the viaduct entirely of concrete, there were fears that the end result would be a monstrosity. However, the finished viaduct with its 21 arches, each spanning 15 metres, bearing a track some 30 metres above the valley floor, put paid to these anxieties. Not only magnificent but durable, the concrete construction has withstood atrocious weather for well over a century with few signs of wear. The viaduct is familiar to many as the one featured in Harry Potter films, used by the Hogwarts Express.

It was at Glen Finnan that Bonnie Prince Charlie (1720–88) raised his standard in 1745. He was the grandson of King James II, exiled after the Battle of the Boyne in 1690. James had been unpopular for being Catholic and pro-French and because he fervently supported the notion that he had a God-given right to rule. Thus his grandson expected at least Catholic and French support, if not divine intervention. Initially, when his standard was raised, it was only a few Highlanders that turned up. Just as hope was fading, some of the clans came to join him en masse, sufficient for an army that would take Edinburgh and embarrass the red-coated Hanoverian forces.

With Scotland conquered, many of his supporters were keen to draw a line under the lightning campaign, but Bonnie Prince Charlie wanted to take England too. With false promises of French support, he persuaded his men to go on. They got as far as Derby before a weary lack of purpose forced a retreat. The episode ended in the Battle of Culloden in 1746, the last to be fought on British soil. Although the Prince escaped, more than 1,200 of his men died in less than an hour at the hands of a vengeful English force.

Almost 200 years later, during the Second World War, the Highlands again became a place for fighting men to show unquestioning bravery. When ordinary armed forces were faring badly, Winston Churchill ordered the formation of an elite corps who would undergo rigorous training before being unleashed as a guerrilla force. Between Glenfinnan and the sea was one of the centres for this, Inverailort House. Here Simon Fraser, 17th Lord Lovat (1911–95), a celebrated commando officer, helped set up the first Highland special training centre. (One of his ancestors, the 11th Lord Lovat, fought for the Jacobites at Culloden, having changed sides, and was afterwards executed for treason.)

Inverailort was ideally placed as it was remote and yet enjoyed rail access to bring in men, equipment and ammunition. And the surrounding landscape, prohibited to the public during the conflict, was an ideal setting for war games – many of which involved live ammunition. Men were brought here from all over the country to master the black arts of hand-to-hand combat, knife fighting, sabotage, demolition, field work and survival skills.

Finally our rail journey finished at Mallaig, where the 'Road to the Isles' and the West Highland Railway both come to an end. But before heading home we boarded a ferry to Skye to pick up on an odd reference in Bradshaw. 'At Kilmuir … Florence MacDonald, the Prince Charles heroine is buried.'

After Culloden Bonnie Prince Charlie took refuge in the Outer Hebrides, hoping for a passage to France. Eventually he happened upon Flora MacDonald (1722–90), aged 24. Despite some misgivings Flora pledged her help and asked her stepfather, the local commander, for a pass to the mainland for herself, a boat's crew, a manservant and a maid named as Betty Burke. 'Betty' was in fact the prince in disguise. The boat sailed to Skye, after which the prince crossed to Raasay and boarded a ship for France.

Flora MacDonald was soon arrested, not least because local people had noticed that the gait of Betty Burke did not appear to be that of an Irish spinning maid. Flora was imprisoned in the Tower of London but was soon permitted to live outside its grim walls until in 1747, after a general amnesty, she was released.

Her act was one of charity, she insisted, rather than conviction. She later married and emigrated to America shortly before the War of Independence. After five years she returned to Skye, and on the voyage revealed her characteristic mettle by refusing to leave the deck when privateers attacked her ship. Her name resonates with the virtues of honour and courage that run like a thread through Highland history.

JOURNEY

7

RAILWAYS MADE FOR TRADE

From Newcastle to Melton Mowbray

For railway enthusiasts the journey to the north-east is something of a pilgrimage. It was here that George Stephenson (1781–1848), father of the railways, was born and brought up. And it's in this area that much of his pioneering work was done. Newcastle was already an important coal-mining area before the age of the train. Other early endeavours in the Industrial Revolution were also clustered in this northern corner of England. Although these enterprises preceded the railways, all benefited from improved transport links when they arrived.

Travelling between Newcastle and Melton Mowbray you're taken from industrial urban to distinctly rural, a stark contrast visible from a train carriage window. The railways transformed not only the cities, but the countryside as well.

George Stephenson was the son of a miner and before he became an engine man he worked in the colliery himself. His only son Robert was born into these humble circumstances too. One of George's earliest inventions was a safety lamp for miners, ultimately overshadowed by one unveiled by Sir Humphrey Davy at about the same time.

On discovering he had a talent for engineering he soon got into the business of building tracks and, later, steam locomotives. Until the coal industry was revolutionised by his inventions, coal from Newcastle was shovelled on to ships docked in the Tyne to be transported to London. Ultimately the train would do the job quicker and more cheaply, while rail also criss-crossed the complex of collieries, taking on some of the more back-breaking tasks. Nowhere was the invention of railway steam locomotives more welcome than among working men of the north-east.

Robert Stephenson who, unlike his father, enjoyed a formal education, joined with others to set up a family locomotive works near the station in Newcastle as early as 1823. It was here that Locomotion No 1, the first locomotive to operate on a public railway, was built. The Forth Street Works, as they were known locally, went on to export locomotives to developing railways all over the world. When he died in 1859 Robert Stephenson's company was the biggest employer on Tyneside.

For Bradshaw the might of the coal industry was something to shout about. 'Coal, the true riches of Newcastle, was first worked here in 1260 but the produce was scanty till steam power was used in 1714. Within a circle of eight to ten miles more than 50 important collieries are open among which are the Hetton, Hartley, Wallsend and other familiar

ROBERT STEPHENSON SHARED HIS FATHER'S FLAIR FOR ENGINEERING AND DESIGN, AND HIS COMPANY EXPORTED LOCOMOTIVES FROM NEWCASTLE TO ALL OVER THE GLOBE.

names employing 10,000 to 15,000 hands. High-main coal is got from a rich bed six ft thick, nearly 200 fathoms beneath the surface. The great northern field of which this is the centre, covers about 500 square miles in Northumberland and Durham and may be 1,800 ft deep. Many and various calculations have been made by practical men and geologists as to the extent of supply but all agree that it will take some hundreds if not thousands of years to exhaust it.'

The promise of job security proved false for mining communities. For one village in particular, perched on the sea cliffs near the mouth of the Tyne, the coal mining industry and the cliffs gave out long before the coal seams. Until 40 years ago Marsden was home to 700 people with homes, a school, a miners' institute, a Methodist chapel and a railway line with a station. The post office doubled as a general store and its

ST HILDA'S COLLIERY IN SOUTH SHIELDS WAS ONE OF NUMEROUS MINES IN THE NORTH EAST THAT OPERATED MORE EFFICIENTLY WITH THE BENEFITS OF NEW TECHNOLOGY AFTER THE INDUSTRIAL REVOLUTION.

front room was sometimes a doctor's and a dentist's surgery. Men from the village worked in the nearby colliery from its opening in 1878 until its closure 90 years later, after the surface coal was exhausted.

Amenities were basic. Returning black with dirt from a day's labour, the most a man could hope for was a bath in a tub in front of the fire. Once a week a horse and cart came to the village to collect the contents of the earth closets, while rubbish – at the time almost entirely bio-degradable – was tossed over the cliffs into the sea.

Food was grown on allotments or pulled from the waves. And it was the sea that once nourished the people here that finally proved to be their nemesis. Constant rock falls brought the cliff edge ever closer to the village. Anxious residents were soon complaining that they could fish from their back gardens because the sea was so close. Hopes that the small

DESPITE THE ADVENT OF THE MECHANICAL AGE, BOYS LIKE THESE WERE STILL EXPECTED TO GO DOWN THE PITS FROM AN EARLY AGE, SACRIFICING THEIR CHILDHOOD FOR THE SAKE OF THE INDUSTRY.

community would survive the closure of the colliery in 1968 were soon dashed when it became obvious the sea wasn't about to halt its forward march. First it became a ghost village. Now most of it has vanished.

Village and pit were built in the lee of Souter lighthouse. Opened in 1871 to protect ships from a notorious stretch of rocks, it was the first lighthouse to use a form of electricity. Its mechanics were designed by Sunderland-born Joseph Swann (1828–1914), who continued honing the uses of electricity until in 1879 he produced the first incandescent light bulb. Although it was decommissioned in 1988, the building with its distinctive red hoops still stands intact, fortunate to have been sited on the structurally sound Lizard Point rather than the adjoining cliff top. Today it's a tourist attraction owned by the National Trust.

Old Marsden was doomed, but it seems that in the future there may be hope for the coal industry at nearby Whitburn. Professor Paul Younger, an expert in the study of water pollution levels in former mines, believes the days of sending men down into the pits are long gone. Instead he is investigating ways of extracting coal cleanly, economically and safely with new technology. In layman's terms he suggests boring into the mineral seam, igniting the coal within it and using the heat that comes out to generate steam and electricity. Further, he envisages the carbon emitted in the process being captured and returned to the same borehole to be sealed up for ever. If these ideas become a reality they certainly could provide a stepping stone as the country seeks a carbon-free economy.

Given the dire consequences a mighty swell can have off this coast, it is perhaps not surprising to discover that the first lifeboat was pioneered at our next stop in South Shields. Bradshaw first alerted us to this fact. 'At South Shields may be seen, in the church, a model of Greathead's first life boat, invented and used in 1790.' Bradshaw is referring to St Hilda's Church and to boat-builder Henry Greathead (1757–1818), the man credited with the creation of a boat capable of rescuing stranded crews in high seas.

The quest for a lifeboat design began in earnest in 1789 after the loss of the *Adventure*, a Newcastle ship wrecked at the mouth of the Tyne. Thousands of spectators gathered to watch the demise of ship and crew, who fell from the rigging one by one just 300 yards from the shore. None of the horrified onlookers would take to a boat and attempt a rescue, as they were certain they too would be lost. Subsequently a

IF THESE IDEAS BECOME A REALITY THEY CERTAINLY COULD PROVIDE A STEPPING STONE AS THE COUNTRY SEEKS A CARBON-FREE ECONOMY

committee was formed which offered a prize for a boat design 'calculated to brave the dangers of the sea, particularly of broken water'.

A design by William Wouldhave, the parish clerk, was forged in copper, made buoyant with the use of cork. Its chief advantage was that it could not be capsized, but the competition organisers disliked the copper aspect of the model. Greathead's boat was made of wood but floated bottom up if it was capsized.

Wouldhave was granted one guinea for his idea, while Greathead was given the contract for making the boat. In the end he incorporated cork cladding from Wouldhave's model and further added a curved keel. It was rowed with 10 short oars and could carry 20 people. The 'Original' served for 40 years before being wrecked on rocks. Greathead went on to build more than 30 lifeboats, but his claim to have invented them was

PREVIOUS PAGE: **WAGONS ROLLED AT ST HILDA'S COLLIERY UNTIL ITS CLOSURE IN 1940 AFTER A 130-YEAR HISTORY, WITH 2,000 MEN EMPLOYED THERE DURING ITS HEYDAY.**

BELOW: **THE 'ORIGINAL' SERVED AS THE RESCUE CRAFT OF THE TYNE LIFEBOAT SOCIETY FOR 40 YEARS.**

challenged both by Wouldhave and by Essex man Lionel Lukin, who believed his drawings of an 'unimmergible boat' predated Greathead's by at least five years.

Lifeboats certainly played their part in the story of South Shields, because of its position. The unstable sandbars near the mouth of the Tyne proved a perpetual hazard to shipping. And it was shipping, along with coal, that made it a boom town. Its population increased from 12,000 in 1801 to 75,000 by the 1860s.

Its history goes back much earlier than that, though, and the banks of the Tyne are littered with Roman remains, including two very well preserved Roman forts, Arbeia at South Shields and Segedunum at nearby Wallsend. Moreover, Hadrian's Wall, built by the Romans to keep out the Picts of Scotland, is still evident here, although much of its stonework has been recycled in other projects including the thirteenth-century Tynemouth Priory. It wasn't until the middle of the nineteenth century that the first steps to preserve the Roman wall were taken. It is now recognised as a world heritage site, which means its stones can no longer be used for local road-building projects as they were throughout the eighteenth century.

Hadrian's Wall was not the only piece of heritage that was almost lost in the region. The tradition of rapper sword dancing is still alive and well in the north-east despite decades of negligible interest in it. It sounds like something modern, but in fact rapper sword dancing is so old its origins are unknown. It is surely related to other sword dances that are known to have existed in Yorkshire and across Europe.

It is widely thought to have had two 'revivals', the first when conditions for miners both above and below ground were grim. In the colliery village of South Hetton, for example, there were five water taps to serve 190 houses in 1842. Fifty years on and there was but one toilet for 154 houses. Living was hard, but the result was a close-knit community that sought to make the most of its limited leisure time. Rapper sword dancing, with its camaraderie and its competition, became an antidote to the misery of working life. The next revival came after the Second World War when a group of university students recalled the dances for public consumption.

The rappers are flexible lengths of steel – although in olden days greensticks would have sufficed. Moving to a fast beat, the performers dance acrobatically and wield the rappers with alarming speed, bringing

ALL THOUGHTS OF MINING MISERY ARE BANISHED BY THE SPECTACULAR SIGHT OF THE NORMAN CASTLE AND 900-YEAR-OLD CATHEDRAL

them together with loud clashes to form different patterns. The Forster family from the village of High Spen, just across the border in County Durham, are continuing a tradition begun in 1926 by ancestor Fred Forster, who taught a group of local children how to dance. A year later, calling themselves the Blue Diamonds, the group won the junior sword section of the North of England Musical Tournament. His grandson and other members of the family happily don costumes of nineteenth-century miners to perform the dances today.

With the onward journey to Durham, however, all thoughts of mining misery are banished by the spectacular sight of the Norman castle and 900-year-old cathedral, towering over a wooded horseshoe bend in the River Wear. Bradshaw says of Durham: 'From all the neighbouring points of view, its appearance is unique and striking and the public edifices exhibit a great degree of magnificence. The centre of eminence is occupied by the cathedral and the castle.'

Although the surrounding area had numerous collieries, Durham itself played little part in the Industrial Revolution. However, it had already

ABOVE: THE BLUE DIAMONDS OF HIGH SPEN, JUNIOR CHAMPION RAPPER SWORD DANCERS IN 1927 AND AN INSPIRATION TO THOSE CONTINUING THE TRADITION TODAY.

OVERLEAF: DURHAM CATHEDRAL WAS COMPLETED BY THE MIDDLE OF THE TWELFTH CENTURY AND IS A PRISTINE AND MONUMENTAL EXAMPLE OF NORMAN ARCHITECTURE THAT HAS BECOME AN ICON OF THE NORTH EAST.

been an important military and ecclesiastical centre for many centuries, as its fine medieval buildings testify. Its religious significance goes back to 995, when the body of St Cuthbert, 300 years after his death, finally found a permanent resting place. Durham became a place of pilgrimage, and after the Conquest the Normans built the huge castle and cathedral, from where the bishops of Durham wielded great power.

One episode of ecclesiastical history that is barely remembered now, but which may ring a few bells, concerned one of Durham's bishops in the middle of the nineteenth century, who was at the centre of an expenses scandal. Bradshaw identified the nub of it when he said: 'In 1856 an Act of Parliament was obtained to enable to Bishops of London and Durham to retire from their sees with handsome pensions.'

Already handsomely paid, the Bishop of Durham, Edward Maltby (1770–1859), asked for such a large sum that Liberal politician William Gladstone (1809–98) accused him of simony, or profiteering from spiritual things. Although the pensions were grudgingly agreed in

INSIDE DURHAM CATHEDRAL THE DECOR REMAINS A TRIBUTE TO THE ARMY OF ARTISANS WHO WORKED THERE DURING ITS CREATION, WITH ONLY BASIC TOOLS TO HAND.

Parliament, the money Maltby received with his fellow bishop and his prospective role as statesman remained a matter for concern.

Hansard, the Parliamentary handbook, records a vitriolic attack by George Hadfield, MP for Sheffield between 1852 and 1874, on the subject, in which he refers to the two bishops receiving 'nearly £1,000,000 of the revenue of the church while there were 10,000 clergymen of that very church each receiving a sum not exceeding £100 per annum'. The injustice was not to be endured, he said, in a speech which came to this contemptuous climax: 'Would not the fact of these two right reverend Prelates, after having received nearly £1,000,000 from the state, and coming to the house and asking for retiring pensions to the amount of £10,500 a year, be canvassed in every pothouse in the country, and be made the subject of the song of the scoffer and the mockery of the drunkard?'

Today the amounts translate to an income of more than £67,000,000 paid while the Bishop was in post and £700,000 a year in the form of a pension. The MP's rage mirrors that of many over more recent stories of money-grubbing by elected and unelected Parliamentarians. In fairness, Maltby was the first regular bishop after a long line of 'prince-bishops' who wielded extraordinary power. Perhaps he expected financial recompense for waiving the right to raise an army, hold his own parliament and mint his own coins.

As the train head south, next on the line came Darlington, in North Yorkshire, a place of pilgrimage for railway historians. It was here in the 1820s that George Stephenson began laying rails to link the Darlington collieries with the river at Stockton-on-Tees. Opened in 1825, it is given the accolade of being the first purpose-built, locomotive-driven freight railway.

The Stockton & Darlington Railway began its life in 1821 the same way as any other, with an Act of Parliament. Its owner Edward Pease (1757–1868) initially conceived it as track with wagons drawn by horses like many others. But George Stephenson persuaded him that 'one locomotive was worth 50 horses'. When Pease saw an early prototype steam engine in action, he knew Stephenson was right.

A new Act of Parliament was sought that would allow the use of 'loco-motive or moveable engines', which caused some concern among the uninitiated. It also permitted the transport of passengers, although no one believed that would be anything other than a distraction from the real business of hauling coal.

NEXT ON THE LINE CAME DARLINGTON, IN NORTH YORKSHIRE, A PLACE OF PILGRIMAGE FOR RAILWAY HISTORIANS

Although it was expensive, steam traction was reliable, and the idea attracted interest from numerous investors. At first the Stockton & Darlington Railway was open to anyone who paid to use the line. It meant trains ran on a whim on the same tracks used by horse-drawn loads. Fights often broke out when rival operators argued over rights of way. In 1833 horses and rival operators were evicted when the S&DR became sole operator. Parallel tracks were laid so trains could travel in opposite directions, and a signalling system of sorts was installed.

Its smooth running became a model for other railways to mimic. Among the early companies to follow suit was the Whitby & Pickering Railway, which began in 1836. It was to Whitby, over to the east on the Yorkshire coast, that our journey took us next.

Whitby was once an important port – in 1828 it ranked seventh in England. It was here that Captain James Cook (1728–79) was born, and it was in a former Whitby collier, the *Endeavour*, that he explored Australia and the South Seas. Bradshaw clearly liked it in Whitby, writing: 'There are, among the watering places of England, few that have been more greatly benefited than Whitby from railway communication or that have become better adapted for the reception of visitors.'

For Bradshaw roles are reversed in Whitby. Here, instead of him quoting others, it is his book that is mentioned in Bram Stoker's *Dracula*, albeit years after his death. 'Dracula consults his Bradshaw guide before the 9.30 goods train to King's Cross from Whitby station, in one of his 50 coffins ...'

As well as the station, there are numerous other Dracula-linked landmarks to spot in Whitby, including Dracula's Seat, with its stunning view across Whitby Bay, the Tate Sands, where Dracula jumped from ship to shore as a black dog, and the Royal Hotel, where Dracula spent his first night in England.

Author Bram Stoker (1847–1912) visited Whitby during a career spent writing, reviewing and acting as agent for actor Henry Irving. It's said he was told a grisly tale about a shipwreck which took place some years previously and resulted in a cargo of coffins being loosed into the sea. The following day, apparently, horrified Whitby folk were confronted with the sight of decomposing bodies scattered along the beach. The drama of the east Yorkshire coast combined with Stoker's fertile imagination to create the rest of a story which was published in 1897 but remained relatively unknown until it attracted the attention of early Hollywood film-makers.

BEYOND SHEER HEIGHTS AND GOTHIC HORROR, WHITBY IS ALSO KNOWN FOR A GEMSTONE

Stoker clearly shared Bradshaw's affection for the ancient town with its romantic abbey ruins. According to Bradshaw, 'Whitby has long been admired for the peculiarity of its position and the grandeur of its coast scenery. To the eastward the cliffs rise abruptly, nearly 200 ft above the sea, and towards the south present a succession of bold headlands. To the north the views along the coast are not less imposing.'

Beyond sheer heights and Gothic horror, Whitby is also known for a gemstone which was immensely popular in Victorian times. Jet is one of two British gemstones and it is found only in a seven-mile stretch of coastline around Whitby. It comes from fossilised monkey puzzle trees.

Jet came into fashion after the death of Prince Albert in 1861, after which Queen Victoria would only countenance the wearing of black jewellery at court. Jet became so popular that there were more than 200 workshops spread throughout Whitby in the 1870s, with a combined turnover of £3 million. One firm alone employed 1,700 people. Craftsmen from all over Europe arrived to cash in on the trend for coal-coloured artefacts. The largest piece of jet ever found in Whitby is about 12 feet long.

ABOVE: **JET WORKSHOPS WERE BIG BUSINESS DURING VICTORIAN TIMES IN WHITBY, WHERE THE GEMSTONE IS FOUND.**

OVERLEAF: **MYSTERIOUS WHITBY FAMOUSLY FEATURED IN BRAM STOKER'S 1897 NOVEL, DRACULA.**

From Whitby we turned back inland and travelled past the Cleveland Hills on our way to Harrogate which, like Whitby, has retained much of its Victorian flavour.

Another Victorian trend emerges at Harrogate, for it was here that the first Turkish bath in Britain was built – and it's still in marvellous order. A Turkish bath usually has three rooms, each with air heated to different temperatures, and a plunge pool. It was opened to the public at a time when cleanliness was not high on many people's agenda.

The man usually credited with bringing the Turkish bath to Britain is David Urquhart (1805–77), a Scottish diplomat, MP for Stafford and public opponent of Russia's political ambitions, including its threat to the Ottoman Empire. To counter this, Urquhart sought to popularise Turkish culture. He was briefly secretary at the British consulate in Constantinople (now Istanbul), and he describes the baths he saw there in his book *The Pillars of Hercules*, published in 1850. They were the kind of baths the Romans would recognise.

Having suffered periods of ill health which were alleviated by different forms of hydrotherapy, Urquhart was in no doubt that people would benefit from use of the baths. There was, he said, 'a chapter [in his book] which, if the reader will peruse it with diligence and apply with care, may prolong his life, fortify his body, diminish his ailments, augment his enjoyments, and improve his temper: then having found something beneficial to himself, he may be prompted to do something to secure the like for his fellow-creatures.'

It was his firm belief that baths like this should be freely available to the public. Victorians embraced the principle of Turkish baths, but many built during the era closed down in the twentieth century and of those that remain several are at risk of closure.

Our journey through northern Britain then took us to the forerunner of today's recycling businesses at Batley, between Leeds and Huddersfield in West Yorkshire.

Benjamin Law (1773–1837) first began using discarded wool for blankets, coats, carpets and fertiliser back in 1813. He blended it with new wool at a time when the Napoleonic Wars had left the country short of raw materials. Before long, wool waste was being brought to Batley from all over the world to be ground up into a gritty, fibrous dust known as 'shoddy'. Shoddy was particularly sought after for the making of military uniforms. Later Law's nephews worked out how to incorporate tailor's

clippings, and the by-product was called 'mungo'. By 1860 Batley was producing around 7,000 tons of shoddy and mungo per year.

Batley's railway station, which opened in 1848, serving the main line to Leeds and Huddersfield and several branch lines, was ideally suited to this industry, as in those days it had eight platforms upon which wool and textiles could be off-loaded.

Law's contribution to the local economy is recalled on his gravestone, which reads: '[his] invention of shoddy converted Batley from an industrial village into a busy manufacturing town'. And in the Yorkshire tradition of 'waste not, want not' the mills that once produced material across the region are now themselves being recycled, into offices and shopping centres.

Another commercial interest that boomed with the railways is the rhubarb-growing industry at nearby Woodlesford, south-east of Leeds on the River Aire. The railway reached here in 1840 as trains forged through on the North Midland Line between Derby and Leeds. Rhubarb crops were loaded on for distribution across the country.

After Woodlesford became an unmanned halt in 1970 the station was demolished. By then the 'rhubarb specials' that once took the morning crop down the line, destination London, were already a distant memory. When production was at its peak before 1939, incredibly, 200 tons of rhubarb would be carried daily on the railways.

Rhubarb was grown in heated sheds in the dark, 'forcing' an early and tender crop. A business that started in 1877, it used shoddy as fertiliser and coal to heat the growing sheds, and both were transported there by train. But the nation's love for rhubarb declined with the introduction of an increasing variety of succulent foreign fruits. Only a handful of farms remain in business.

Our journey then took us through the coal-mining areas of Wakefield and Barnsley and on to the southern tip of Yorkshire and to Sheffield. Strangely, this vibrant city appears to have once been unusually class-ridden. One of the first things we learnt on arrival was that when the station was built in 1845 it had separate entrances for different classes of traveller.

Recognised by Bradshaw as the 'great seat of the cutlery trade', Sheffield had been famous for cutlery making since the fourteenth century. Following the invention of the steel-making process in the eighteenth century, Sheffield became Britain's steel capital – and soon it wasn't just cutlery. Bradshaw lists the products that emerged from Sheffield in Victorian times. 'Knives, forks, razors, Britannia metal, Sheffield plate, scythes, garden implements, files, screws, other tools, stoves, fenders as well as engines, railway springs and buffers – steel being the basis of nearly all.'

On the strength of its steel industry, at the beginning of the twentieth century Sheffield was the world's tenth largest city. 'Made in Sheffield' was seen on cutlery used all over the world and, in the arms race that preceded the First World War, the armour plating for Britain's new Dreadnoughts was mostly made in Sheffield.

From Sheffield it's a short train journey south to Nottingham, whose main product could not be more different. What Sheffield was for steel, Nottingham was for stockings and lace. For centuries 'the Queen of the Midlands' had been a hosiery town, and in 1589 a local man, the Rev. William Lee, invented the stocking-frame, which enabled stockings to be made far more quickly than they could be knitted by hand. Even so it remained a cottage industry, until the Industrial Revolution.

Bradshaw said of Nottingham, 'Silk, cotton stockings and bobbin-net lace are the staple manufactures. Until recently the bobbins were usually worked upon frames rented from the employers but this to a great extent has been altered since the introduction of the round frames, which are now generally confined to factories.'

With the Industrial Revolution came the power-loom and the flying shuttle, and crafts like weaving and lace-making moved into factories, to be done mechanically. The stocking-frame was also adapted, so that lace-making too was mechanised. It was now that Nottingham came to be closely associated with cotton-spinning.

The move into factories meant low pay and terrible conditions for working people, whose resentment ultimately boiled over. Nottingham became the birthplace of the movement that tried to stop the Industrial Revolution in its tracks.

In 1811, while Britain was still suffering the privations caused by the Napoleonic Wars, a radical group known as the Luddites was formed. Taking their name from the probably fictional Ned Ludd, or King Ludd, they set out to destroy the technology that they believed was threatening their livelihoods. Groups of men burst into factories and smashed up the machinery, in particular the 'wide frames', which could make stockings in large quantities and far more cheaply

WHAT SHEFFIELD WAS FOR STEEL, NOTTINGHAM WAS FOR STOCKINGS AND LACE

than could a skilled craftsman. The Luddite movement spread from Nottingham throughout the north, attracting such enormous levels of support that the army was at times called in to quell unrest. Frustrated by this secretive but effective army of the poor, the government resorted to making machine breaking a capital offence, and men were consequently hanged or transported for Luddite activity. By 1817, as the wealth of the nation improved, the movement had died out.

From Nottingham we headed south-east on the last leg of the journey. The end of the line is Melton Mowbray in Leicestershire, a town solidly rural and traditional in character. Bradshaw described Melton Mowbray as 'the centre of a famous hunting country. Horses are bred here; its pork pies and Stilton cheese are also valuable productions.' Today Melton Mowbray remains the headquarters of hunting, the Quorn, Cottesmore and Belvoir all hunting in the vicinity, while the cheese made there includes both Stilton and Red Leicester.

Stilton cheese is a delicacy made only in Leicestershire, Nottinghamshire and Derbyshire, and has European Union Protected Designation of Origin status, like Parma ham. It means that cheese made anywhere else can't be called Stilton. The local cheese industry had a notable spin-off. The excess whey from cheese production led to the keeping of pigs on a large scale – and the development of the pork pie industry.

There is also a link between pork pies and hunting. Pigs were slaughtered in the autumn and winter, the hunting seasons. And the pies that were produced afterwards were popular with the hunt servant, who would pop one into his pocket before trekking around the countryside in the wake of the hunt. The tasty snacks soon came to the notice of the huntsmen, who began taking pork pies of their own.

As early as 1831 the Leeds to London stagecoach was being used to take Melton Mowbray pork pies to London for sale. The arrival of the railways took production to another level, with new bakehouses springing up close to the station. With the age of refrigeration, the brand went global.

It's another example of how railway innovation boosted everyday business in city, town and village. Since the railway's inception, some associated trades have come and gone. Others, like the humble pork pie, have been robust enough to stand the test of time.

R. Thames

LONDON & WINDSOR

Horton

Perry Oaks

Barracks

Stanwell

Hatton

Stanwell Moor

West Bedfont

Drilling Ground

Wyrardsbury

SHIRE

Bishopsgate

Runney Mead

STAINES

17

Windsor & S.W. Sta. Railway

East Bedfont

Feltham Station

Feltham

Egham

River Thames

Ashford

Hanworth

Obelisk

Penton Hook

Thorpe

M

Littleton

Charlton

Kenton Parks

Trottsworth

Thorpe

Laleham

Upper Halliford

15

Sunbury

R. Thames

Hampton Race Co.

West Moulsey

St Ann's Hill

CHERTSEY

21

Halliford

Walton on Thames

River Mole

Sandgate

Shepperton

Andrew New Gr.

Oatlands Park

Hersham Gr.

Westend

Botley's Park

Addlestone

Weybridge

19

STATION

Otter

Southwood

Ottershaw Park

River Wey

St Georges Hill

Chobham

Bourn Brook

Basingstoke Canal

R. Mole

Cobham Street

Cobham 26

Byfleet

22

Wisley

Cobham Court

Woking Heath

Pirford Green

Junction Canal

WESTERN

Horsell

JUNCTION STATION

Hill

S

Pirford

U

Kingsland Gr.

Wey River

Ripley Gr.

Martyrs Gr.

Mays Gr.

ded. London Metropolis &c.

Woking 24

Ripley

Ockham

Fetcham Common

GODALMING BRANCH

SOUTH

Send Marsh

Eastwick

Sutton Gr.

Wenham

Send

Little Bookham

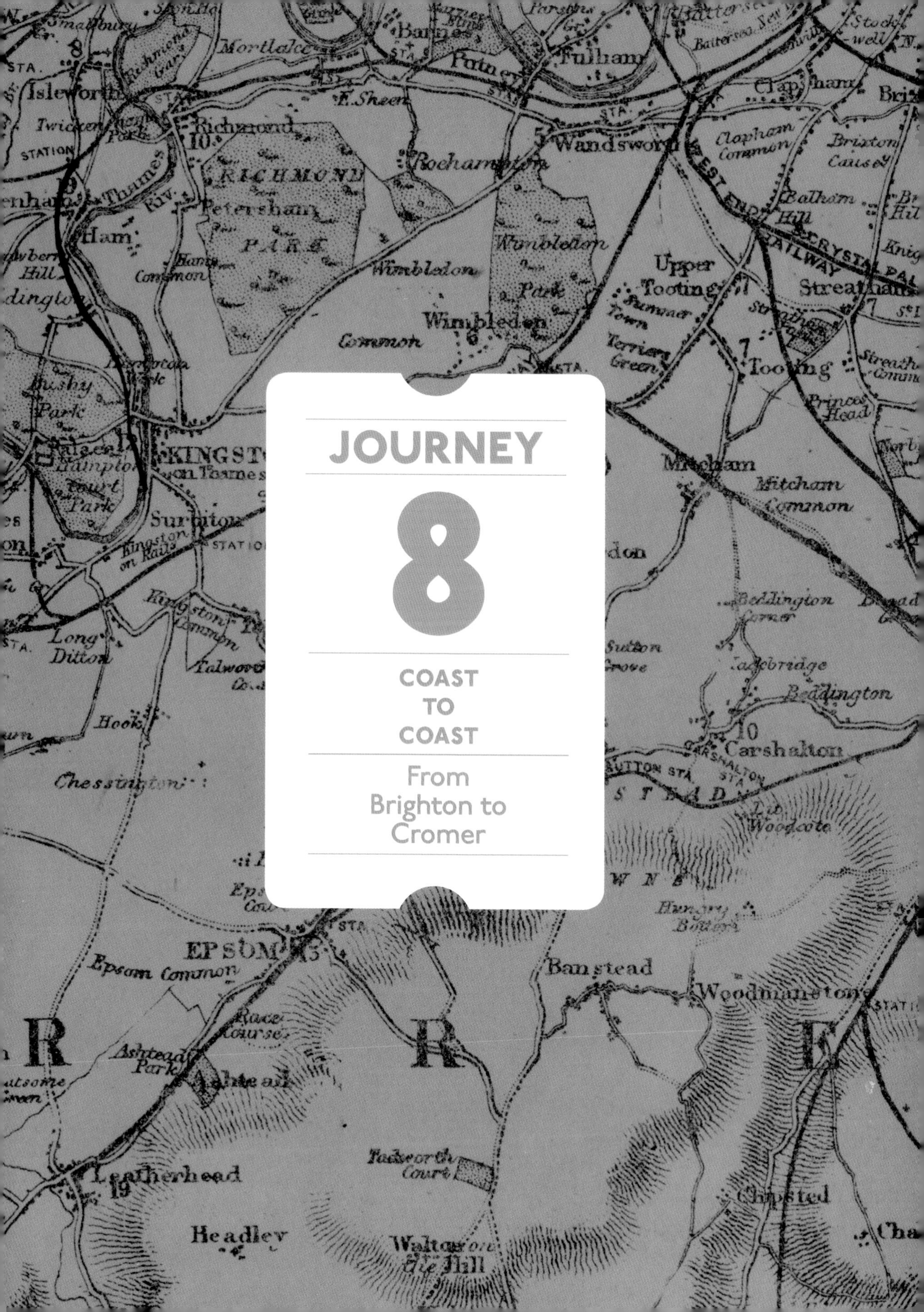

JOURNEY 8

COAST TO COAST

From Brighton to Cromer

Britain's railways were revolutionary. They gave power to ordinary people who at last had a chance to, quite literally, broaden their horizons. Rather than being confined to a single neighbourhood people could visit, or even move to and commute from, coast and countryside. This was especially true of the new middle classes, created by the Industrial Revolution.

For example, the line between Brighton and London was mostly used by passenger trains transporting commuters, shoppers, workers and sports enthusiasts. As technology improved, the journey times were slashed, enticing still more people on to the train. In Bradshaw's day the journey took one and a half hours. By 1865 that had reduced to 75 minutes and today it can be close to 50 minutes.

Bradshaw was acutely aware of the changes afoot. 'Merchants who formerly made Dulwich or Dalston the boundaries of their suburban residences now have got their mansion on the south coast, and still get in less time, by a less expensive conveyance, to their counting houses in the city.'

There was a flipside to the railways that led to financial ruin for many. Although most of these stories are in the shadow of history, this route shines a light on a few.

Brighton was in many ways defined by the Royal Pavilion, a former farmhouse refashioned in 1822 by John Nash (1752–1835), the designer of London's Regent Street. He was acting at the behest of the future George IV (1762–1830), whose patronage made Brighton popular. He first rented the farmouse, in 1783, then bought it and had it transformed.

The Pavilion's onion domes and exotic spires were a nod to India, a country whose importance in terms of trade was escalating. Inside it was sumptuous, a measure of George's extraordinary self-indulgence that ultimately led him into ill health and terrible debt. The planned gardens which were to be in similarly elaborate style were never built.

On the face of it George came to Brighton to take advantage of the benefits of sea bathing, made popular after 1750 by prescription of local doctor Richard Russell. In fact, he was shadowing his mistress Maria Fitzherbert, who had a house there. Fitzherbert was a Catholic, so marriage was out of the question for the heir to the British throne. He later married Caroline of Brunswick and they honeymooned in Brighton. But he so loathed her that she was barred from his coronation in 1821 and afterwards the marriage was dissolved by Parliament.

BRIGHTON'S ROYAL PAVILION, GEORGE IV'S FOLLY, IS OVERPOWERINGLY OSTENTATIOUS, ALTHOUGH IT HELPED TO CHANGE THE TOWN'S FORTUNES FOR THE BETTER.

George's death in 1830 came on the cusp of the railway revolution. Within 20 years the trains transformed Brighton from a royal playground to a busy resort. Queen Victoria had no love for the place or the Pavilion, and in 1850 she sold the bloated palace to Brighton's municipal authority for a fraction of its cost. Later, during the First World War, it was used as a military hospital. Hundreds of Indian soldiers who had been wounded on the Western Front were brought there. It was hoped that the décor and ambience would make them feel at home and aid their recovery.

Bradshaw seems to have shared Queen Victoria's view of the building. 'The Pavilion which rises with domes and minarets, and is fretted with greater variety than taste … erected for George IV after a fanciful oriental model, which, despite its supposed resemblance to the Moscow Kremlin, has had no precedent before or since.'

With his description of the Brighton sea-front he also gives us a few more clues about why Queen Victoria so disliked the town, referring to 'scores of laughing, chubby, thoughtless children, skilled manifestly in the

BELOW: THE WEST PIER WAS CONSIDERED THE MOST ATTRACTIVE OF BRIGHTON'S THREE PIERS UNTIL IT WAS DESTROYED BY FIRE.

OVERLEAF: CRYSTAL PALACE WAS A TRIUMPH OF VICTORIAN ENGINEERING, FIRST SITED IN LONDON'S HYDE PARK AND LATER RELOCATED TO SYDENHAM, WHERE IT STOOD FOR 80 YEARS BEFORE BEING WRECKED IN A BLAZE.

art of ingeniously tormenting maids, tutors, governesses, and mammas; prawn sellers and shellfish hawkers a few, and flymen a multitude, all idly vociferating, whilst intent upon their customary constitutional walk, the morning habitués of the promenade swing lustily past. Let us mingle with the throng and obtain a closer intimacy with the principal features of the place … for amusements, there is no provincial town in the kingdom that can offer such a variety of assembly and concert-rooms, libraries, bazaars, and other expedients for slaughtering our common enemy – time.'

Clearly the train link opened in 1841 had brought an influx of 'commoners' to Brighton. Nor was its arrival entirely good news for commerce in the town. Until the advent of the train Brighton was an essential staging post on the quickest route between London and Paris. Ferries pulled alongside the chain pier, which had been built in 1823 and looked like a stunted suspension bridge, to transport people to Dieppe on the other side of the Channel and onward to the French capital.

When the railway reached nearby Newhaven in 1847, however, its deep-water port was immediately a better option for cross-channel ferries. The chain pier was then used for leisure purposes. As the science of pier building improved, Brighton got not one but two more piers to the west, although only a lone example, the Palace Pier, remains open today. The chain pier was washed away by a storm in 1896, and the West Pier, designed by Victorian architect Eugenius Birch (1816–84) and acclaimed as the most magnificent, was left a skeleton after an arson attack and later succumbed to wind and fire.

Brighton also boasts the oldest aquarium and, along the sea-front, the longest serving electric railway in the world, the brainchild of Magnus Volks (1851–1937). Opened in 1883, it was the first electric railway in the world for public use. For a few years around the turn of the century the line was linked to another Volks creation, the Seashore Railway, which ran all the way from Brighton to Rottingdean on rails built under the sea. Passengers travelled in a tramcar perched on high stilts, which led to the railway being known as 'Daddy Long Legs'. Sadly the Seashore Railway closed in 1901 to make way for sea defences.

Volks also installed electricity in his Brighton house in 1880 and later built an electric car. The Grand Hotel was built in 1864. All these and more are indicators of the lively, outward-looking and affluent resort that Brighton became in the last half of the nineteenth century. The aquarium and sea-front railway are still operational.

PASSENGERS TRAVELLED IN A TRAMCAR PERCHED ON HIGH STILTS, WHICH LED TO THE RAILWAY BEING KNOWN AS 'DADDY LONG LEGS'

On its way from Brighton the London train climbs a valley and then tunnels through the South Downs before continuing north to Haywards Heath and Crawley. When the railway arrived, each of these towns was already well established, with a long history, but elsewhere the line brought sudden changes in status.

Southern Britain was rapidly criss-crossed with railway lines, making small towns out of villages and major commercial centres out of small towns. Two places on the London to Brighton line fall into this category. Gatwick was barely a village when the aerodrome opened in 1936, but since its modernisation and expansion in the 1950s it has been one of Britain's main airports and now has 30 million visitors a year flying to 200 world-wide destinations from its single runway. Further north the line bypassed hilly Reigate, and where it crossed the Guildford to Tonbridge line nearby, the town of Redhill grew so fast that it soon rivalled its senior neighbour in size and commercial importance.

Six miles east of Redhill on the line towards Tonbridge and Ashford is Godstone, where firestone was once quarried. It was used for buildings, in furnaces and as a bed in glass-making. As the 'good stone' quarried here had no grain, it could be cut in any direction. Once the quarry enjoyed a monopoly, but it was killed off in about 1860 by a revolution in transport which led to the arrival of cheaper stone from elsewhere. The quarry caves still contain the original tram lines that brought loaded wagons to the surface. In fact the lines have an older history than that. Before being installed underground they were part of the Croydon, Merstham & Godstone Iron Railway, a horse-drawn tramway that operated between 1803 and 1838, and was then supplanted by the railway.

Continuing north from Redhill, the railway eventually takes us into south London and through Croydon to Sydenham. Here we reach the site of the Crystal Palace, an elegant glass citadel that symbolised the shining hopes and aspirations of the Victorian age.

An immense glazed building, designed by Sir Joseph Paxton (1801–65), was constructed in Hyde Park at the bidding of Prince Albert in 1851 for the Great Exhibition, showcasing Britain's contribution to the Industrial Revolution and cutting-edge technology from the rest of the world. Its construction was made possible by the removal of a tax on glass and the advances in glass manufacturing techniques that followed.

But the Hyde Park exhibition was temporary. In 1854 the magnificent structure was dismantled and reconstructed across London in another

park at Sydenham. Seeking to enhance its reputation, the London, Brighton & South Coast Railway paid for the move, confident that it would recoup costs as passengers used the trains to flock there.

The building remained an exhibition centre and was also used for plays and concerts. The public loved it. Even Bradshaw seems uncharacteristically poetic... 'But when the train approaches the spot where the brilliant and fairy fabric, in the midst of the most enchanting scenery, is revealed suddenly to the eye, the impression produced solicits our warmest admiration ... the view of which we may envy the Brighton Railway traveller who enjoys the sight daily in virtue of his season ticket.' It was, the guide insists, 'the most wonderful work human hands and mind have yet achieved'.

The hunch by the rail company about increased passenger numbers paid off, but it couldn't then raise the capital to extend railway lines.

ABOVE: **PREHISTORY WAS A NEW SCIENCE FOR THE VICTORIANS. THE CREATURES CONSTRUCTED AT CRYSTAL PALACE WERE INTERPRETATIONS OF RECENTLY UNEARTHED SKELETONS.**

OVERLEAF: **BURLINGTON ARCADE OPENED IN 1819, OFFERING LONDON SHOPPERS LUXURY, CHOICE AND SECURITY.**

Instead it encouraged the West End of London & Crystal Palace Railway to build a branch line from its station in Sydenham to Crystal Palace itself.

More than 112,000 people visited Crystal Palace by train in a single day in 1859. Inside there were 13,000 exhibits in a building that measured 1,858 feet in length. The square footage inside the glass walls was six times that of St Paul's Cathedral.

Next to the palace were grounds almost as large as Hyde Park, among which were dotted one of its most popular features, life-size models of dinosaurs. This was an early attempt to reconstruct a species recognised by scientists through skeletal excavation in an age when the Bible's version of creation held sway. Created by Professor Richard Owen, the 33 models were built from brick and artificial stone on a framework of iron. Not entirely accurate in their interpretation, they were modelled on partial skeletons that had been discovered and nonetheless pre-dated Charles Darwin's 1859 book *On the Origin of Species* by several years. They represented a bold effort at understanding a distant history with no precedent to follow.

As time went on the popularity of the palace inevitably waned. The 1911 Festival of Empire marked the last of its glory days. The event was swiftly followed by its bankruptcy, and the Crystal Palace was ultimately bought for the nation, to be used as a naval training establishment during the First World War. Finally, disaster struck in 1936 when a small office fire was fanned by the wind into an all-consuming blaze. The Crystal Palace was destroyed by night in a conflagration that could be seen from eight counties.

The park remains, and on and around an island in the lake children can still find excitement in the one feature of the Crystal Palace that's not extinct – the dinosaurs.

Trains from Brighton to London terminate at London Bridge or Victoria, while you can also change at Clapham Junction and arrive at Waterloo. Thanks to the underground services all London stations are highly accessible. Waterloo station was opened in 1848 by the London & South Western Railway, not as a terminal but a stop on a through line. It grew into a jumble of stations, platforms and services until a major refurbishment took place in the first decade of the twentieth century. Among the trains that departed from Waterloo before and after the rebuild was the 'stiffs express', as it was known among railway workers. It was a service run especially for the dead, heading from London to Brookwood Cemetery in Surrey.

The London Necropolis Company, which ran it, was set up in 1850 when the sudden growth in building throughout the capital meant that land for burial was in short supply. The company hit on the idea of ferrying coffins to an out-of-city cemetery where there was plenty of space and which family and friends knew would not be ploughed up by developers within a few years. They found a suitable site at Brookwood, between Woking and Farnborough. When it opened in 1854, the 2,000-acre cemetery was the largest in the world.

At Waterloo a special station was built, designed by Sir William Tite, easily accessible from the company's building in Westminster Bridge Road. Every day an express train departed for Brookwood, bearing coffins and associated mourners, for whom there were three classes of ticket. At Brookwood the cemetery had its own branch line from Necropolis Junction and two stations, one for the Anglican section and one for the Nonconformists. As time went by, the odd golfer was found among the grieving, taking advantage of the service to reach the nearby West Hill Golf Club.

While the cemetery remains, the London Necropolis Company was largely erased in the Second World War, except for the frontage of its administrative offices in the Westminster Bridge Road.

Commuters apart, people using stations in Bradshaw's day were more likely to be shoppers than mourners, because the railways allowed ordinary people easy access of the city. They could refer to Bradshaw's guide, which had plenty of recommendations, including the stylish Burlington Arcade off Piccadilly next to the Royal Academy. 'The visitor should not omit to visit the Burlington arcade, the prettiest gallery in London. It is a facsimile of a portion of the Palais Royal, but the tradesmen who occupy these shops are of a less wealthy class and the place is considered as the fashionable gentleman's lounge.'

It is indeed as elegant as the French palace and, although not as large, it is certainly extremely long. The forerunner of the modern shopping mall, Burlington Arcade was conceived by Lord George Cavendish, ostensibly to make the shopping experience more pleasurable for his wife. Designer Samuel Ware envisaged 'a Piazza for all Hardware, Wearing Apparel and Articles not Offensive in appearance nor smell'.

Since its opening in 1819 the Arcade has been patrolled by Beadles, liveried officers in frock-coats and braided top hats. These were initially drawn from Lord Cavendish's own regiment, the 10th Hussars, to enhance the safety of shoppers. They did so by enforcing the Arcade code, which meant no whistling, singing, playing of musical instruments, running, carrying of large parcels, opening of umbrellas or pushing of prams. Today four beadles continue to uphold the traditional values of Burlington Arcade. As a private police force, which incidentally pre-dates the Metropolitan Police, they have full authority to eject shoppers who fail to comply.

The choice of shopping venues in London now is colossal, and the best way to visit them is by travelling on the underground. On 30 July 1900, the Central London Railway – now called the Central Line –

THE ARMAMENTS FACTORY AT ENFIELD ESTABLISHED IN 1816 WAS OPEN TO ANYONE WHO SECURED A GOVERNMENT ORDER PERMITTING A VISIT.

opened between Bank and Shepherd's Bush. It was nicknamed the 'twopenny tube' for its flat fare and tunnels, and 'the tube' came to be applied to all undergrounds.

The maze of underground tunnels underfoot has often inhibited development in London. However, it didn't prevent the installation of a splendid Masonic temple within the Great Eastern Hotel, which had been built in 1884 near Liverpool Street station as a railway hotel. The lavish Grecian temple was added in 1912 and featured 12 different types of marble and a mahogany throne. Its cost was a cool £50,000, equivalent to about £4 million today, but it had been sealed off until builders discovered it behind a false wall in 1997.

One of the routes that radiate out of London is the line from Liverpool Street towards Harlow and Stansted. About half-way to Harlow, close to the station of Enfield Lock and the River Lea Navigation, is the site of the Royal Small Arms Factory. A housing estate now stands in its place, but this was once the most eminent gun manufacturer in the world. It was so famous that it became something of a tourist attraction. Bradshaw notes: 'The environs of Enfield are exceedingly pretty and the scenery quite picturesque. A visit should be made to the Government Arms factory, an order for which must be previously obtained from the ordenance [sic] office, London.'

The first arms factory was established at Enfield in 1816 by a government concerned at the price and quality of weapons on the open market. The nearby canal solved the problem of water supply needed for steam engines. Every element of the guns was made by hand. The original factory was substantially enlarged in 1854 in response to the Crimean War. It was then that American engineering techniques for mass production, first seen in Britain at the Great Exhibition, were installed.

In time it became more than a factory, as shops, housing, a school and other facilities grew up around it. The station at Enfield Lock opened in 1855, when it was called Ordnance Factory. In 1860 a workforce of 1,000 was producing on average 1,744 rifles every week. By 1887 the workforce had increased by 140 per cent to cope with demand. After learning a trade at the small arms factory apprentices could reasonably hope to get a job anywhere, because their experience was so highly valued.

Guns produced there took the name Enfield or its first two letters – En. Thus the most famous of its products today are probably the Lee-Enfield

A HOUSING
ESTATE NOW
STANDS IN ITS
PLACE, BUT
THIS WAS ONCE
THE MOST
EMINENT GUN
MANUFACTURER
IN THE WORLD

rifle, Bren light machine-guns and Sten submachine-guns. Its guns have played a part in every major war or armed skirmish that Britain has taken part in during the past 200 years.

Our route continued around the edge of Essex, through Bishop's Stortford and Saffron Walden towards Newmarket. We were heading into some of England's flattest landscapes, so perhaps it's no surprise that Newmarket became the beating heart of horse racing. However, although it was the first venue for regular horse racing, a prejudice against middle-class visitors arriving by rail nearly caused the town to be sidelined.

Until the age of rail travel Newmarket was accustomed to having only aristocrats as race-goers. The influential Jockey Club, which is still based there, assumed that its future lay with society's elite. When the Great Eastern Railway scheduled excursion trains to a station near Newmarket, the Jockey Club's response was to arrange races with a start and finish so far apart that only the monied few who could accompany the riders on horseback or in carriages would watch.

However, rival race tracks were keen to seize the initiative offered by the railways. Horses were transported for miles to make races more competitive. Spectators were welcomed by the hundred. Soon Newmarket found itself on the back foot as owners sought to race at courses most conveniently reached by train. By 1847 the Jockey Club was actively supporting plans for a rail link to its track. Afterwards 'race specials', often double the length of a normal train, were laid on to Newmarket from numerous major cities. Train-travelling politicians were in the habit of attending big races – then racing back to the Houses of Parliament for an evening debate.

On the main line from London and on similarly flat ground lies Cambridge, crowned by its university buildings. 'The University of Cambridge is second to no other in Europe,' states Bradshaw. 'On approaching the town, whether by rail or otherwise, the first object that meets the eye is the Chapel of King's College.'

Although the railway penetrated Cambridge in 1845, the station was built some distance from the city. Rumour had it that this was to make it harder for male students to jump on the train for assignations in London. That may be speculation, but it is true that university dons retained the right to search the station for undergraduates and had an Act of Parliament passed so they could ask railway companies to ban students from travelling even if they had a valid ticket. Nor would the university

UNTIL THE AGE OF RAIL TRAVEL NEWMARKET WAS ACCUSTOMED TO HAVING ONLY ARISTOCRATS AS RACE-GOERS

countenance trains running on a Sunday through Cambridge station. This rule stayed in place until 1908.

However, the authorities at Cambridge were more forward-thinking when it came to football. Records show that in the sixteenth century football or something like it was being played at Cambridge, and in the nineteenth century it was the public school sport of choice. However, there was scant regard for an opponent's well-being as players used hands as well as feet, and body checks, kicking and tripping to win. What's more, each team played according to its own set of rules.

In 1848 a meeting of University players was held in Cambridge which resulted in a definitive set of rules being agreed. Copies were pinned to the trees surrounding Parker's Piece, the park in the middle of Cambridge which was a favourite spot for games. Although not universally accepted, the Cambridge rules did help to impose some order on an otherwise unruly and often violent game. (Games between 'town' and 'gown' were particu-

CAMBRIDGE UNIVERSITY'S FOOTBALL CLUB WAS ONE OF THE FIRST TO ADOPT NEW RULES THAT TOOK HAND BALLS, BODY CHECKS AND HIGH KICKS OUT OF THE GAME.

ELY
IT'S QUICKER BY RAIL
ILLUSTRATED BOOKLET FREE FROM L·N·E·R OFFICES AND AGENCIES
OR INFORMATION BUREAU, I MINSTER PLACE, ELY, CAMBRIDGESHIRE

JARROLD & SONS, LTD, NORWICH & LONDON   Printed in Great Britain   1940   Published by the LONDON & NORTH EASTERN RAILWAY

larly feisty affairs.) They became the foundation of the rules drawn up in 1863 by the newly founded Football Association.

Railways also played a part in popularising the game, by taking teams across the country for matches and supporters to games.

As the line heads further into the Fens the land is not only flat but low-lying. The Norman founders of the immense Ely cathedral sited it on the highest piece land in the region, and its vast tower with its magnificent octagonal lantern can be seen from many miles away. The surrounding land was at best marshy, at worst underwater, and in the seventeenth century the first attempts at reclamation began. In 1670 Dutchman Cornelius Vermuyden constructed enormous drains that wiped out parts of the traditional wetlands.

The drainage was not entirely successful, and wind-powered pumps were installed to finish the job. Once drained of water, however, the peaty bottom of the fens shrank and the fields became lower still. After rivers burst their banks the fens were underwater once more. Only when coal-powered steam engines were introduced did man finally overcome nature. According to Bradshaw, 'The productive and remunerative farming of the Fens of Norfolk is one of the greatest triumphs of steam, for that was the effective agent employed to give value to, or rather to create, this extensive territory. Even within a recent period land estimated at £3 or £4 an acre has been enhanced in value, not only one hundred percent but even one hundred fold.'

As sluices were built to back high tides and help drain excess rainfall, more of the Fens were conquered. The land turned over to agriculture was so productive that the region has become known as the breadbasket of England.

The station at King's Lynn on the Norfolk coast is the terminus of the Fen Line from Cambridge. King's Lynn was one of the few towns to feel the pinch when the railway turned up in the town in 1846. The once bustling port went into decline when coal was then transported by rail rather than sea. But the town made a swift recovery as the railway shifted produce and seafood to London and welcomed train-loads of tourists.

King's Lynn sits on The Wash, an extensive area of estuaries, marshes and tidal mud flats. For centuries the ambitious have dreamed of reclaiming land from the sea there. According to Bradshaw, 'Here since 1850 works on a large scale have been carried out for reclaiming part of The Wash but its practicality is doubtful.' Now hopes of extending the

THE LANDMARK CATHEDRAL AT ELY, BUILT IN NORMAN TIMES BY BENEDICTINE MONKS, CAN BE SEEN FOR MILES AND ITS AWESOME SILHOUETTE WAS AN INSPIRATION FOR PILGRIMS.

land at the expense of the sea have come to an end with the realisation that, left untouched, the salt marshes provide a natural buffer to coastal erosion by exhausting the power of the waves. Consequently the area remains as it has always been, and a perfect habitat for wading birds and seals. Our journey then took us east across Norfolk to Norwich, which was linked to the national railway grid in 1845. Already its pre-eminence in the textile industry had been lost, probably because other mill towns had been quicker to join up with the railways.

Norwich maintained a measure of magnificence, though, as Bradshaw reveals. 'The prospect of the city from a little distance is both imposing and beautiful. The massive walls of the old castle crowning the summit of the hill form the central object in view; the lofty spire of the cathedral and those of the numerous parish churches rising in all directions, give it an air of great magnificence and, mixed with this architectural grandeur, is much more than the usual share of rural scenery … many large spaces laid out as gardens or planted with fruit trees.'

Norwich was home to Gurney's Bank, founded in 1770 by a respected Quaker family, the fate of which became inextricably linked with that of the railways. The bank was highly regarded, as Bradshaw confirms. 'On Bank Plain is Gurney's Bank, established by an old Norfolk family, equally known for their good works and philanthropy.' Prisoner reformer Elizabeth Fry (1780–1845) was born into the Gurney family.

Through a subsidiary – Overend, Gurney & Company – the bank was drawn into 'railway mania', which amounted to feverish share buying followed by a financial crash. For, while the railways frequently brought prosperity, investment in some other railway schemes spelled ruin for a number of people and institutions. For this reason the railway companies had a dubious reputation.

There were two bouts of 'railway mania'. The first was in the 1840s when there was a headlong rush to exploit the riches that railways were thought to yield. But lines and locomotives were costly to build. Those that became operational weren't always profitable. People lost money after investing in plans that failed to become reality or companies that couldn't sustain services.

It was a similar story in the 1860s when Overend, Gurney & Company was heavily committed in railway investments. Creditors panicked and rushed to withdraw their savings. The bank went into liquidation in June 1866 owing about £11 million – that's equivalent to about £1 billion today.

THE AREA REMAINS AS IT HAS ALWAYS BEEN, AND A PERFECT HABITAT FOR WADING BIRDS AND SEALS

RIGHT: COLMAN'S MUSTARD WAS ESTABLISHED IN NORWICH IN 1823 AND MADE HISTORY 55 YEARS LATER BY STARTING CONTRACT FARMING.

OVERLEAF: CROMER'S GOLDEN AGE HAS GONE AND ITS FIGHT FOR A SHARE OF THE TOURIST SHILLING IS MADE MORE ARDUOUS BY THE LOSS OF RAIL SERVICES.

LMS CROMER

GEM OF THE NORFOLK COAS

GUIDES ON APPLICATION AT L·N·E·R OR LMS STATION, ENQUIRY OFFICE OR ADVE

NER

OCIATION. CROMER

LONDON LITHOGRAPHIC C? LONDON S.E

Overend, Gurney & Co. were among 200 companies that failed in the crisis. Writer Charles Dickens laid the blame at the door of the overly ambitious railway companies and a government which had allowed them to perpetuate chaos. Happily, Gurney's of Norwich survived and merged with others to form Barclay's Bank in 1896.

Investors might have done better putting their money with another Norwich firm, J. & J. Colman, the mustard makers who have been in business since 1823. Colman's initiated contract farming in 1878, an agreement that meant the farmer was assured of a buyer for his crops while the buyer was certain of supplies for his company.

By the end of the nineteenth century Colman's was such a huge concern that it had its own railway system serving its warehouses and factory, and its own station. The company also provided a school for employees' children from 1857 and a company nurse from 1864. Since 1866, the year it was awarded a Royal Warrant, the mustard has been sold with its hallmark red and yellow packaging.

Due north of Norwich lies the charming coastal town of Cromer. Once a small fishing village, it was not connected with the rest of Britain by rail until 1877, but when it was discovered by Britain's holidaymakers its streets and beaches were soon filled. Most sampled Cromer crab, for which the resort is famous.

Trippers, who could disembark at three stations from destinations across the Midlands and the North, walked on the promenade, which was in fact a massive sea wall installed by the Victorians to fend off coastal erosion. For later generations this has meant major maintenance costs and the growing realisation that defences don't stop erosion but move the problem on to a different section of coast. As the battle against the encroaching sea continues, in areas away from towns authorities have been compelled to take the attitude 'let it be'.

Like Brighton at the start of the journey, Cromer was propelled into the public's affection in the age of the train. Along the way there are numerous examples of how financial disaster followed in the wake of the railways: a bankrupt business here, a squeezed industry there. The trump card played by the railways was always the arrival of visitors. Brighton, which still has a vibrant railway service, continues to prosper. Cromer, where rail services have been cut, must battle harder for its share of the tourist trade.

LONDON

Plaislow · E. Ham · Roding R.

River Lea · East Ham Level · Plaistow

Hyde Park · VICTORIA DOCKS · WOOLWICH · NORTH WOOLWICH RAIL STA · Plum

Battersea Park · Isle of Dogs · Greenwich Marsh · Dock Yard · Arsenal · NORTH

LEWISHAM · Surrey Canal · Kent Road · 9 STA · WOOLWICH · Plum

Battersea · Battersea New Town · Clapham · 7 Charlton · East Wickham

Camberwell · Peckham · Black Heath STA · 8 Eltham · Welling

N. Brixton · Denmark Hill · Peckham Rye Mainland · 6 Lee · Welling

Clapham · Brixton · Herne Hill · Red Post Hill · LONDON & CROYDON RAILWAY · Lewisham · 8 Eltham · Blen

Clapham Common · Brixton Cause · Dulwich · College · Bushey Gr. · Eltham Place · Southend

Balham Hill · Brixton Hill · Knights Hill · Dulwich Common · Forest Hill · Mottingham

Upper Tooting · CRYSTAL PALACE RAILWAY · Streatham · 6 · Norwood Cemetery · Norwood · Sydenham · Southend · Belmount · Foots Cray

Tooting · Streatham Common · Penge · CRYSTAL PALACE · Beckenham Place · BROMLEY · 10½ Chiselhurst · Foots Cray

Mitcham · Mitcham Common · Thornton Heath · Woodside · EASTERN RAILWAY · Beckenham · Elm End · Bickley · Wickham · Southborough

Beddington Corner · Broad Green · CROYDON · 10 · Shirley · Pickhurst · Hayes · Keston · Brasted

Carshalton · Woodcote · CROYDON RAILWAY · Wickham St. · West Wickham · Addington · Boston · 15 · Farnborough

Woodmansterne · STATION · Sanderstead · Schollon · Leaves Gr. · Down · Keston

Coulsdon · Warlingham · Farley · Chelsham · Knockholt Beeches

Chipstead · Chaldon · Caterham · Tatsfield

10

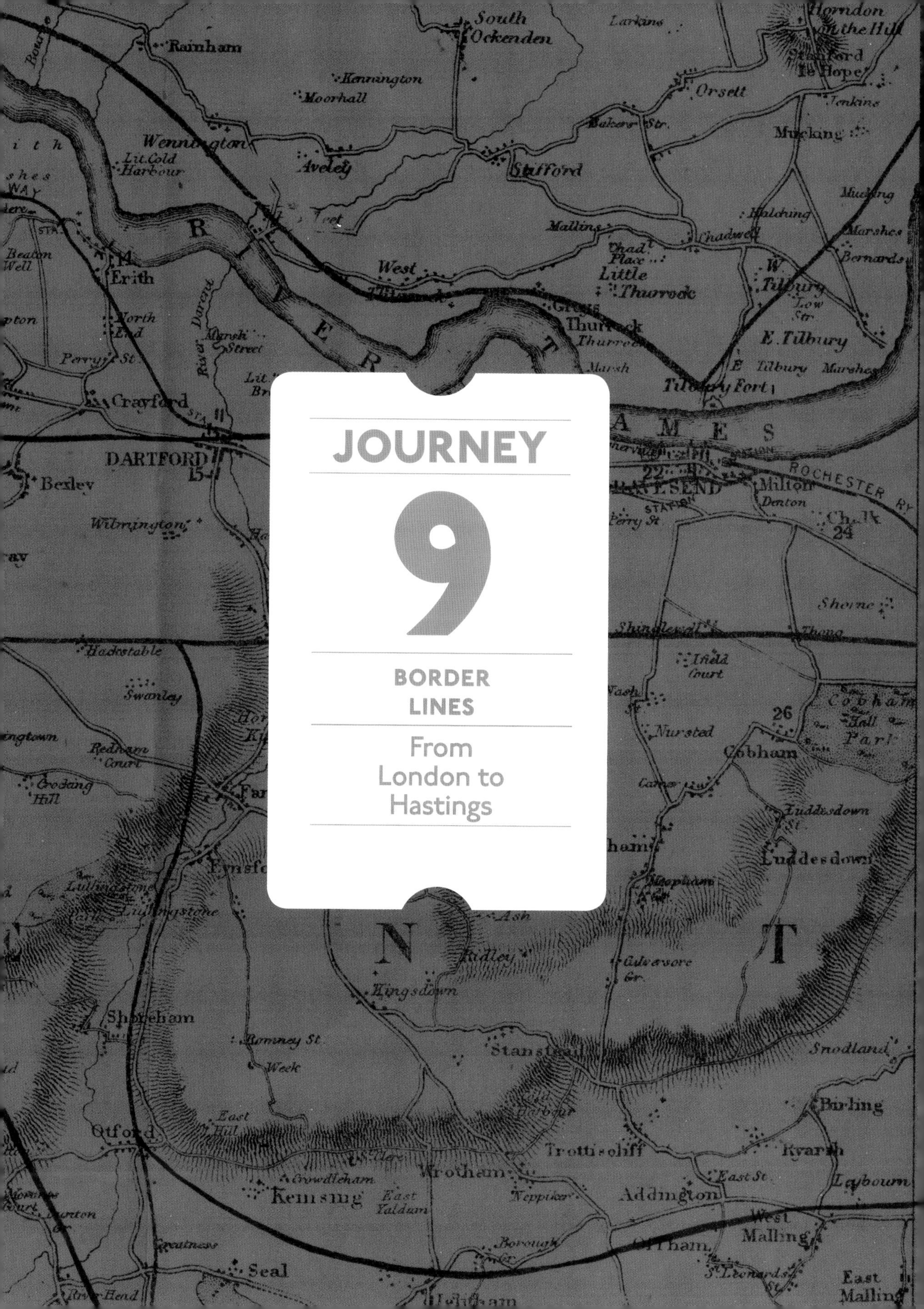

JOURNEY

9

BORDER LINES

From London to Hastings

Kent is a county of contrasts. On the one hand it is like London's allotment, with a history of growing food and fruit aplenty on its fertile fields. Yet throughout history it has also been England's first line of defence. In the nineteenth century, an era when again England's enemies were close by in Europe, it was Kent that was specially fortified to keep them at bay.

There are few ways to better illuminate the light and shade of south-east England than a train journey from London. And any trip heading towards Kent from the capital traditionally began at London Bridge station, which receives fulsome praise from Bradshaw. 'The platforms are spacious and extensive; the wooden roofs over them are light and airy; and the plates of glass diffuse sufficient light to every part of the vast area …'

Those words would be enough to make today's commuters who pass through the station choke on their cappuccinos. It's now dark, over-crowded and quite confusing thanks to a 1970s rebuild. The current multimillion pound redevelopment should see it transformed again into something light and airy.

London Bridge station was the terminal for the city's first railway line heading south-east. Unlike most other railways around the country, this three-and-a-half-mile stretch was built with passengers rather than cargo in mind. The line travelled on viaducts through heavily popu-lated districts, in turn spawning colonies that lived and worked in the 878 railway arches beneath. It opened in 1836, and within 20 years there were 10 million passengers using the line, travelling between London and the suburb of Greenwich.

Not everyone, though, saw the railways as something that would last. A writer in the *Quarterly Review* declared: 'Can anything be more palpably ridiculous than the prospect held out of locomotives travel-ling twice as fast as stage coaches? … we will back Old Father Thames against the Greenwich railway for any sum.'

Three years before it became the terminal on this early railway, Greenwich already had another historic role to play in the history of transport. It became home in 1833 to the influential time ball installed at the Royal Observatory, which had been built on the highest point in Greenwich Park in 1675.

The time ball had been invented by a Royal Navy captain in 1829 and was first in action at Portsmouth Harbour. Its purpose was to give

LONDON BRIDGE STATION, WHICH OPENED FIVE YEARS AFTER THE THAMES BRIDGE, WAS INITIALLY PRAISED FOR BEING SPACIOUS, LIGHT AND AIRY.

passing ships an accurate time, which in turn would help them determine longitude and thus their position.

At Greenwich the distinctive red ball straddles a pole perched on top of the Observatory. Each day at lunchtime the ball is hoisted to the top of the pole and then, at exactly 1 p.m., it is released, falling to the bottom of the pole within easy view of London's shipping. Although midday seems a more significant moment in time, 1 p.m. was traditionally the time when mariners worked out longitude by the position of the sun. Time balls acted like a bridge between sundials and accurate clocks. After radio time signals were introduced in the 1920s they were largely obsolete.

The time ball at Greenwich has particular importance as this location was chosen as the prime meridian of the world in 1884. The prime meridian is the starting point for different time zones. It was an obvious choice because the US had already established its time zones in accordance with Greenwich, as had many of the existing sea charts.

Bradshaw highlights another Greenwich tradition that sadly no longer exists. 'Approaching Greenwich reach, where large quantities of whitebait are caught in the season … Whitebait dinners form the chief attraction to the taverns adjacent, and here Her Majesty's ministers for the time being regale themselves annually on that fish; the season is from May to the latter end of July when parliament generally closes for the season.'

The ministerial whitebait dinners haven't been held since 1894, the last being on August 15 at the invitation of the Prime Minister.

For railway buffs there's a recently opened line in London linking north and south. This addition to the network brought new life to a tunnel built under the Thames by Marc Isambard Brunel, with the help of his son Isambard Kingdom. When it opened in 1843 the Wapping to Rotherhithe tunnel was the first ever built under a river. Its construction was an arduous process which took almost 20 years, during which time a deluge of river water nearly claimed Marc Brunel's life. Following the accident he invented a tunnel shield to protect workers from collapse, and the associated perils of drowning. This device, which kept the exposed face to a minimum and allowed the newly dug section to be shored up, is still used today in underwater tunnelling. Despite that, it was still a dreary task, with sewage from the Thames seeping through the tunnel walls and dangerously compromising workers' health.

THE TIME BALL
AT GREENWICH
HAS PARTICULAR
IMPORTANCE AS
THIS LOCATION
WAS CHOSEN
AS THE PRIME
MERIDIAN OF THE
WORLD IN 1884

The original plan to use the tunnel for carriages was abandoned because money ran out before the approaches could be completed. Nevertheless it was initially a popular attraction as a pedestrian tunnel, housing underground shops and stalls, until it got a reputation for thievery and prostitution. In 1865 it was taken over by the East London Railway Company, who built a railway through it linking existing lines north and south of the river. This was eventually absorbed into the underground system as the East London line, and has recently been revamped as an overground line for London's 2012 Olympics. The history of the tunnel can be studied at a museum in the original engine house at Rotherhithe built to hold the machinery that pumped water out of the tunnel.

To continue our journey into Kent we decided that instead of using the slower Victorian line that still exists, we would take the High Speed Link from St Pancras to Kent, opened in 2007 and the first domestic line of its kind in the country. Michael was transport minister when the plans were initially drawn up. Getting the tunnel off or under the ground was a huge struggle and one of which Michael jokes he still bears the scars.

Chatham and its historic dockyard on the Medway are just 40 minutes from St Pancras station, saving us 20 minutes or more on the London Bridge route.

Ever since Henry VIII set up the dockyard there in the early sixteenth century Chatham has been famous as a place where ships, including Nelson's *Victory*, were built, repaired and maintained. But in the nineteenth century, with the threat from Europe looming, there was a major escalation of scale. The dockyard was made five times its original size and a narrow-gauge railway was installed to move men and equipment around it. There was no doubt in anyone's mind at the time that a strong navy could deter would-be invaders and maintain the British Empire.

Bradshaw was admiring, if not entirely accurate: 'The Dockyard was commenced by Queen Elizabeth,' he states, 'and is about a mile long. It contains six buildings, slips, wet and dry docks. Rope House 1,140 ft long. Blacksmith's shops. Steam saw-mills, oar and block machinery by Brunel.'

Although the dockyard is now open only as a museum, its rope-making facilities are still operational and remain unrivalled. Rope has been made

GETTING THE TUNNEL OFF OR UNDER THE GROUND WAS A HUGE STRUGGLE AND ONE OF WHICH MICHAEL JOKES HE STILL BEARS THE SCARS

RIGHT: CHATHAM DOCKYARD HAS A PROUD HISTORY FROM WHEN THE ROYAL NAVY'S 'WOODEN WALLS' WERE BRITAIN'S BEST DEFENCE, THROUGH TWO WORLD WARS UNTIL ITS CLOSURE.

OVERLEAF: WHILE HOP-PICKING IS NO MORE IN KENT THANKS TO MACHINES, GRAPE-PICKING, HERE AT THE TENTERDEN VINEYARD PARK, IS FIRMLY ON THE AGENDA AS THE COUNTY WINS ACCLAIMS FOR ITS WINES.

on the site since 1618. After 1826 the process was mechanised with steam-powered machines positioned in a rope-walk building that is about a quarter of a mile in length, to accommodate laying the longest rope. Some of the kit from that era is still in use today. However, the rope that's made there now isn't for the Royal Navy but is used for sailing ships. Being made of natural fibres, it's also perfect for zoos, where it is used to help cage animals who try to gnaw to freedom.

To protect Chatham docks a number of brick-lined ditches were built, known as 'the lines'. More than a mile long and reinforced by two square redoubts, they were once the site of mock battles staged by servicemen at Chatham.

A few miles to the south on the old line to Maidstone is the village of Aylesford, which in Bradshaw's day was known entirely for its hop production. Hops were used to preserve and flavour beer. The arrival of the trains in Kent's hop grounds solved a seasonal labour shortage for farmers there, as they carried women and children from London's East End on 'hopping specials'. These city folk would set about the annual harvest, staying in 'hopping huts' and being rewarded with food and some wages. Although they rose at dawn, they got fresh air and exercise, which were widely believed to improve their health and that of the children. The evenings were the most popular time, with dinner, usually cooked on a camp fire, and a sing-song. At weekends extra trains were laid on so that the pickers could be joined by family and friends.

By the twentieth century hop picking attracted some 250,000 men, women and children to Kent at harvest time. Most thought of it as a holiday with pay, but it was not universally popular. Writer George Orwell (1903–50) was unhappy with the wages and conditions and insisted: 'Hop picking is in the category of things that are great fun when they are over.'

After the Second World War machines were brought in to replace labourers, and London's East Enders found other places to holiday. The hop farms that remain in business use their crops for herbal remedies and decoration rather than brewing. It's usually imported hops that go into beers these days.

From Aylesford the line continues into Maidstone, further up the River Medway. When a railway was first proposed for Maidstone there was a barrage of opposition, led by the mayor, who suggested it would be 'ruined as a commercial town'. Consequently the main line to Dover was built six miles to the south of the town. Of course, it was a mam-

moth mistake. Within a few years there was a branch line to Maidstone and it was directly linked to London by rail after 1874. Immediately trains were transporting a new innovation in paper from the mills of Maidstone to some of the highest and most influential houses in the land. James Whatman (1702–59) was a craftsman who developed a more even product called 'wove' paper to replace the rough stuff that had existed before. His son, also called James, introduced further refinements, to make it whiter and smoother than ever.

Wove paper was used by painters J.M.W. Turner and Thomas Gainsborough, poet William Blake, Napoleon, who wrote his will on it, and Queen Victoria. It was even selected for the document recording the peace treaty between the US and Japan that ended the Second World War.

An hour and a train change later we were in the spa town of Tunbridge Wells, in genteel commuter country to the south-west. Along with nearby Tonbridge, it became a centre for the manufacture of leather cricket balls which were then shipped across the country by rail.

The advent of railways changed the face of cricket in other ways too. At the beginning of the nineteenth century cricket was a game for the aristocracy and their staff only. By the end of the century it was open to all, with village and county games played by the most talented rather than the richest men. For the first time teams could travel considerable distances for matches in a matter of hours rather than days.

We continued down a branch line from Ashford – the major railway junction in the region – to Canterbury, not least because Bradshaw waxes lyrical about the trip. '[At Ashford] the line branches off to Canterbury, Whitstable, Sandwich, Deal, Ramsgate and Margate and from the accommodation it affords to the towns through which it passes and the exquisite beauty of the scenery along its route, will not suffer in any comparison with any line of similar length in the kingdom. It follows throughout the meanderings of the River Stour and traversing the most fertile districts in the country, has one uninterrupted panorama of luxuriant fertility … Thence the windings of the Stour, spanned ever and anon by some rustic bridge of wood or stone, enhances the romantic beauty of the landscape and we seem to be for many miles treading the sylvan labyrinth of a miniature Rhine-land.'

At Canterbury Bradshaw was once again bowled over, this time by the numerous medieval features of a city he branded 'exquisitely beautiful'.

AT CANTERBURY BRADSHAW WAS ONCE AGAIN BOWLED OVER, THIS TIME BY THE NUMEROUS MEDIEVAL FEATURES OF A CITY HE BRANDED 'EXQUISITELY BEAUTIFUL'

Unfortunately, Canterbury was extensively bombed during the Second World War and much of what he saw was turned to dust.

Canterbury was a victim of the raids carried out in April and June 1942 that became known as the Baedeker Blitz. Baedeker was the name of a tourist guide that featured Britain and was available in Germany. Frustrated by Royal Air Force raids on its own historic cities and towns, the Germans pledged to target every British city marked with three stars in the Baedeker guide. Exeter, Norwich, Bath and York were subjected to terrifying raids after the historic ports of Lübeck and Rostock were bombed. Canterbury was attacked after Cologne was substantially

CANTERBURY

FREQUENT TRAINS & CHEAP FARES

SOUTHERN RAILWAY

destroyed. Both the Luftwaffe and the Royal Air Force were deliberately targeting civilians in undefended cities rather than military targets, in the hope of destroying morale.

It's a lesser known fact that the first railway season tickets were issued at Canterbury in 1834 for people regularly visiting the beach at Whitstable from there during the summer months. The trippers were travelling on the six-mile 'Crab and Winkle' line, so named because it shared the same two first letters as destinations Canterbury and Whitstable, and to underline the fact that the shellfish industry was in full swing at the coast.

The line, another George and Robert Stephenson production, was built as early as 1830 and led to a new harbour being built in Whitstable. It was open several months before the Liverpool & Manchester railway. However, the line involved steep gradients and initially the carriages were pulled by ropes reeled in and out by two stationary, steam-driven winding engines along the route. As such, it's mostly under the radar of the railway record books.

Even today the catch at Whitstable usually includes whelks, the poor man's oyster, which was a staple dish on the bar of London pubs. We met the West family, fourth-generation whelk fishermen, whose great-grandfather came to Whitstable from Norfolk in 1901, bringing with him the innovation of the whelk pot that dramatically improved catches.

Further east down the branch line from Ashford is the resort of Margate, where sea bathing first became popular. Bradshaw clearly gets a measure of the town. 'There is not in the whole range of our seaside physiology a more lively, bustling place than this said Margate; albeit by those who are fettered down to cold formalities and regard laughter as a positive breech of good-breeding, it is pronounced to be essentially and irredeemably vulgar. The streets are always a scene of continued excitement, and troops of roguish ruddy cheeked urchins escorted by their mammas traverse every thoroughfare …

'In short for those who do not go to the coast for retirement and who like to have an atmosphere of London life surrounding them at the seaside there is no place where their desires can be so easily and comprehensively gratified as here.'

After the railway arrived in Margate in 1846, people came in their droves, convinced that a dip in the sea was something of a cure-all. The

LEFT: DESPITE EXTENSIVE BOMBING DURING THE SECOND WORLD WAR, CANTERBURY CATHEDRAL'S STAINED GLASS WINDOWS, WHICH DATE BACK FOR CENTURIES, ESCAPED TOTAL DESTRUCTION.

OVERLEAF: MARGATE WAS A POPULAR DESTINATION FOR TRIPPERS KEEN TO TAKE ADVANTAGE OF ITS BRACING AIR AND REFRESHING SEA WATERS FOR HEALTH REASONS.

Royal Sea Bathing Hospital had already been established in Margate for 50 years, to provide swimming for the less well off. It was, however, an era before the concept of swimming costumes. For this reason there were bathing machines on hand to protect everyone's finer feelings.

Bathing machines were in effect wooden carts that could be hired by bathers. Getting into the machine on the beach, the swimmer would disrobe away from prying eyes. The machine was then propelled into the water, sometimes by hand but usually under horsepower. At the required depth the cart came to a halt and the bather dropped out, seaward side, to swim at leisure, usually naked. A bather indicated that his swim was finished by waving a flag to attract the attention of the machine operator.

Margate Quaker and glove maker Benjamin Beale (c.1717--75) claimed to have invented the bathing machine. In fact, it's likely that they adapted an existing machine by attaching a canvas awning at one end which could be pulled down to the water encasing the swimmer in a small area.

As the railways brought in day-trippers, the necessity for bathing machines became not only to keep men and women apart but also

THE NECESSITY FOR BATHING MACHINES BECAME NOT ONLY TO KEEP MEN AND WOMEN APART BUT ALSO TO SEPERATE THE UPPER CLASSES FROM THE MIDDLE CLASSSES

WHEN SWIMMING COSTUMES BECAME COMMONPLACE, BATHERS WERE RELEASED FROM THE CONFINES OF BATHING MACHINES WHICH WERE USED PREVIOUSLY TO SPARE THE BLUSHES OF NAKED SWIMMERS WHEN THEY ENTERED THE WATER.

to separate the upper classes from the middle classes and to keep both away from the workers. By the 1880s swimming costumes were being widely used, which diminished demand for bathing machines. However, they are frequently seen on postcards from numerous British resorts at the turn of the twentieth century and are thought to have been in sporadic use as late as 1927.

Five minutes' walk from the sea front is something else that Margate kept under wraps in the early part of the nineteenth century. The Shell Grotto was discovered under farmland in 1835 by James Newlove, who immediately set about making a commercial success of his discovery.

Since the first visitors descended into the grotto two years later the jury has been out about who built it and why. Inside there are some 4.6 million shells arranged in mosaics, patterned or depicting trees and symbols. These are not exotic shells imported from a far-flung beach, but the highly familiar ones from cockles, whelks, mussels and oysters.

But why go to so much trouble? Some people maintain that the grotto was a Regency folly, while others believe it to be a smugglers' retreat. The most recent theory is that it was a temple linked to sun worship. But no one knows for sure. Attempts to carbon date the shells have failed because they are covered with years of pollution given off by Victorian lamps which once lit the way for visitors.

Along the coast of fortress Kent are the Roman remains at Richborough, dating from the first invasion in AD43. Bradshaw tells the traveller to watch out for the site from the train as it heads across Sandwich flats past the hamlet of Saltpans. 'At this spot the memorable ruins of Richborough come fully into sight; and shortly after the train sweeps around the sandy hill on which they stand. This was a celebrated Roman station … the remains of an amphitheatre are still very apparent. In the centre of the great quadrangle is the celebrated prostrate cross, built to commemorate the introduction of Christianity into England. It is placed on the top of an immense heathen altar and marks the spot on which Augustin preached the gospel. No monument in the kingdom equals this simple cross in interest yet few have been treated with greater neglect.'

Of course, the departure of the Romans and the introduction of Christianity are separated by 200 years, but Richborough continued to be important long after the Roman settlements had disappeared, probably thanks to its key defensive position.

Less well known is the First World War port developed at Richborough from 1916, taking advantage of its rail links. Acting as a secret supply base and encampment, it was known as 'Q' and was the last that countless British soldiers saw of England before setting off for the trenches. On 10 February 1918 a cross-channel ferry began between Richborough and Calais, the first roll-on, roll-off design. A further 60 miles of track were also laid at the port for transporting locomotives and wagons with heavy guns and tanks to ships.

At the end of the war the port silted up and the camps which once held men preparing for war were deserted. The ferries, though, were taken to Harwich and began running regular services to Zeebrugge in the 1920s.

From Richborough the line continues south and reaches the coast at Deal. Here, according to Bradshaw, the railway helped to transform a notorious smugglers' haunt into a respectable Victorian seaside town. 'This town stands close to the sea shore which is a bold and open beach being defended by an extensive wall of stones and pebbles which the sea has thrown up. Deal was formerly a rough looking irregular sailor-like place, full of narrow streets and shops with multifarious articles termed slops or marine stores. It is however much improved and is now resorted to for sea bathing, especially on account of its good repute for moderate charges.'

A mile down the coast is Walmer Castle, built by Henry VIII to repel French and Spanish invasions. Although it dates from the 1530s, because of its circular keep it is often mistaken for one of the Martello towers built around the south and east coasts in the early nineteenth century as protection against a Napoleonic invasion. They took their inspiration and name from a rounded castle in Corsica that had defied the might of the British navy in 1794. Each of the 74 Martello towers was armed with a cannon. At Walmer Castle, in 1801, with Napoleon's great army encamped near Calais, poised to invade, Admiral Horatio Nelson discussed his plan of action with William Pitt.

Today Walmer Castle is the official residence of the Lord Warden of the Cinque Ports. This is the name for a confederation of towns that banded together for defensive and economic purposes perhaps as early as Norman times. (The towns were Dover, Sandwich, Hythe, Romney and Hastings.) Its wardens have included the Duke of Wellington, who died in an armchair there in 1852, Sir Winston Churchill, W.H. Smith and the Queen Mother, the only woman to have held the office.

RIGHT: DEAL WAS ANOTHER KENT SEASIDE TOWN TO BENEFIT FROM THE ARRIVAL OF RAIL SERVICES. AN INFLUX OF VISITORS CHANGED IT FROM SMUGGLERS' HAUNT TO RESPECTED RESORT.

OVERLEAF: DEAL, PICTURED HERE FROM ITS PIER, OFFERED AMPLE OPPORTUNITIES FOR LEISURE SEEKERS.

Deal did apparently witness one successful invasion. It is claimed locally that between the lifeboat station and the pier is the very spot where Julius Caesar first set foot on land in 55BC.

Today, in common with Greenwich, Deal also has its own operational time ball, the first to be operated by a direct signal via the railway telegraph.

Nearby Folkestone was also rejuvenated by the arrival of the railway, which makes a spectacular entry through carved cliffs to give passengers a stunning water's-edge experience. It was transformed from fishing village to cross-channel port after 1847, when the the South Eastern Railway invested in a new harbour that brought trade and tourism to the town.

Ultimately the railways brought the possibility of a channel tunnel into life. Talk of a tunnel dates back to 1802 when French mining engineer Albert Mathieu put forward his design. A year later, the first English design was proposed by Henri Mottray. But it wasn't until the 1880s that it became a serious prospect. Once again it was the South Eastern Railway putting up the cash. Although tunneling began, fears that the French would use it to invade prompted Parliament to put a stop to the project. Another attempt begun in the 1970s faltered for lack of investment.

The tunnel that's in operation today was started in 1988 and plunges some 75 metres below the sea bed. First used in 1994, it is an engineering feat of distinction. A desire to hold Europe at bay has by now been replaced by the economic necessity of reaching out to our neighbours. However, just as the canals suffered as the original railways flourished, the ports have taken a pummelling because of the cross-channel rail link.

Three miles west of Folkestone, and once served by a branch line through Hythe, is the beginning of another major line of defence. Between 1804 and 1809, when an invasion by Napoleon again seemed imminent, the Royal Military Canal was dug from there to Winchelsea in a 28-mile arc along the inland edge of Romney Marsh.

Meanwhile, as if to symbolise Kent's dual role, the very stretch of coast behind which the canal curves is now the site of one of the county's best-loved tourist attractions: the miniature railway that runs for 13 miles across the marsh. The brainchild of two wealthy racing drivers who were also railway enthusiasts, it was opened between Hythe and New Romney in 1927 and extended to Dungeness in 1828. One of its stations is at Dymchurch, where Edith Nesbit, the author of *The Railway Children*, was born, and where two Martello towers can be seen.

11220. - DEAL. VIEW FROM PIER.

The next part of the journey took us back to Ashford and off down a different line to the south-west. Perhaps inadvertently, while travelling on a similar route Bradshaw identifies a possible new industry for Kent. 'The main line on leaving Ashford makes a gradual approach towards the coast, swerving slightly to the south east and having on each side a delightful champaign [sic] country.'

Indeed, the chalk downs of the south coast are mirrored across the channel in the region that makes champagne. The climate is also similar. Now, for the first time, Kent is gaining a reputation for the sparkling wines it produces. Using Pinot Noir, Chardonnay and Pinot Meunier grapes, Kent's wine makers are winning international prizes for flavour, colour and bouquet. The amount of land devoted to vineyards has increased by almost 50 per cent in five years. By 2014 the Kent harvest is likely to produce at least 3 million bottles of still and sparkling wine.

The line from Ashford bridges the Royal Military Canal and heads across the western side of Romney Marsh and the Isle of Oxney and out of the county. Once in Sussex it again crosses the canal before reaching Rye. Like its neighbour Winchelsea, Rye was once a thriving medieval port and made an additional member of the Cinque Ports, but is now some way inland.

All enquiries to PR 300 Information Bureau, Hastings

HASTINGS
AND ST. LEONARDS
BRITISH RAILWAYS

Fast and Frequent Service of Trains from London

LESS A BATTLEGROUND, MORE A PLAYGROUND, HASTINGS WAS TRANSFORMED WITH THE ARRIVAL OF THE TRAIN AND BEGAN CATERING FOR HOLIDAYMAKERS WHILE MAINTAINING ITS BEACH-BASED FISHING FLEET.

Our final destination on this journey is Hastings, whose name will always be associated with the last successful invasion of England. In fact it was six miles away, at what is now called Battle, that William the Conqueror defeated King Harold, but it was at Hastings that he prepared his forces for action after landing at Pevensey.

The most westerly of the Cinque Ports, Hastings too fell on hard times after its harbour silted up. However, early in the nineteenth century it became a genteel watering place. Then came the railway in 1851, and the town prepared itself for change. Bradshaw remarked approvingly, 'The openness of the coast and smoothness of the beach have long made Hastings a favourite and recommended resort. The shore is not abrupt and the water almost always limpid and of that beautiful hue so inviting to bathers … A very efficient substitute for a trip to Madeira.'

Today it is not the colour of the sea that catches a visitor's eye but the way the beach has been transformed into a boat park. Indeed, Hastings claims to have the largest beach-based fishing fleet in England.

The boats are pulled up after each trip on to an area of beach known as the Stade, which was greatly improved thanks to the building of a groyne and a harbour at the end of the nineteenth century to shield it from shingle movement. Fishing gear was traditionally stored in the net shops, unusually tall, narrow buildings coated in tar to protect them from the elements. Of necessity the boats must be small, and that means the system of fishing is guaranteed to be sustainable.

The south-eastern corner of Britain has evolved from keeping the rest of the world out to actively beckoning people in. Without doubt railways helped bridge the gap between the no-nonsense Napoleonic rebuff carefully constructed around Kent and beyond at the beginning of the nineteenth century to the breaking down of borders that has been taking place increasingly since the railways came on the scene.

Some 170 years after it was published, Bradshaw had again proved invaluable in guiding us on our journey through Britain. With it we'd marvelled at the extraordinary Victorian achievements, but also celebrated what's still so exciting about modern Britain. With the last of our journeys at an end and the team finally heading back to their homes, it was with surprising relish that our thoughts turned to where we could go next …

USING PINOT NOIR, CHARDONNAY AND PINOT MEUNIER GRAPES, KENT'S WINE MAKERS ARE WINNING INTERNATIONAL PRIZES

INDEX

PICTURE CREDITS

GREAT
VICTORIAN
RAILWAY
JOURNEYS

KAREN FARRINGTON

WILLIAM
COLLINS

ACKNOWLEDGEMENTS

To write a book about Victorian railways is to chart the changes that transformed Britain from rural idyll to industrial powerhouse. It required extensive reading of published and internet resources. Among the most inspirational books that I used were *A Historical Dictionary of Railways in the British Isles* by David Wragg, *The Age of Steam* by Thomas Crump, *Along Country Lines* by Paul Atterbury, *Ironing the Land* by Kevin O'Connor, *On the Slow Train* by Michael Williams, *Eleven Minutes Late* by Matthew Engel, *Bradshaw's Railway Map 1907*, re-published by Old House Books and *A Book of Railway Journeys*, an anthology compiled by Ludovic Kennedy. On the internet Grace's Guide was a beacon, as were all the superb websites hosted by heritage lines too numerous to mention.

First and foremost, my thanks to everyone at talkbackTHAMES who has supported this book from start to finish. Without the help and advice of John Comerford and Jay Taylor this book would not have been possible. Lucy Butler generously shared her knowledge with me, helping greatly by supplying photographs and interpreting research material. Jacqueline Moreton, Esther Johnson and Cat Ledger provided invaluable back-up. Pam Cavannagh at the BBC once again kept us all on track. And special thanks to Michael Portillo for his support.

Biggest thanks, however, go to Nick Constable for ceaseless support and encouragement. Thanks also to Lewis, Conor and Annie for their consideration.

Karen Farrington
November 2011

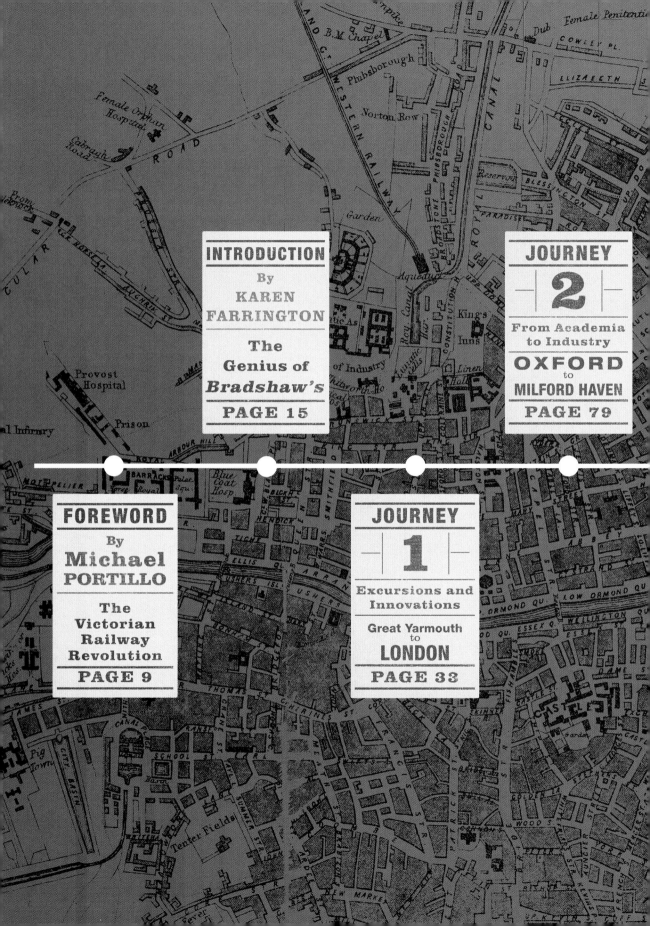

THE SOLENT

Sowley Pond

Gurnet Bay

Thorney Bay

Lr Cocklee
Ben Street

Newtown River

Elmsworth

Stugwell

Nort

East Hampstead

PARKHURST
FOREST

Lower Hampstead

Newtown

Ningwood Common

Upper
Watchingwell

Hurst Castle

Black Rock

YARMOUTH

Thorley

Thorley St.

Shalfleet

Lr Watchingwell

Forest Side

Norton

WIGHT

Swainstone

NEW

Freshwater Ho.

Wilmingwood
Green

L W

Dog
Kennel

Freshwater

Red Lion

Afton House

Calbourn

Attan Farm

Tapnell Farm

Churchills

Westover

Rawridge

Bowcomb

Freshwater Gate

Attan Down

Chessells

Lynch

Gallibury Down

Idlcombe

Nedds

Shalcomb

Mottistone
Down

Brixton
Down

Gatco

Compton Bay

Bradlee

Down

Lemerston
Down

Chille
St

Brook Ledge

Mottestone

Lynch

MED

N

Brook Chine

MEE

Drapers

Brighstone

Shorewell

Chilton
Green

Bull Rock

Grange

Brixton

Ros

Chilton Chine

Smallbroon

Billingham
House

Grange Chine

Sutton

Baines Chine

Brixton

Chine

Kingston

Cowlease Chine

Atherfield
Gr

Strou

Bay

Atherfield Rocks

Whale Chine

Chale

Walpen Chine

Chale

Blackgang Chine

Bay

FOREWORD

By Michael PORTILLO

The Victorian Railway Revolution

Since 2009, when I started making televised train journeys using *Bradshaw's Handbook*, I have tried to imagine what impact and impression the arrival of the railways made on British society. Of course every generation since has experienced technological change, which has, if anything, grown faster. As we look back over twenty years, most of us can no longer understand how we lived without mobile phones and the internet. Similarly, a Victorian by the 1850s must have struggled to recall the days when he or she had had to travel by coach, never able to exceed the speed of a horse. There had been a revolution in communications, perhaps similar in scope to the one that we are experiencing today.

But on top of that, Britain underwent a physical metamorphosis. Where before, country lanes meandered, now embankments, tunnels and viaducts scythed through the landscape. Stations sprouted up, resembling Italian palaces, French châteaux or even Gothic cathedrals. Fearsome locomotives belching fire and steam frightened the horses as they sliced through city centres, or engulfed fields in flame as stray sparks set light to hay or stubble.

I remember being in awe and fear of steam locomotives. They were so big and noisy. Their wheels towered above me (especially when I was a boy, of course) and they were given to highly unpredictable behaviour, suddenly releasing clouds of water vapour with a hiss that made me jump. How did the Victorian middle classes in their finery, how did genteel ladies, cope with their sudden proximity to these roaring fireboxes, with being brought face to face with the industrial revolution?

How could they adapt to speed? At the Rainhill trials to choose a source of traction for the Manchester to Liverpool railway, Stephenson's *Rocket* reached 30 miles per hour, a velocity previously unseen and hard even to imagine. The potency of the technology took some getting used to. At the inauguration of that line in 1830, William Huskisson MP, former President of the Board of Trade, left his carriage to greet the Prime Minister, the Duke of Wellington. The *Rocket*, running on the parallel track, struck him as he tried to scramble out of its path. A train transported him to the vicarage at Eccles where he died of his injuries.

When Isambard Kingdom Brunel opened his epic Box tunnel on the Great Western Railway, Dionysius Lardner, a professor of astronomy, was on hand to warn that if the brakes failed the train

PREVIOUS PAGE: Bradshaw's map of the Isle of Wight.

On an engine from the Downpatrick Heritage Steam Railway.

would accelerate and the passengers suffocate; and some at least believed him and alighted before the tunnel to continue their journey by more traditional means.

At the beginning of the nineteenth century William Blake wrote of 'dark Satanic Mills'. The railways greatly accelerated the industrial revolution. George Bradshaw was enthusiastic about the railways, and the *Handbook* describes with admiration the dimensions of stations, tunnels and bridges. But the book's depictions of iron-smelting furnaces lighting up the night sky sometimes bring the fires of Hell to mind. Bradshaw's awareness of the social consequences of the industrial revolution suggests that Victorians saw that progress had brought both paradise and inferno.

Of Merthyr Tydfil the *Handbook* says:

> Visitors should see the furnaces by night, when the red glare of the flames produces an uncommonly striking effect. Indeed, the town is best visited at that time, for by day it will be found dirty... Cholera and fever are of course at home here ... We do hope that proper measures will be taken by those who draw enormous wealth from these [iron and coal] works to improve the condition of the people.

Quakers like Bradshaw tended to believe strongly that the industrialist owed a duty of care to his workers and their families.

To judge from the Great Western works at Swindon, railway magnates were appropriately paternalistic, housing the employees in model dwellings and supplying free rail travel for a family summer holiday in Devon or Cornwall. Many thousands would depart on charter trains, turning Swindon for a week into a virtual ghost town.

Train travel vastly broadened the horizons of working-class people. The mid-nineteenth century saw an enormous growth in travel and in resorts. As the railway navvies levelled the land, the railways levelled society. Those of modest means, who before train travel might scarcely have travelled beyond a 15-mile radius of home, could leave the smoke and grime of city life and enjoy the 'salubrious' (to use a favourite Bradshaw word) sea or mountain air. Town dwellers could for the first time enjoy fresh sea fish and a range of perishable farm products.

The railways threw up some interesting questions of etiquette, and drove social change. The usual requirement that ladies be chaperoned was difficult to enforce on trains. The new freedoms offered by rail travel contributed to increasing equality between the sexes. Nonetheless, women sometimes journeyed in fear, especially in compartments on trains that had no corridor. Some ladies secreted pins in their mouths as a way to deal with male passengers who in the darkness of a tunnel might attempt to steal a kiss!

Any worries that travelling by train was not ladylike were dismissed when Queen Victoria herself took to the tracks in 1842. Although she was nervous of travelling at high speed, she became a frequent railway passenger. The train conveyed her to Windsor, Osborne House and Balmoral. In 1882 it carried her to Nice, on the first of her nine visits to the Riviera. As though to emphasise how thoroughly the railway had entered national life, after her death on the Isle of Wight a train brought the Queen's coffin home to Windsor.

Her lifetime covers most of the railway building that was done in this country. Poignantly, the last link of the West Highland line between Fort William and Mallaig (since made famous by the Harry Potter films) opened in 1901, the year of the Queen's death. So, if you take a train today, it is extremely likely that you will travel on a route laid down in her day.

British national self-confidence reached its zenith in the Victorian era. The empire was vast and, to Bradshaw's mind, the greatest that the world had ever seen. London was the biggest city on earth and Manchester could take cotton from India, turn it into manufactured garments and sell them back in India below the cost of local products. No hint of colonial guilt affected our patriotic pride.

That Britain was the first country to open an inter-city railway, that geniuses like Brunel and the Stephensons achieved engineering wonders, were evidence of the superiority of British ingenuity, science and entrepreneurship.

As today I travel along Victorian track beds I try to imagine the awe and pride that railways then inspired. Actually, if I look out the carriage window at the stations and viaducts that Victorian engineers erected, imagining it is very easy.

Michael Portillo
2012

INTRODUCTION

By
KAREN
FARRINGTON

The
Genius of
Bradshaw's

W hen Queen Victoria came to the throne trains had already been running for a dozen years, with modest services along variously sized tracks that amounted to less than 300 miles in length. By then farmers no longer believed trains would set fire to crops or frighten horses to madness, although the sight of a steam engine, rare and awesome, was still sufficiently thrilling to move waving children to the track side.

However, in 1837 a tipping point was fast approaching. During Victoria's reign there was a headlong rush towards railway building that careered out of control, with profit rather than common sense at its heart.

With the rampant growth of railways, regimented tracks treated towns and fields with the same disdain as they splintered into an arbitrary network that reached from city to coast. The UK map was scored with lines that linked one town to the next – or sometimes bypassed entire populations for the sake of a country halt, depending

PREVIOUS PAGE: Bradshaw's map of Oxford.

Restored Caledonian Railway 0-6-0 steam engine 828 steams along the Strathspey Railway track between Broomhill and Boat of Garten.

on local politics. Before Victoria's death in 1901 some 18,670 miles of track were on the ground.

One man had the vision to pull the hotchpotch of strands together to make sense of Britain's railways for the travelling public. George Bradshaw was an engraver in Manchester whose first major work was a map of British canals, rivers and railways, published in 1830. In 1838 he began producing railway timetables which, four years later, began appearing as a monthly guide.

One of the first challenges Bradshaw faced was the time lag between, say, London and the West Country, which amounted to some 10 minutes, with separate communities setting their watches by their own calculations of sunrise and sunset. Engineer Isambard Kingdom Brunel had already identified the problem and insisted on standardising clock faces across the Great Western Railway network, using 'railway time'. Bradshaw picked up the baton and made 'railway time' uniform for the whole of Britain for the purposes of his timetabling.

Eventually Bradshaw's publishing stable included a *Continental Railway Guide* and a *Railway Manual, Shareholders' Guide*. But it was the monthly guides that were best sellers and, after Bradshaw's untimely death in 1853 from cholera, the publication continued to appear under his name. Indeed, it was published until 1961.

George Bradshaw,
c. 1850s.

The station clock at
Crowcombe Heathfield
on the West Somerset
railway line.

This book focuses on another Bradshaw publication, *Bradshaw's Tourist Handbook*, published in 1866. Inside its pages lies a lyrical image of Britain as it was 150 years ago. There are both hearty recommendations and dire warnings for the Victorian explorer embarking on long-distance domestic journeys. For example, *Bradshaw's* gives an emphatic thumbs-up to Gravesend, with a description that would make any casual reader want to hop on a train and visit:

> Gravesend is one of the most pleasantly situated and easily attained of all the places thronged upon the margin of the Thames. It is, moreover, a capital starting point for a series of excursions through the finest parts of Kent and has, besides, in its own immediate neighbourhood some tempting allurements to the summer excursionist in the way of attractive scenery and venerable buildings.

But Cornwall, which today might be considered the brighter prospect of the two for travellers, is altogether less impressive through nineteenth-century eyes:

> Cornwall, from its soil, appearance and climate, is one of the least inviting of the English counties. A ridge of bare and rugged hills intermixed with bleak moors runs through the midst of its whole length and exhibits the appearance of a dreary waste.

As intriguing as these descriptive passages are the accompanying advertisements, for 'Davis's Patent Excelsior Knife Cleaner' and 'Morison's Pills – a cure for all curable diseases'. The 1866 fares for day trips and holidays are also advertised.

Excursions were a joyful hallmark of the Victorian age. Many people had more leisure time and spare income than ever before and they broadened their horizons by travelling across the country or the Channel to new resorts and to attend great occasions like exhibitions and major sporting events. For the railway companies, dedicated trains to resorts or events were a profitable way to use idle stock at off-peak times.

To travel to Dublin via Liverpool from Hull in 1866 cost the first-class passenger 43 shillings. It was 10 shillings less in second class. Return tickets to the Continent via Calais from London were £2 first class and £1 10 shillings in second. Meanwhile, a first-class ticket from Nottingham to Windermere was priced at 42 shillings, and 10 shillings less again for those in second class.

The virtues of Bradshaw's guides in all their forms have long been recognised. Journalist and travel writer Charles Larcom Graves (1856–1944) penned the following verse, reflecting his own cosy association.

When books are pow'rless to beguile
And papers only stir my bile,
For solace and relief I flee
To Bradshaw or the ABC
And find the best of recreations
In studying the names of stations.

Certainly in those days before the advent of through tickets, *Bradshaw's Monthly Railway Guide* was an often-consulted bible for travellers who industriously sought arrival and departure times during detailed journey planning.

No doubt the tripper clutching a Bradshaw guide would feel a rush of nerves as well as excitement in boarding the train, for the notion that railways were dangerous took a long while to subside and railway safety standards were poor by comparison with today. To compound matters, railway companies were reluctant to spend money on even basic safety measures, preferring to reward their shareholders rather than to protect their passengers and staff. Accordingly, brightly painted engines were kept whistle clean but might not be fitted with an adequate number of brakes. The prospect of a rail crash in Victorian times and death by technology invariably filled travellers with fear.

It wasn't until 1875 that a Royal Commission on Railway Accidents was established. It fostered trials on different braking systems, with American-designed systems coming out on top. However, not all railway casualties were linked to crashes, according to railway writer and Royal Commission member William Mitchell Acworth.

Passengers tried to jump on and off trains moving at full speed with absolute recklessness. Again and again it is recorded, 'injured, jumped out after his hat', 'fell off, riding on the side of a wagon', 'skull broken, riding on the top of the carriage, came into collision with a bridge', 'guard's head struck against a bridge, attempting to remove a passenger who had improperly seated himself outside', 'fell out of a third class carriage while pushing and jostling with a friend'.

'SERIOUS ACCIDENTS ... HAPPENED TO PERSONS WHO JUMPED OFF WHEN THE CARRIAGES WERE GOING AT SPEED, GENERALLY AFTER THEIR HATS'

'Of all the serious accidents reported to the Board of Trade,' writes one authority, *'twenty-two happened to persons who jumped off when the carriages were going at speed, generally after their hats, and five persons were run over when lying either drunk or asleep upon the line.'*

Putting aside the dread of disaster, there was a lot of general discomfort to overcome, even for those travelling in first class. With as few as four wheels per carriage in the early days of rail, there was no sense of a rhythmic lull, more a violent vibration. Moreover, for decades carriages were unheated, although foot-warmers were available at a price on most routes. Initially only first-class travellers were permitted their use.

Until the mid-1840s third-class passengers were transported in open wagons that were sometimes attached to goods trains. In winter passengers were typically underdressed while subject to wind and rain,

'A Train of the First Class (top) and a Train of the Second Class (bottom)' from *Coloured View of the Liverpool & Manchester Railway*, engraved by S. G. Hughes and published by Ackermann & Co., London in 1832/33.

THE STAPLEHURST RAIL DISASTER

Author Charles Dickens showed remarkable presence of mind after he was involved in the Staplehurst disaster, but later he wrote about the long-term after-effects he suffered.

Charles Dickens (1812–1870) in middle age.

On 9 June 1865 Dickens was returning from France aboard the boat train, heading for Charing Cross. Along the way, at Staplehurst in Kent, track was being renewed on a railway bridge by a group of 'gangers' or 'waymen', employed by the thousand across the country to repair and maintain track. (The remains of line-side huts where equipment was stored and tea was brewed for this unsung army are sometimes still visible today.)

The train was known as 'the tidal', because its timing varied with the tide that brought the ferries to their berth. According to foreman John Benge's calculations, it would roll into view at 5.20 p.m. In fact, the train was two hours earlier than that and was bearing down on the fractured bridge at a speed of 50 mph. It was impossible to return the necessary track to its position in time.

With rails missing, the locomotive ploughed into the mud lying 10 feet below. The first coach almost went after it but lurched to a halt, balanced precariously between engine and bridge. Its coupling with the rest of the train snapped and another five coaches, travelling with momentum, piled into the gap, landing at all angles.

Ten passengers died and 49 people were injured. Dickens, who was in the first carriage, was uninjured and climbed out of the window. The author tended the wounded as best he could. One man died in his arms and he saw several other dead bodies as he picked his way cautiously through the injured, offering water and brandy.

He wrote about the shocking experience in a letter:

> *No imagination can conceive the ruin, or the extraordinary weights under which people were lying, or the complications into which they were twisted among iron and wood, and mud and water.*
>
> *I have a – I don't know what to call it – constitutional presence of mind and was*

The Staplehurst Rail Disaster: Dickens, Ellen Ternan and her mother escaped unhurt, but he suffered psychologically to the end of his life.

not in the least flustered at the time ... But, in writing these scanty words of recollection, I feel the shakes and am obliged to stop.

The crash left him at a low ebb. Three years later he wrote:

To this hour I have sudden rushes of terror, even when riding in a Hansom cab, which are perfectly unreasonable but quite insurmountable ... my reading secretary and companion knows so well when one of these momentary seizures comes upon me in a railway carriage that he instantly produces a dram of brandy which rallies the blood to the heart and generally prevails.

Dickens died five years later, on the anniversary of the Staplehurst crash.

TO THIS HOUR I HAVE SUDDEN RUSHES OF TERROR, EVEN WHEN RIDING IN A HANSOM CAB, WHICH ARE PERFECTLY UNREASONABLE BUT QUITE INSURMOUNTABLE

and might even suffer exposure. Travelling inside carriages modelled on stagecoaches was not without its disadvantages either.

If the atmosphere in the small railway compartments became fetid it was tempting to open the window. However, passengers risked being enveloped in smuts and steam from the engine rather than enjoying the bracing fresh air they'd sought. The question of whether or not to open windows on stuffy journeys was often the cause of fall-outs between passengers.

Borrowing an American idea, railway companies began to introduce more luxuriously appointed accommodation with restaurant facilities from the 1880s. Self-contained sleepers were on the rails from 1873. However, the first train with a corridor running its entire length wasn't introduced until 1892. Until then lavatories were simply not available to third-class travellers, and guards were sometimes compelled to clamber along the outside of moving carriages.

The Comfort of the Pullman Coach of a late-Victorian Passenger Train by Harry Green (b. 1920).

An electric signal for railways invented by a Mr King of Paxton, Derbyshire and exhibited at the Crystal Palace Electric Exhibition in 1882. The signal worked by passing electricity through a series of signal-posts placed along a railway line, which would activate a clock hand demonstrating the length of time elapsing between trains.

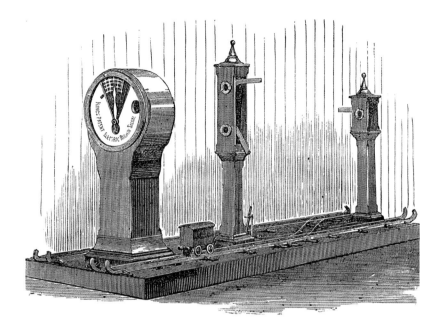

There's no doubt that railways were evolving throughout the Victorian era, although not as quickly as some had hoped. Bigger engines were soon hauling more carriages, increasing capacity and cutting costs. However, they weren't going much faster than early models. Until braking issues were resolved drivers were compelled to travel more slowly than they might have liked.

Steel rails were introduced at a junction outside Derby by the Midland Rail Company in 1857. They replaced wrought-iron rails that were so subject to wear and tear they were renewed every six months. Ten years later the steel rails, which carried about 500 trains daily, were still in use. Steel rails enhanced the comfort of passengers, too, making for a smoother ride, and soon steel was used in bridges and in locomotive manufacture after industrial advances made it cheap to produce.

If safety was a worry for passengers it was an even bigger issue among railway staff. In the 1870s an average of 750 railway employees were killed each year as managers turned a blind eye to even basic safety measures. However, advances in signalling did mean there were fewer collisions.

In early railway history, signalling was rudimentary and varied between companies. Alarmingly, two red discs on a hand-held wand indicated the line was 'all clear' on the Great Western while the same signal meant 'danger' on the London & Birmingham. Although flag-wavers were placed along busy lines, most drivers could only hope to stop in time if they saw danger ahead and could muster sufficient braking power.

A system of 'blocks' was then devised. Tracks were divided into a series of blocks and a train was only given permission to proceed if the block ahead was empty. At first signallers allowed 10 minutes between trains – although they still could not be sure the line ahead was empty. The number of trains permitted to run was duly curtailed. Soon railway managers pushed for the time gap to be reduced and, as a consequence, the number of accidents increased again.

The introduction of the telegraph brought about automatic signalling, in use from the 1840s. Soon the rail-side flag waver was replaced by a signalman who had his own dedicated space at the station. Typically, a weather-boarded box stood in a commanding position at one end of the platform after the 1860s, and by 1900 there were more than 13,000 in use all over Britain.

When he was president of the Board of Trade in the mid-1840s, William Gladstone set about involving government in the higgledy-piggledy railway administration. However, railway companies were staunchly opposed to sharing profits and power with government and used their political leverage to scotch the plans. Eventually, the Railway Clearing House (RCH) was instituted in 1842 to sort out who owed what to whom as a result of long-distance railway journeys. Railway companies were invited to join, although the RCH didn't achieve national coverage for more than 20 years.

Mostly the RCH accountants relied on honesty. However, an army of some 500 men were regularly dispatched to sit at key railway junctions noting every carriage and wagon that went by. For such perilous work they were relatively poorly paid, out in all weathers, and worked 13-hour shifts. High standards were generally expected of railway workers, as the 1856 rulebook issued by the Taff Vale Company reveals.

Every person is to come on duty daily, clean in his person and clothes, shaved, and his shoes blacked.

It is urgently requested every person … on Sunday and Holy Days, when he is not required on duty that he will attend a place of worship; as it will be the means of promotion when vacancies occur.

EVERY PERSON IS TO COME ON DUTY DAILY, CLEAN IN HIS PERSON AND CLOTHES, SHAVED, AND HIS SHOES BLACKED

William Ewart Gladstone (1809–1898).

(In addition, singing, whistling, laughing and political activity were banned. No one could become a stationmaster unless he was married, and all staff had to salute officers and directors.)

The difference in gauges across the networks was another issue that needed a national view. Confusion reigned at Gloucester station, where the broad-gauge Great Western Railway met the rest. Every passenger, animal and pound of freight had to make a change. Brunel had proved his broad gauge was superior when it came to speed, hauling an 80-ton load at almost 60 mph on one occasion. But the Royal Commission established to investigate railway gauges thought there was more to the argument than mere speed. It was cheaper to make a broad gauge narrow than vice versa, and there was already much more standard gauge on the ground than broad. Consequently, standard gauge was required by law in all railways built after 1846,

'Gauge War': an 1845 cartoon by Angus Reach on the conflict between the broad gauge of the Great Western Railway and the narrow gauge.

THE BROAD GAUGE AND THE NARROW GAUGE.

although the Great Western Railway didn't say farewell to its wide lines entirely until 1892.

The railways gave impetus to ship building, dock trade, harbours, hotels and the leisure industry. They modified everyone's lives and existing businesses beyond recognition.

Immense changes were made in the postal system, for example. Before the advent of the railways letters and parcels were transported with comparative speed by horse-drawn mail coaches that travelled across the nation. However, it was soon apparent that trains would do the same job more quickly and soon mail coaches became second-rate alternatives to rail.

Enterprising postal chiefs soon realised that trains could not only deliver the mail more rapidly but could be used as travelling sorting offices to further speed the progress of the post. As early as 1838 mail was sorted in a moving train, on this occasion a carriage made from a converted horse-box, on the Grand Junction Railway. The idea was seized upon by other services and incorporated into trains. These were first known as Railway Post Offices and later as Travelling Post Offices or TPOs.

From 1852 the mail bag pick-up apparatus became a common sight at the side of main lines. Aboard the train, postal workers secured letters inside leather pouches weighing anything between 20 and 60 lb (9–27 kg). These were attached to hinged metal arms that could swing out through open doors, dangling the pouch a few feet above the ground and several feet from the side of the carriage. A robust line-side net then scooped up the pouch and the metal arm retracted. To pass mail to a train, a postman positioned similar leather pouches in nets by the tracks so an arm from the train could 'catch' them and toss them through the open doors into the train.

Today it seems an old-fashioned and inefficient way to exchange mail, yet the system was used throughout Victorian times and well into the twentieth century, until 1971.

Throughout the era, the volume of post continued to increase thanks to a uniformity imposed by Sir Rowland Hill, who published his pamphlet *Post Office Reform* in the year Victoria came to the throne. Hill saw that, thanks to the railways, mail could be distributed

with increasing ease across the nation. If the cost was kept low more people than ever would use the service, he predicted. By 1840 the Penny Black stamp, bearing the profile of Queen Victoria and snipped from a sheet with scissors, came into use. Within a few years the first Christmas card was sent. By the mid-1850s pillar boxes were appearing on street corners to aid the collection of mail, and by Victoria's death there were some 32,500 pillar boxes in the UK. Without the age of the train, it is difficult to see how the postal service would have proliferated.

There were victims that fell to the age of rail, including stagecoaches, a sound road system built by Turnpike Trusts that eventually went out of the business, numerous ancient sites ploughed up for rail beds, and the rural economy. But the trains brought progress apace. At Victoria's death, *The Times* contemplated the achievements won in her lifetime and in its first breath addressed the expansion of railways.

> *Viewing that reign in its incidents, what a chronicle it offers of great national achievement, startling inventions and progress in every direction.*
>
> *The first railway was constructed before Victoria came to the throne but the universal development in the appliance of steam and electricity took place in her time and it profoundly altered the conditions of political and social life.*

More than just a method of getting from A to B, the railways imbued the country from top to bottom with a sense of 'can do' that had for the most part been sorely lacking. No aspect of life was left untouched by trains, and the interwoven railway lines that webbed the country were springboards for still more social and economic progress in the twentieth century.

There's an argument to say that every train trip of the nineteenth century fell into the bracket of 'great Victorian railway journeys', for there were sights, sounds, smells and tastes that are rarely re-created today. More than a series of sentimental journeys in pastoral England, the following five expeditions echo the eccentricities and evolution of Victorian railways, glimpsing an age of lines and locomotives the legacy of which is still evident today.

JOURNEY

1

Excursions and Innovations

Great Yarmouth to LONDON

In Victorian times Great Yarmouth was fabled for two commodities: herring and holidays. The fishing industry was established long before the era began, peopled in part by Scottish fishermen who had sailed down with their families to live on the sandy promontory and exploit the shimmering shoals of the North Sea. Fish were then salted, barrelled and sent across the country.

Initially, the town was bounded by walls and fishermen lived cheek by jowl with one another, crammed into streets known as The Rows. For decades it was The Rows that gave Yarmouth its defining features, and they expanded to fill every available inch. Several wider roads ran roughly parallel with the waterfront. Narrower passages extended from those roads at right angles, creating a medieval grid that incorporated housing for rich and poor alike.

The Rows were so narrow that a law was passed to ensure doors opened inwards rather than outwards, to avoid injury to passers-by. Daylight and privacy were at a premium for the inhabitants. Drains that acted as open sewers ran down The Rows, with good community health dependent on prevailing winds and driving rain to drive the steady outpouring of sewage into the sea.

Author Charles Dickens was struck by the bunched-up quaintness:

A Row is a long, narrow lane or alley quite straight, or as nearly as maybe, with houses on each side, both of which you can sometimes touch at once with the fingertips of each hand, by stretching out your arms to their full extent.

Now and then the houses overhang and even join above your head, converting the row so far into a sort of tunnel or tubular passage. Many picturesque old bits of domestic architecture are to be found among the rows. In some rows there is little more than a blank wall for the double boundary. In others the houses retreat into tiny square courts where washing and clear starching was done.

Eventually Yarmouth's population outgrew the confines of the thirteenth-century town walls and, led by the example of wealthy merchants, spilled over on to nearby land formed when the seaways silted up.

Bradshaw's guidebook mentions to the town's fishing industry, also making reference to The Rows:

PREVIOUS PAGE: **The Great Western Railway Terminus at Paddington Station.**

RIGHT: **Great Yarmouth, Row Number 60, 1908.**

OVERLEAF: **A steam train passes Weybourne windmill on the North Norfolk Railway connecting Sheringham with Holt.**

The old town contains about 150 streets or passages, locally called rows, extending from east to west, in which many remains of antiquity may still be traced ... the inhabitants are chiefly engaged in the mackerel, herring or deep sea fisheries which are here prosecuted to a very great extent with much success.

The Jetty, Great Yarmouth

Yet it makes little reference to the holiday trade which was by then beginning to boom. Great Yarmouth had long been a destination for a few well-heeled tourists who enjoyed the fresh air and the perceived benefits of sea water.

It was the arrival of trains that fired up the holiday trade, with trippers coming from London and other cities to sample the delights

IT WAS THE
ARRIVAL OF
TRAINS THAT
FIRED UP THE
HOLIDAY TRADE,
WITH TRIPPERS
COMING FROM
LONDON AND
OTHER CITIES
TO SAMPLE THE
DELIGHTS OF THE
EAST COAST

of the east coast. Without the onset of train travel, it's doubtful that the national passion for a trip to the seaside would ever have taken root, for travel by coach was slow and expensive by comparison. The town's first station, known as Yarmouth Vauxhall, opened in 1844, and so popular was Great Yarmouth as a destination that one estimate insists more than 80,000 people visited the resort just two years after that station opened.

Great Yarmouth was once served by four separate train lines, and a clutch of town centre stations and no fewer than 17 other stations were spread around the borough. It was such a popular destination that the Great Eastern Railway produced postcards featuring views of Great Yarmouth to sell to its passengers.

When a suspension bridge collapsed on 2 May 1845, killing 79, the dead surely included some of the new influx of tourists. People had gathered on the bridge to watch a clown in a barrel being towed down the River Bure by a team of geese. As the barrel passed under the bridge they rushed for the other side to catch more of the spectacle, causing supporting chains to snap. Scores of people, mostly women and children, were hurled into the river and local men took to their boats to save them.

According to an account in the *Norwich Gazette*, tragedy on a far greater scale was averted:

> *It can be easily imagined that a mass of people thus precipitated into water, five feet deep, would have but a small chance of saving themselves; and but for the prompt assistance which was afforded, few, very few, would have escaped. Boats and wherries were immediately in motion and from 20 to 30 with gallant crews, were soon among the drowning people, picking them up with wonderful rapidity. Many were put on the shore in their wet clothes who went directly home, and no account was taken of the number thus saved.*

The tombstone of nine-year-old bridge disaster victim Thomas Beloe, in nearby St Nicholas' Churchyard, depicts the tragedy. In fact saving lives became something of a theme for Great Yarmouth, with local boat-builder James Beeching winning the 100 guinea first prize in an 1851 competition to find the best self-righting lifeboat.

THE SELF-RIGHTING LIFEBOAT

Lifeboat design was still in its infancy in the Victorian era and the 1851 competition was launched to design a new and better boat. It had several stated aims. Lifeboats of the future needed to be lighter in construction than previous models so that they could more easily be launched from the beach. They also needed to be cheaper to make so that more could be produced. With such generous prize money on offer the competition attracted 280 entries from across Britain, Europe and even the USA.

Following adjustments, and with inspiration taken from other designs submitted for judging, the Beeching lifeboat became the basis of the longstanding Norfolk and Suffolk class of boats. Throughout the second half of the nineteenth century the design was improved, but the Beeching boat's enduring feature was its buoyancy, with air-filled cases at the bow and stern and cork cladding. It effectively discharged the seawater which frequently swamped small, open boats through valved tubes, and an iron keel acted as ballast. It was stable, self-righting, fast, robust and comparatively roomy. Boats like this saved countless hundreds of lives during the remainder of the century.

A self-righting boat like Beeching's was popular with lifeboat men. Analysis of the number of capsizes between 1852 and 1874 showed their instincts were probably right. In that time, 35 self-righters rolled with the loss of 25 men out of a total of 401. At the same time 8 non-self-righters capsized, killing 87 men out of 140.

A lifeboat rests on its carriage, c. 1880.

However, a train from Great Yarmouth heading for Norwich was involved in a night-time collision on 10 September 1874 in which 25 people died and 50 were injured. It occurred after a signalling error had allowed a 14-coach mail train to rush headlong on a single track into the 13-coach passenger train from Yarmouth. Although the fronts of both trains were smashed to smithereens, the rear coaches were left relatively unscathed. One account of the accident ends with an odd incident that perplexed everyone who witnessed the wreckage:

George Bidder (1806–1868).

> It would be difficult to conceive of a more violent collision … yet it is said that two gentlemen in the last carriage of one of the trains, finding it at a sudden standstill close to the place to which they were going, supposed it had stopped for some unimportant cause and concluded to take advantage of a happy chance which left them almost at the doors of their homes. They accordingly got out and hurried away in the rain, learning only the next morning of the catastrophe in which they had been unconscious participants.

The Great Eastern main line from Yarmouth heads to Reedham, distinguished by one of four swing bridges in the area. This bridge across the River Yare, and the one at Somerleyton – on the branch line that connects Reedham with Lowestoft – spanning the River Waveney were financed by Sir Samuel Morton Peto, entrepreneur and engineering enthusiast.

Both bridges are made from a stout collection of wrought iron, brick, cast steel and timber. When it is in place for trains, the bridge ends rest on piers by the river banks. If it is open for river traffic then the bridge pivots on a central pier using cast steel wheels with a diameter of 16 inches. The load of the open bridge is shouldered by two truss girders.

Even today the bridges are an object of wonder. The man who built the bridges, George Bidder, was equally remarkable. The son of a Devon stonemason, his natural ability with maths manifested itself before he could read or write and his father had him perform in shows around the country for money, under the title of 'a calculating boy'. Fortunately, his potential was spotted by two benefactors, who ultimately paid for his education. In adulthood he teamed up with the

The Reedham railway swing bridge crossing the River Yare.

great Robert Stephenson to work on major railway projects at home and abroad. Perhaps his proudest achievement was to build London's Victoria docks.

The man who financed the swing bridges has a story that perhaps even exceeds that of Bidder. Sir Samuel Morton Peto was born in Woking, Surrey, to a tenant farmer. After two years at boarding school he was made an apprentice to his builder uncle, Henry Peto. In 1830 he took over the business with his cousin Thomas Grissell, and together they changed the landscape of London by building the Houses of Parliament, Trafalgar Square and Nelson's Column, among other landmarks. The business then became involved in building railways.

After he bought Somerleyton Hall in 1844, Peto invested heavily in the area, fashioning Lowestoft into a thriving port and town. He built the railway line to it from Reedham, which opened in 1847 after some two years in construction.

ABOVE: **Somerleyton Hall, the home of Samuel Peto.**

OVERLEAF: **The inauguration of the Great Industrial Exhibition of 1851.**

However, his partner Grissell was becoming nervous about what he perceived as reckless risks taken by Peto in pursuit of railway contracts. The partnership was dissolved and Peto began business anew with his brother-in-law Edward Betts in 1846. They also worked with engineer Thomas Brassey, a millionaire railway builder and civil engineer credited with an enormous number of projects. Previously Brassey had worked with George Stephenson and his acolyte Joseph Locke, and by the time he died Brassey had built a sixth of the railways in Britain and half of those in France.

The trio of Peto, Betts and Brassey built numerous railways at home and abroad. Peto earned the gratitude of Prince Albert by ensuring there were suitable rail links to the Great Exhibition at Crystal Palace in 1851. However, one of the most significant contributions Peto – with Betts and Brassey – made to history was to build a rail link in the Crimea, where Britain was at war with Russia.

In a conflict ignited by Russian occupation of Turkish territories, British hopes of a swift victory were confounded by climate and disease. However, Britain and her allies got back on the front foot with the first strategic use of railways, built and paid for by Peto. A railway line to ferry men and supplies to the front line was in operation by 1855. Five months later the British target, Sebastopol, had fallen.

That same year Peto was given a baronetcy, and for 20 years he was an MP. But in 1866 his riskier ventures caught up with him as the frenzied speculation in railway building known as 'railway mania' reached its third crescendo and brought down a bank, Overend, Gurney & Company, to which Peto was deeply committed. With the bank entering liquidation in 1866 owing about £11 million, he was declared bankrupt. Peto moved to Budapest, hoping to spark railway building there, but he met with no success. He moved back to Britain but died in obscurity in 1889.

Peto had shouldered a lot of the small East Anglian lines into existence. In 1862 many of the small, east coast companies, including the Norfolk Railway, Eastern Union Railway, East Norfolk Railway, Newmarket & Chesterford Railway, Harwich Railway and the East Suffolk Railway, were mopped up by the Great Eastern Railway, along with the more major Eastern Counties Railway. Although they were now officially all one company, it took years for the competitive habit between lines to fall by the wayside.

The branch line to Lowestoft was not the only one to extend from the railway that linked Great Yarmouth to Ipswich. As Lowestoft's fortunes increased, so Southwold further down the coast became the poorer. A lack of railway line was clearly a factor in any future prosperity the town might enjoy, so local people clubbed together to buy shares in the Southwold Railway Company that would join the main line at Halesworth.

After protracted negotiations, a 3-foot gauge was chosen for the route, which had a single track that ran for nearly nine miles. It opened on 24 September 1879. The locomotives that used the line were limited to a speed of 16 mph and before long it was quicker to cycle there than take the train. Coupled with a reputation for unreliability and a laissez-faire attitude among station staff, the line became something of a laughing stock and the subject of jokey postcards.

But there was plenty to recommend Southwold, including an attractive North Sea coastline and its proximity to Dunwich, the medieval city that was reclaimed by the sea after a series of violent storms. Victorian curiosity was piqued about the city, which by all accounts at one time had 52 churches, city walls, a Royal palace and a mint. In 1900 the railway carried 10,000 passengers, 90,000 tons of minerals and 600 tons of merchandise. It finally closed in 1929 in the face of fierce competition from buses.

Another branch line further south at Ipswich led to Felixstowe, today the nation's biggest commercial port, which had its fate and fortunes defined by one man.

George Tomline was an enormously wealthy MP who made his home at nearby Orwell Park, named for the River Orwell, in Suffolk. After rebuilding the house he furnished it with fine art, an extensive library and even an observatory. He was known as 'Colonel Tomline' but the title was the result of a loose association with a regiment rather than distinguished military service.

Tomline conceived the plan for a railway line that would leave the main Great Eastern Railway at Westerfield and would head for Felixstowe via Orwell Park. On the face of it there was naked self-interest in having his own railway station. However, Tomline maintained his motive was to provide work for hard-pressed local people.

The odds were stacked in his favour from the outset. Following a concerted campaign of purchasing he already owned most of the land needed for the route. When it applied for parliamentary approval in 1875, his company was called the Felixstowe Railway & Pier Company. Within two years (and at a cost of £14,000) the line had opened with three locomotives, 19 passenger carriages and 15 goods wagons on the line. At Felixstowe he built a beach-side station, which was not only on land he owned but was as far away as possible from the Ordnance Hotel, owned by Ipswich brewery magnate John Chevallier Cobbold – a man Tomline apparently detested.

Within two years of its opening, the running of the line was given over to the Great Eastern Railway – but it wasn't the end of the story

as far as Tomline and Felixstowe were concerned. In 1884 his company was renamed the Felixstowe Dock & Railway Company, having secured the necessary permissions for construction work that would provide moorings, warehousing and railway sidings. Although Tomline gave up his interest in the railway three years later he maintained a link with the dock, which finally opened in 1886, three years before his death. Since then it has grown beyond all expectation.

Felixstowe finally got a town-centre railway station in 1898, courtesy of the Great Eastern Railway.

Midway between Ipswich and Colchester, Suffolk gives way to Essex, although the slow pace of rural life remained the same. When the Great Eastern main line crossed the River Stour on the Essex and Suffolk border it bisected an area known today as Constable Country. It contains, of course, the vistas that inspired artist John Constable. Some of his most famous works, including *The Haywain* and *Flatford Mill*, were painted here near his boyhood home of East Bergholt in Suffolk.

Constable died in 1837, the year Victoria came to the throne. During his lifetime his paintings were more popular in France than ever they were in England. Both he and fellow artist J. M. W. Turner were lambasted by critics of the day for being safe and unadventurous in their work. But Constable insisted he would rather be a poor man in England than a rich one overseas and stayed to forge a living in the only way he knew how.

His inspiration was nature, and his pictures often betrayed the first intrusions of the Industrial Age into rural life. Although he didn't always live there, it was Suffolk scenes he was perpetually drawn to paint. 'I should paint my own places best,' he wrote. 'Painting is but another word for feeling.' An indisputably Romantic painter, his rich use of colour arguably laid the foundations for future trends in art.

The tallest Tudor gatehouse ever built lies further down the line, marking the half-way point between Colchester and Chelmsford. Aside from its architectural glory, Layer Marney Tower has two striking claims to fame. The first is that it was owned from 1835 by Quintin Dick, an MP made notorious by his practice of buying votes. Indeed,

RIGHT: Layer Marney Tower, a Tudor palace damaged by the Great English Earthquake of 1884.

there's some speculation that he spent more money bribing his constituents than any other MP of the era. The son of an Irish linen merchant, Dick spent a total of 43 years as an MP, representing five different constituencies.

The tower's second claim to fame is that it and surrounding buildings built during the reign of King Henry VIII were badly damaged in the Great English Earthquake of 1884, which had its epicentre near Colchester. Afterwards a report in *The Builder* magazine stated the author's belief that the attractive monument was beyond repair: 'The outlay needed to restore the tower to anything like a sound and habitable condition would be so large that the chance of the work ever being done appears remote indeed.'

However, the tower was repaired, thanks to the efforts of the then owners, brother and sister Alfred and Kezia Peache, who re-floored and re-roofed the gatehouse, and created the garden to the south of the tower. Layer Marney Tower was one of an estimated 1,200 buildings damaged by the earthquake, which struck on 22 April and measured 4.6 on the Richter scale. There were conflicting reports about a possible death toll, ranging from none to five. The earthquake sent waves crashing on to the coastline where numerous small boats were destroyed.

From the main east coast line it eventually became possible to forge across country by branch line to Southend. It wasn't the earliest line built to the resort, however, nor would it be the busiest. Contractors Brassey, Betts and Peto built the first railway into Southend from London, although plans to site the station at the town's pier head were vetoed on grounds of nuisance. It was the last stop on a line that went via Tilbury and Forest Gate to either Bishopsgate or Fenchurch Street. Primarily managed by the London, Tilbury & Southend Railway Company, the line was known locally as the LTS.

After the railway was opened there was extensive development in the town, providing houses large and small at Clifftown. Samuel Morton Peto was once again a moving force in the plans. The homes were completed in 1870 and, a decade later, a newly designed tank engine went into operation on the LTS which could haul more people at faster speeds than ever before. For the first time people could live in Southend while working in London with ease, thanks to the train. Thus Southend became an early commuter town, as well as being the closest resort to London.

But its reputation was mainly thanks to the attractions of the seaside. In 1871 the law was changed to permit Bank Holidays – days when the banks were officially shut so no trading could take place. And, thanks to its closeness to London, the train brought in hordes of trippers to Southend for days out, particularly on the popular Bank Holiday that fell on the first Monday in August – initially known as St Lubbock's day for the Liberal political and banker Sir John Lubbock who drove the necessary Act through Parliament.

An early wooden pier in the town, dating from 1830, was now beginning to show its age. Maintenance and repair bills were high. Its original purpose had been as a landing stage for boats bringing a few tourists from London. Now there were scores more tourists and the pleasure principle was about to take precedence.

Plans drawn up for a new iron pier included an electric railway to run its length. When it opened in 1890 there was a pavilion at the shore end that hosted concerts as well as the popular pier railway to entertain the crowds. According to the National Piers Society, £10,000 of the £80,000 costs was spent on the new electric railway. Notwithstanding, there was only a single engine on the three-quarter-mile-long track. Its 13-horsepower motor was powered by the pier's own generator. Three years later a passing loop was installed and a second three-car train went into service.

Still it wasn't sufficient capacity for the relentless number of trippers, particularly from East London, that made their way to Southend. Although a second generator was added in 1899 to help power two more trains, it wasn't until the Southend Corporation built its own generating station in 1902 that the four trains could be extended to cater for more passengers. The pier generators were then scrapped.

The pier was continually extended, first to provide an access point for passing steamers, and secondly to accommodate holidaymakers. The final addition in 1929 brought the length to 2,360 yards (1.34 miles or 2,158 metres), making it the longest pleasure pier in the world.

Between Southend and London the landscape was largely lush and green in Victorian times, although the capital itself was becoming a spaghetti-mess of railway lines. Along with other railway builders,

NOW THERE WERE SCORES MORE TOURISTS AND THE PLEASURE PRINCIPLE WAS ABOUT TO TAKE PRECEDENCE

Great Eastern Railways was committed to developing suburban lines around London. One of them, terminating at Ongar, led to the Royal Gunpowder Mills at Waltham Abbey. Initially a cloth mill, it is thought gunpowder was made there using saltpetre from the middle of the sixteenth century.

The site was taken under government control in 1787 to secure supply, and production stepped up from the middle of the nineteenth century to supply arms for the Crimean War, the Indian Mutiny and, later, the Boer War. It also became central to weapons science and technology. In 1865 a patent was granted for gun cotton, a new if somewhat unstable explosive, which was then produced at Waltham Abbey. It was also the focus of production for cordite, a smokeless alternative to gunpowder pioneered in 1889.

A network of railways crossed the site after a building programme escalated during the Crimean War at a time when steam could provide the necessary power for production. The rails were for wagons which were gently pushed rather than towed – a nod to the volatile cargo aboard. Initially the gauge of the rails was 2 ft 3 in.

Her Majesty's Gunpowder Mills at Waltham Abbey.

In 1862 at Crewe, John Ramsbottom, chief engineer of the London & North Western Railway, proved the versatility of an 18-inch gauge for industrial trains, which could run not only up to but into warehouses. Eventually the gauge at Waltham Abbey was changed, so when production went into overdrive during the First World War the factory was at its most efficient.

Freight across the Great Eastern Railway was for years dominated by food. In addition to fish from the east coast there were vegetables – linking the fortunes of the railway company inextricably to the wealth of the harvest. There was also milk, which first travelled in churns hoisted into ventilated vans to keep it as fresh as it could be for thirsty city folk. This way the train service made a significant contribution to the health of the nation, supplying fresh food to cities at comparatively low costs.

In the same way (but in the opposite direction), railways carried newspapers fast and efficiently into rural areas, improving education and awareness everywhere in a way that was once confined to cities.

In 1847 the Eastern Counties Railway began to build a depot at Stratford where its locomotives were made. It was extended time and again throughout its history until it became a maze of track and workshops. In 1891, when it was under the aegis of the Great Eastern Railway, a new record was set there for building a locomotive. It took just nine hours and 47 minutes to produce a tender engine from scratch, complete with coat of grey primer. As a sign of the frantic railway times, the locomotive was dispatched immediately on coal runs, and covered 36,000 miles before returning to Stratford for its final coat of paint. Its working life lasted for 40 years and it ran through 1,127,000 miles before being scrapped.

When *Bradshaw's* was written in 1866, the terminus of the Great Eastern line was Bishopsgate in Shoreditch. The guidebook calls it 'one of the handsomest (externally) in London'. It was opened in 1840 by the Eastern Counties Railway and its name was changed from Shoreditch to Bishopsgate in 1847.

When Eastern Counties Railways amalgamated with other lines to form Great Eastern Railways, the new company found its two options for terminals – Bishopsgate and Fenchurch Street Stations – were not sufficiently large and set about building Liverpool Street Station and its approach tunnel, which opened in 1874.

An engraving of Bishopsgate Street by Gustav Doré, 1872.

IT TOOK JUST NINE HOURS AND 47 MINUTES TO PRODUCE A TENDER ENGINE FROM SCRATCH, COMPLETE WITH COAT OF GREY PRIMER

Railway carriages at
Weybourne Station on the
North Norfolk Railway.

Nowhere in Britain has the railway map changed more than in London, not least due to the Blitz in the Second World War. In 1866 it was possible to jump on a North London line train at Fenchurch Street or Bow, within moments of getting off a Great Eastern line train.

This is a route that became infamous in 1864 for being the scene of Britain's first train murder. The victim was 69-year-old Thomas Briggs, a senior clerk at the City bank Messrs Robarts, Curtis & Co. On Saturday 9 July he had worked as he always did until 3 p.m. and then visited a niece in Peckham before making his way home by train.

No one knows just what happened in the first-class carriage of the 9.50 p.m. Fenchurch Street service. It was, in common with many other carriages, sealed off from other travellers. There were six seats, three on each side, and two doors in a design reminiscent of stagecoaches. Subsequent passengers found the empty seats covered in blood and an abandoned bag, stick and hat. Almost simultaneously, a train driver travelling in the other direction saw a body lying between the tracks. After he raised the alarm the badly injured Mr Briggs was carried to a nearby tavern but he died later from severe head injuries.

There was a public outcry at the killing, although crimes like theft and even assault had been carried out on trains almost since their inception. Now, however, a sense of peril accompanied train travel as never before.

At first there seemed little for detectives to go on. Mr Briggs's family identified the stick and bag as his but the hat was not, and his own hat was missing. Cash was left in his pocket but his gold watch and chain were gone.

A wave of scandalised press coverage yielded the first clue. It alerted a London silversmith, appropriately called John Death, who told police he had been asked to swap Mr Briggs's watch chain for another, and described the customer making the request. Later, a Hansom driver confirmed that a box with the name Death written on it was at his house, brought there by a German tailor, Franz Muller, who had been engaged to his daughter. The Hansom driver obligingly produced a photo of Muller and the silversmith confirmed him to be the watch-chain man.

Before a warrant could be issued for his arrest, Muller had boarded the sailing ship *Victoria* bound for New York in anticipation of a new life in America. Detective Inspector Richard Tanner, along with his material witnesses, soon booked tickets aboard the steamship *City of*

HORRID MURDER

OF

A GENTLEMAN,

IN A

RAILWAY CARRIAGE.

Another base and dreadful murder,
  Now again, alas, has been,
One of the most atrocious murders
  It is, as ever yet was seen;
Poor Thomas Briggs, how sad to mention,
  Was in a first-class railway carriage slain,
Between Old Ford and Hackney Wick,
  Which caused excitement, care and pain.

Oh, listen to this railway murder
  Poor Briggs received the fatal wound,
Between Old Ford Bridge and Hackney Wick
  And very near great London town.

They found a hat in the railway carriage,
  Made in Crawford-street, St. Marylebone,
In which poor Thomas Briggs was riding,
  On his journey to his home ;
Alas, poor man, he little thought
  That he would be deprived of life,
In the railway carriage, by a villain,
  At ten o'clock that fatal night.

Oh, little did he think they'd kill him,
  He had no thought he was to die,
Upon that fatal Saturday evening,
  On the 9th day of July ;
The villains in the carriage slew him,
  For plunder Thomas Briggs was killed,
In a first-class carriage they did rob him,
  And all around his blood was spilled.

Thomas Briggs was a faithful servant,
  To Robarts, Lubbock and Company,
Three hundred pounds rewards is offered,
  Soon may the murderer taken be,

2 E

And brought to justice for the dreadful
  Deed he done, as we may hear,
And glad we are there is before us,
  A clue to the wicked murderer.

They have traced his watch-chain in the city,
  The very key, as we are told,
Stole from poor Briggs that fatal evening,
  Albert curb, with swivel seal in gold.
Robbed of nearly all that he possessed,
  He was, upon that fatal night,
Between Old Ford and Hackney Wick,
  In the Railway Carriage in daylight.

This sad affair has caused excitement,
  Far and near, for miles around,
And thousands to the spot are going
  From all around great London town.
And on the spot they look with horror,
  Where poor Thomas Briggs was killed,
They view with grief, with pain and sorrow,
  Where his crimson blood was spilled.

Oh, God above, look down from Heaven,
  Point the murdering villains out,
Let stern justice close pursue them,
  Never let them roam about ;
On him, or them, we all are certain,
  Has on the brow the mark of Cain,
Thus ends the brutal horrid murder,
  Which has caused such grief and pain.

On that fatal Saturday evening,
  They left him in his crimson gore,
July the 9th, in a railway carriage,
  Eighteen hundred and sixty-four.

A report, taking the form of verse, on the murder of Thomas Briggs in a railway carriage on 9 July 1864.

Manchester, easily beating the *Victoria* to its destination. In fact, the Metropolitan Police party had to wait four weeks for it to catch up. When the police finally approached Muller on the dockside he asked, 'What's the matter?'

A swift search established he was in possession of Mr Briggs's watch and remodelled hat. At the time, relations between Britain and America – torn by civil war – were strained. Nonetheless, a judge agreed to extradite Muller and he was soon brought back to England.

Muller maintained his innocence throughout his Old Bailey trial and claimed he bought the watch and hat on the London dockside. He was small, mild-mannered and apparently lacked a motive. There were also witnesses to say Mr Briggs was seated with not one but two men on the night he was killed. But the jury took just 15 minutes to find Muller guilty.

Despite pleas for clemency from the Prussian King Wilhelm I, Muller was publicly hanged at Newgate Prison just four months after the crime. Later the prison chaplain claimed his final words were 'I did it'. Still, his death nearly resulted in a riot, with many Londoners filled with doubt about the verdict.

The savage killing of Thomas Briggs resulted in new legislation, introduced in 1868, which made communication cords compulsory on trains. Although open carriages were still viewed unfavourably it was felt Mr Briggs's life could have been saved if the train driver only knew he had been in difficulties.

In 1897 an American journalist, Stephen Crane, travelled on the Scotch Express between London and Glasgow, and revealed that, some 30 years after the death of Mr Briggs, communication cords were causing unforeseen difficulties. The problem arose when dining cars came into use and shared the same alarm system, causing confusion. He wrote:

> ...if one rings for tea, the guard comes to interrupt the murder and that if one is being murdered, the attendant appears with tea. At any rate, the guard was forever being called from his reports and his comfortable seat in the forward end of the luggage van by thrilling alarms. He often prowled the length of the train with hardihood and determination, merely to meet a request for a sandwich.

Moved by Mrs Briggs's plight, spy holes were drilled in carriage partitions by some train companies, and became known as 'Muller lights'. Bizarrely, Mr Briggs's reshaped hat became something of a fashion item.

The North London Railway established a depot on a 10-acre site at Bow in 1853 where it built and repaired its own locomotives for the remainder of the Victorian era. At the time East London was assuming a reputation for poverty and moral decline. Most families

Franz Muller, a German tailor found guilty of the murder of Thomas Briggs and hanged ouside Newgate prison in 1864.

ANNIE BESANT AND THE MATCH GIRLS' STRIKE

Annie Besant, a campaigning social reformer, decided to investigate claims about the ill treatment of match workers at Bryant & May's factory, dangerous conditions and the company's system of fines for petty misdemeanours. She reported what she found after interviewing some of the 'match girls' in her journal, *The Link*, in June 1888 under the headline 'WHITE SLAVERY IN LONDON'.

Annie Besant (1847–1933).

The splendid salary of 4s. is subject to deductions in the shape of fines; if the feet are dirty, or the ground under the bench is left untidy, a fine of 3d. is inflicted; for putting 'burnts' — matches that have caught fire during the work — on the bench 1s. has been forfeited, and one unhappy girl was once fined 2s. 6d for some unknown crime. If a girl leaves four or five matches on her bench when she goes for a fresh 'frame' she is fined 3d., and in some departments a fine of 3d. is inflicted for talking. If a girl is late she is shut out for 'half the day', that is for the morning six hours, and 5d. is deducted out of her day's 8d. One girl was fined 1s. for letting the web twist round a machine in the endeavour to save her fingers from being cut, and was sharply told to take care of the machine, 'never mind your fingers'. Another, who carried out the instructions and lost a finger thereby, was left unsupported while she was helpless. The wage covers the duty of submitting to an occasional blow from a foreman; one, who appears to be a gentleman of variable temper, 'clouts' them 'when he is mad'.

Besant was gravely concerned that working with phosphorus used at the factory – already banned in Sweden and the USA – was causing cancer. (The British government refused a ban on the grounds it would restrain free trade.)

The company's owners, Quakers Francis May and William Bryant, were furious, branding Besant's newspaper claims as lies and hounding those they believed were responsible for talking to her.

When the factory owners forced their employees to sign a statement saying they were happy with working conditions, 1,400 women went on strike with Besant at their head. Their campaign attracted some high-level support, including from the *Pall Mall Gazette*, Catherine

The Bryant & May match factory.

Booth of the Salvation Army and the writer George Bernard Shaw. However, they were also lambasted by others, including *The Times*.

Determined to beat the bosses, the strikers organised themselves as never before. There were marches in both the east and west end of London. There was a strike fund, with each contribution listed in an accounts book. For the first time the London Trades Council – formed in 1860 to represent skilled workers – lent its support, donating £20 to the strike fund and offered to mediate in talks.

A strike headquarters set up in Bow Road to coordinate action and maintain a register of everyone involved. The Strike Register reveals many of the women and girls were of Irish extraction and lived close to one another in nearby slums. Typically, the Irish already felt under attack by the British and British attitudes, and were more inclined to confront the Establishment than many English workers at the time.

After three weeks the company agreed to end the hated fines' system. The strikers were triumphant and infant union movements nationwide were given a boost.

On 27 July 1888 the inaugural meeting of the Union of Women Match Makers was held, with Besant elected as the first secretary. With money left over from the strike fund – as well as the profits from a benefit show held at a London theatre – the union found itself premises and enrolled 666 women. Before the year was out it became known as the Matchmakers' Union. Its story was short-lived as it folded in 1903, but its galvanising effect on the union movement continued for years afterwards.

Moreover, the Salvation Army went on to open its own match factory in East London, using a less harmful phosphorus and paying twice as much as Bryant & May. Bad publicity continued for the company, until in 1901 it announced an end to the use of harmful yellow phosphorus in its production process.

lived in single rooms in largely insanitary conditions. Once, the area was the domain of weavers and their families. Now their cloth-making skills were largely obsolete, although a couple of silk factories remained.

The strike by the match girls was not the only East End story to hit the headlines at the time. Between April 1888 and February 1891 11 women were murdered and mutilated by a man who became known as 'Jack the Ripper'. Despite a massive operation the police failed even to arrest, let alone convict, anyone for the crime.

Staff at the Bow Infirmary Asylum, which stood opposite the Bryant & May factory, felt sure one of their patients, an East European immigrant butcher called Jacob Isenschmid, was the culprit. He had been released from the asylum in 1887, apparently cured. After the fourth murder he was seen with blood on his clothes

OPPOSITE: A steam train on the North Norfolk Railway.

BELOW: Horse-drawn trams and wagons outside the City of London Infirmary.

City of London Infirmary, Bow Road, E.

in a pub close to the scene of the murder. Asylum staff contacted the police but, despite an interview, there was no evidence against him and he remained at large, although he does not appear on present-day lists of suspects.

London's transport systems were changing dramatically. There were new terminals built, usually in grand fashion, on the outskirts of the city centre to receive trains from all corners of the country. But for a while these stood in awkward isolation, although an ever-increasing number of lines were bolted on to the company or network they served, at the expense of London housing. Congestion on London's roads as travellers went between one railway line and the next intensified.

In writing *Dombey and Son*, which appeared in instalments between 1846 and 1848, Dickens described railway building in London.

> *Houses were knocked down; streets broken through and stopped; deep pits and trenches dug in the ground; enormous heaps of earth and clay thrown up; buildings that were undermined and shaking, propped up with great beams of wood ... Hot springs and fiery eruptions, the usual attendance upon earthquakes, lent their contribution of confusion to the scene...*
>
> *In short, the yet unfinished and unopened railroad was in progress; and, from the very core of all this dire disorder, trailed smoothly away upon its mighty course of civilization and improvement.*

In 1863 the notion of one mighty central terminus for all the capital's railways was once again rejected by a House of Lords Select Committee, anxious that no more housing in an already overcrowded city should be sacrificed for the sake of the railways. The following excerpt from *Hansard* reveals the extent of railway schemes laid before the Select Committee the following year.

> *We found that those schemes were of vast magnitude for so limited an area as the metropolitan district. The new railways proposed to be constructed within that area extended over a length of 174 miles in the aggregate, and involved the raising of capital to the amount of about £44,000,000. It was, of course, impossible all that mileage could be*

constructed, or all that capital expended for metropolitan railways, because many of those schemes were necessarily competing schemes. At the same time, my Lords, it must be confessed that there was sufficient cause for considerable alarm among the holders of property in the metropolis, and much reason to apprehend that, if any large number of these lines were sanctioned, the traffic of many important public thoroughfares would be seriously interfered with during the construction of those works. Those schemes, as they came before us, included the construction of no less than four new railway bridges across the Thames, two of them – and these of a very large size – being intended to cross the river below London Bridge.

There was by now an undercurrent of public feeling against the railways as they deposited viaducts, tracks and tunnels at will, altering the complexion of the capital forever. London, perhaps more than any other city, was almost entirely remodelled by the converging transport companies.

As early as 1864 the satirical magazine *Punch* asked plaintively: 'Are there no means of averting the imminent destruction of the little beauty that our capital possesses?' The article went on to say that, given the railway frenzy existing at the time, St Paul's Cathedral might just as well become a railway station.

The graveyard at St Pancras was removed for the sake of the railway. A coaching house that escaped the Great Fire of London in 1666 – in which about 13,500 homes and 87 parish churches were razed to the ground – lying in the shadow of St Paul's was destroyed in 1875 to make way for lines and stations. Hundreds more buildings were flattened to make way for tracks, including Sir Paul Pindar's house in Bishopsgate. Pindar, an ambassador to the Ottoman court for James I, owned a fine house with one of the most distinctive frontages in Victorian London that likewise escaped the Great Fire. In 1890 the house's distinctive Jacobean façade was dismantled in favour of an extension to Liverpool Street Station. Fortunately, the wooden structure found a new home in the Victoria and Albert Museum.

London's population was being squeezed into its outer reaches. Those houses that remained were smeared with smoke as steam trains brought dense and eerie pollution into the city. Only the very rich could resist the onward march of the railways.

THE GRAVEYARD AT ST PANCRAS WAS REMOVED FOR THE SAKE OF THE RAILWAY

CHRONOLOGY OF THE LONDON TERMINALS

1836 **London Bridge Station** was built in primitive form for the London & Greenwich Railway and was soon subject to a rebuild.

1837 **Euston**, operated by the London & North Western Railway.

1838 **Paddington**, still bearing the hallmarks of its designer Brunel, built to receive Great Western Railway services.

1841 **Fenchurch Street**, the smallest of the railway terminals in London, originally constructed for the London & Blackwall Railway, and rebuilt 13 years later in time to accommodate the London, Tilbury & Southend Railway. It was the site of the first station bookstall.

1848 **Waterloo Bridge Station**, as it was called, opened after being linked to the busy outer-city satellite at Nine Elms for the London & South Western Railway.

1852 **King's Cross** opened for the Great Northern Railway on the site of smallpox and fever hospitals. It was designed by Lewis Cubitt along remarkably simple lines save for an Italianate clock turret. A hotel was built to accompany the station and opened two years later.

1858 **Victoria**, named for the nearby street, was the home of London, Brighton & South Coast Railway trains, although it was soon popular with other companies.

1864 **Charing Cross**, arguably the only London station to breach the West End, opened with six wooden platforms for what was initially a limited service to Greenwich and mid-Kent.

1866 **Moorgate** came into being in an extension to the Metropolitan Line and only became a main-line terminus in 1900.

1868 **St Pancras** was built by the Midland Railway after it found King's Cross too expensive. It became remarkable for the railway hotel's vast Gothic frontage.

1874 **Liverpool Street** was built to replace Bishopsgate Station, being closer to the city centre and more user friendly.

1899 **Marylebone** was home to the final main line to enter London, the Great Central, but plans by chairman Sir Edward Watkin to continue expansion with a channel tunnel were never realized.

Railway company managers were powerful people but some left a more distinguished legacy than others.

Sir James Allport spent a career in railways, ending up as the boss of Midland Railways for 27 years, excepting a short spell spent at a shipyard in Jarrow. He was also instrumental in forming the Railway Clearing House, which managed payments between different companies to cover journeys spanning several networks. After his retirement as manager in 1880 he became a director of the company.

Under his leadership, Midland Railway services expanded and the grand station at St Pancras was opened. But he is best remembered for transforming the journeys of third-class passengers. He was the first to realise that, rather than being a hindrance to the railway company, third-class passengers were in fact a valuable asset.

Accordingly, he made third-class carriages much more comfortable and, from 1872, included third-class carriages on every train, charging passengers a penny per mile for a journey. When some angry passengers

PREVIOUS PAGE: *Charing Cross Station*, London, c. 1864, a coloured chromolithograph by the Kell brothers. The station was designed by John Hawkshaw and was the London terminus of the South Eastern Railway.

BELOW: *Seats for Five Persons* by Abraham Solomon (1824–1862).

RATHER
THAN BEING A
HINDRANCE TO
THE RAILWAY
COMPANY,
THIRD-CLASS
PASSENGERS
WERE IN FACT A
VALUABLE ASSET

boycotted Midland Services he scrapped second class, at the same time lowering first-class fares. The result was better revenues for the railway company and a more equitable system of travelling.

For his services to cheaper travel Allport was knighted in 1884. But in his later life it wasn't the gong at the forefront of his mind:

If there is one part of my public life on which I look back with more satisfaction than on anything else, it is with reference to the boon we conferred on third-class travellers. I have felt saddened to see third-class passengers shunted on to a siding in cold and bitter weather – a train containing amongst others many lightly-clad women and children – for the convenience of allowing the more comfortable and warmly-clad passengers to pass them. I have even known third-class trains to be shunted into a siding to allow express goods to pass.

When the rich man travels, or if he lies in bed all day, his capital remains undiminished, and perhaps his income flows in all the same. But when the poor man travels, he has not only to pay his fare, but to sink his capital, for his time is his capital; and if he now consumes only five hours instead of ten in making a journey, he has saved five hours of time for useful labour – useful to himself, his family, and to society. And I think with even more pleasure of the comfort in travelling we have been able to confer on women and children. But it took twenty-five years to get it done.

Not everybody appreciated the boon of cheap travel. An anonymous account, date unknown, tells how one man hitched a ride on the mainline train that ran between Euston and Liverpool. The man in question was apparently a sailor who chose to travel on the 9 p.m. express, for which the first stop was Rugby, some 82 miles up the line.

Mr Smith did not take his seat like an ordinary passenger inside any of the carriages but he travelled underneath one of them and would, no doubt, have concluded his journey to Liverpool in safety but that on the arrival of the train at Rugby the wheel-examiner, seeing a man's legs protruding from under one of the carriages, had the curiosity to make further search and discovered Mr Smith coiled round the brake-rod, a piece of iron not above three inches broad, in a fantastic position.

Mr Smith was immediately uncoiled and being technically in error was detained in custody. The bottom of the carriage was only eighteen inches from the ground and where the engine takes up the water as it travels, Mr Smith was not more than six inches from the trough.

Section of a London Underground station: illustration from *L'Universe illustré*, late 19th century.

Magistrates fined him two shillings and sixpence, or 14 days in jail, expressing wonder at how he endured the ride. He presumably was able to assume the unorthodox position because Euston Station was thronged with people. And for London the transport problem would only get worse.

The answer as far as the Select Committee was concerned was to venture underground. Authorisation for this had been given in 1854 but the project was delayed by concerns about finance.

The world's first underground railway would link Paddington, the terminus of the Great Western Railway services, and Farringdon Street in the City in 1863. Along its four-mile route the existing road was lifted and a trench was dug and lined with bricks. Tracks were laid in the trench before it was enclosed once more and the road replaced. This elementary construction system was called 'cut and cover'. The ground-breaking first line was known as the Metropolitan or 'the Met'.

It was an immediate hit with Londoners, and some 30,000 people travelled on it daily. Nor was it an easy journey for those intrepid travellers. The wagons were initially open and drawn by steam engines. Although the route was amply vented it was nonetheless a smoky and dirty experience, albeit short-lived. The driver and guard, compelled to spend all day in the sulphurous atmosphere, were less fortunate still than the passengers.

In the following months further sections of underground lines were opened and extraordinary chaos was brought to London thoroughfares while construction work was underway. A phalanx of men turned up in the capital to undertake the work, and their reputation for hard living preceded them. Upright Victorians were appalled that heavy drinkers and rough talkers were labouring outside their homes, sharing the same streets.

But navvies – named for the so-called 'navigators' who built Britain's canals in the eighteenth century – were much maligned. If their appearance was ragged it was because the work they did was grindingly hard and dangerous. Many originated in Ireland and escaped to Britain at the time of the Famine. Often left at the margins of society, they developed a culture and even a language of their own. Hundreds had died as railways cut through the country, from both accident and disease. Construction companies frequently viewed the men as alarmingly expendable. Living quarters usually amounted to little more than a turf shack, and they were vulnerable to cold and hunger. Aside from gunpowder, the tools they had at their disposal to complete tremendous feats of engineering amounted to little more than picks and shovels.

Isambard Kingdom Brunel, who was known for being kindly rather than cruel to his workers, expressed no surprise when he was told 131 workers were taken to Bath hospital with serious injuries in less than two years while that part of the Great Western was under construction. 'I think it is a small list, considering the very heavy works and the immense amount of powder used,' he commented.

By the time the underground was being built, conditions had improved for navvies although it was still their muscle-power that

UPRIGHT VICTORIANS WERE APPALLED THAT HEAVY DRINKERS AND ROUGH TALKERS WERE LABOURING OUTSIDE THEIR HOMES

turned the blueprint for the London underground into a reality. In 1868 the second underground railway opened, the District Line, and plans were afoot to link the two. The much-heralded Circle Line, which would finally provide a link between the major railway stations, was opened in its entirety by 1884.

Two years later, further up the Thames a short-lived cable-hauled train was opened between the Tower of London and Bermondsey. It was so unpopular that it was turned into a pedestrian subway until the opening of Tower Bridge in 1894, after which it was closed for lack of use. Today it still exists as a cable channel.

There was another step change in London's transport in 1890 when electric locomotives replaced steam. Tunnelling expertise was better than ever before too, and it led to the first deep tube running on what is now called the Northern Line. Its carriages were without windows as train operators reckoned there was nothing to see. Passengers relied on a guard to call out the station names.

Along London's Victoria Embankment, built from 1862 for traffic above ground and underground trains below, there's a pink granite monument from the heart of Egypt. Its purpose is to mark Nelson's victory over Napoleon at the Battle of the Nile in 1798. The battle was already a dim and distant memory, though, by the time the monolith was put up 80 years later.

Lying in the sand at Heliopolis, the 68-foot-tall monument, weighing 180 tons, was given to the British in 1819 by Mehemet Ali, the Albanian-born Egyptian leader who had himself fought against Napoleon. It was a somewhat belated gesture of thanks, a mere 21 years after the battle took place. Alas, he didn't come up with a suitable mode of transport. And, for the record, there's no evidence that the monolith, dating back to 1500 bc, has any links with the famous Egyptian queen Cleopatra, despite being commonly known as 'Cleopatra's Needle'.

Its transfer between countries didn't take place until 1877, when two bold Victorians grappled with the logistics. They were Sir William Wilson, who sponsored the operation, and engineer John Dixon, who designed a ship that would carry the stone from Egypt to Britain. Looking like an early container ship, its boxy appearance seemed

the ideal solution to the problem of protecting the monument in the heaving seas of the Bay of Biscay.

But on 14 October 1877 the operation looked doomed to failure. The ship, called *Cleopatra* in honour of its cargo, seemed to be sinking. Worse still, six men dispatched in a rowing boat from the tug towing it to rescue its crew were lost. Eventually, the crew of the *Cleopatra* were pulled to safety and the monument was abandoned to its fate. However, against the odds, it survived the storm and was later spotted by another ship which towed it to safety.

When the monument was finally put up by the River Thames it was guarded by two faux sphinxes and perched atop a time capsule containing, among other things, a portrait of Queen Victoria, pictures of a dozen beautiful women, a box of cigars, a hydraulic jack and a current copy of *Bradshaw's Monthly Railway Guide*.

Engraving showing the obelisk ship *Cleopatra*, with Cleopatra's Needle aboard, off Westminster Bridge, London, 1878.

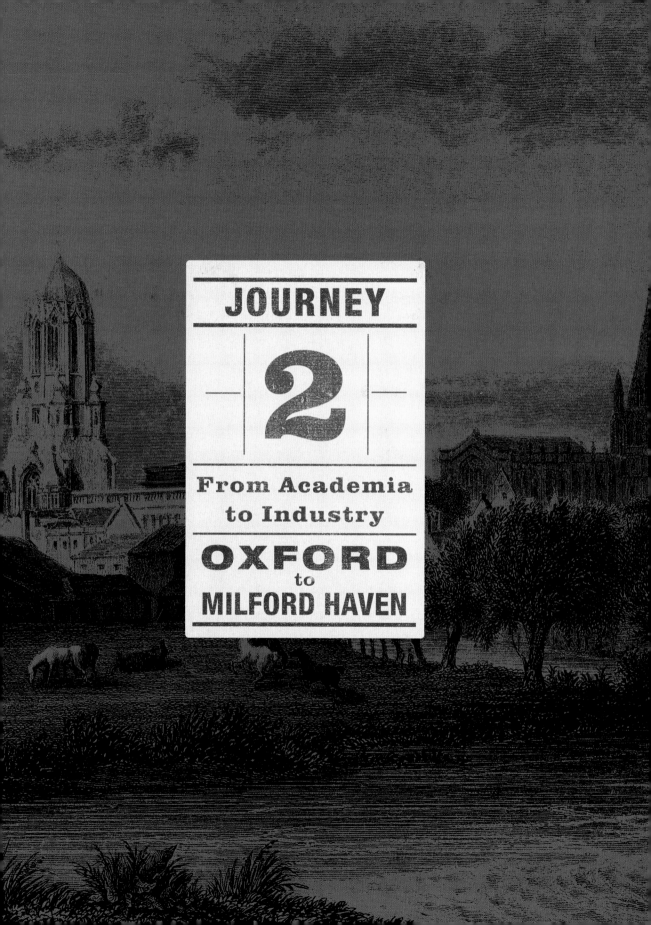

JOURNEY

2

From Academia
to Industry

OXFORD
to
MILFORD HAVEN

W hen it comes to Oxford, Bradshaw's guide is fulsome in praise for its stylish architecture and noble seats of learning, all lying snug in a soft blanket of verdant countryside.

It is situated on a gentle eminence in a rich valley between the rivers Cherwell and Isis and is surrounded by highly cultivated scenery – the prospect being bounded by an amphitheatre of hills.

From the neighbouring heights the city presents a very imposing appearance, from the number and variety of its spires, domes and public edifices while these structures, from their magnitude and splendid architecture, give it on a near approach an air of great magnificence...

The high street in Oxford is justly considered the finest in England from its length and breadth, the number and elegance of its public buildings and its remarkable curvature which, from continually presenting new combinations of magnificent objects to the eye, produces an uncommonly striking effect.

Perhaps all of this is to be expected from a city that has led education worldwide since the era of King Alfred. Yet, for all its elaborate grandeur, Oxford's reputation lay elsewhere for the majority of ordinary Victorians – for it was once as celebrated for its sausages as it was for its honours degrees.

Even *Bradshaw's* makes reference to the meatier side of Oxford's fame, almost in the same breath as speaking about its visible charms. 'Oxford has long been famous for good sausages and brawn.' If there's any doubt about the status of the city's sausages, then one only has to refer to Mrs Beeton's cookbook, one of the few publications as popular as *Bradshaw's*, to be certain.

Next to Queen Victoria, cookbook icon Mrs Isabella Beeton remains the most prominent woman of the nineteenth century. Mrs Beeton was the original domestic goddess — an orchestrator of recipes, an authority on cookery techniques and a fount of kitchen knowledge. Although she was dead by the age of 28 she left a mark

PREAVIOUS PAGE: A view of Oxford from meadows near the railway station, c. 1840.

Oxford High Street, c. 1890.

that subsequent chefs – connoisseur, celebrity and quirky – have failed to erase.

In fact there were several remarkable facets to Isabella Beeton. She was, for example, the eldest of no fewer than 21 children. Her mother, Elizabeth, had four children before being widowed. Then she married widower Henry Dorling, who also had four children, and with him went on to have a further 13. That Isabella had plenty of hands-on experience in home skills as the oldest child of this immense brood is beyond doubt.

Mrs Beeton's areas of expertise extended beyond child-rearing and cookery. Her most famous tome, *The Book of Household Management*, included sensible advice on how to manage servants, medicines, poisons, animal husbandry and fashion. If that wasn't enough, she was also a talented pianist.

Perhaps strangely, she married a man who, like her, was born in Milk Street, in the City of London. Their mothers had previously been neighbours and friends. Crucially, Samuel Orchart Beeton was a publisher, and Isabella regularly wrote articles on housekeeping and cookery for him. When these were drawn together under one cover by her astute husband and published on Christmas Day 1861, a bestseller that endured for decades was created. Its full title was something of a mouthful, however: *The Book of Household Management Comprising Information for the Mistress, Housekeeper, Cook, Kitchen-maid, Butler, Footman, Coachman, Valet, Upper and under house-maids, Lady's-maid,*

Maid-of-all-work, Laundry-maid, Nurse and nurse-maid, Monthly, wet, and sick nurses, etc. etc. also, sanitary, medical, & legal memoranda; with a history of the origin, properties, and uses of all things connected with home life and comfort.

In it, perhaps for the first time, recipes were documented with exact quantities. From this sound foundation we can glean much about the Victorian diet. The book contains a recipe for Oxford sausages, the aroma of which so often floated around the city's dreamy spires. Mrs Beeton's recipe, which she claims as her own, is as follows:

INGREDIENTS.— 1 lb. of pork, fat and lean, without skin or gristle; 1 lb. of lean veal, 1 lb. of beef suet, ½ lb. of bread crumbs, the rind of ½ lemon, 1 small nutmeg, 6 sage-leaves, 1 teaspoonful of pepper, 2 teaspoonfuls of salt, ½ teaspoonful of savory, ½ teaspoonful of marjoram.

Mode.— Chop the pork, veal, and suet finely together, add the bread crumbs, lemon-peel (which should be well minced), and a small nutmeg grated. Wash and chop the sage-leaves very finely; add these with the remaining ingredients to the sausage-meat, and when thoroughly mixed, either put the meat into skins, or, when wanted for table, form it into little cakes, which should be floured and fried.

Average cost, for this quantity, 2s. 6d.

Sufficient for about 30 moderate-sized sausages.

Seasonable from October to March.

There's been speculation that Mrs Beeton copied recipes rather than created them. Even if that's true, her plagiarism has given subsequent generations a unique view of the Victorian kitchen. Her common sense and forthright thoughts were her own, though:

Dining is the privilege of civilization. The rank which people occupy in the grand scale may be measured by their way of taking their meals, as well as by their way of treating women. The nation which knows how to dine has learnt the leading lesson of progress.

Indeed, progress was the watchword of the Victorian era. The same industrial innovation that was powering trains was also present in the

ABOVE: Isabella Mary Beeton (1836–1865).

OVERLEAF: The Shakespeare Express at Stratford-upon-Avon.

publishing industry. As steam-powered presses produced more books at cheaper-than-before prices, Mrs Beeton's words spread further than ever. In any event, after the railway reached Oxford in 1844 it is safe to assume that the city's sausages of distinction were no longer the preserve of scholars and dons.

Isabella Beeton died in 1865 after giving birth to her fourth child (the two eldest died as infants). Her husband survived her for a dozen years before succumbing to tuberculosis aged 46.

There are two more points of interest about Oxford in *Bradshaw's*. First, the book notes: 'The railways and the meadows around the city were all under water in the floods of 1853.' Secondly, it observes that in 1866 the city returned two MPs to Parliament and another two were elected by the university.

At first glance the fact that the university elite wielded such power seems like a scandal. In fact, voting was far from universal at the time *Bradshaw's* was published. After the much-heralded 1832 Reform Act it was still only one in seven men who were entitled to vote. Only with the 1867 Reform Act – passed a year after our *Bradshaw's* was published – was the vote extended to all male householders in urban areas. An amendment to it meant that more men than ever before could vote in elections after 1884, but that number still only represented six out of every ten men in the UK. Giving women the vote was a largely overlooked issue in Victorian England.

Heading north-west, the Oxford, Worcester & Wolverhampton line, finished by 1853, scythed through some of the country's prettiest scenes. By 1859 a branch line had been built off it from Honeybourne to Stratford-upon-Avon.

For Victorian sightseers a love of Shakespeare put Stratford high on the 'to do' list. *Bradshaw's* sheds considerable light on how the town fared 150 years ago:

> This interesting part of Warwickshire is directly accessible by a branch of the Oxford, Worcester and Wolverhampton line by which means it is within about 100 miles journey by rail from London...

It is a municipal borough but derives its chief importance from being the birthplace of Shakespeare who was born here on 23 April (St George's Day) 1564 in an old-fashioned timbered house, opposite the Falcon, in Henley Street which, after some changes and the risk even of being transferred as it stood to America by a calculating speculation, was at last purchased by the Shakespeare Club and adopted by Government as a tribute to his memory.

Bradshaw's pays tribute to the luxuriant scenery surrounding Stratford but is quickly overcome with Bard fever.

But rich and pleasant as the prospect is, it takes its crowning glory from the immortal poet, the mighty genius whose dust reposes at our feet. It is his genial spirit which pervades and sanctifies the scene and every spot on which the eye can rest claims some association with his life. We tread the very ground that he has trod a thousand times and feel as he has felt...

It also reveals some literary vandalism that occurred a century previously on the outskirts of Stratford:

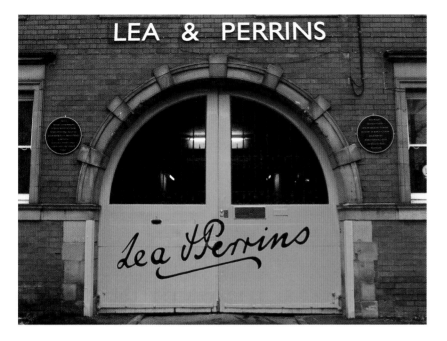

The main entrance to the Lea & Perrins factory in Worcester.

> Ingon House was Shakespeare's at his death, having been bought by him in 1597 ... In 1752 it was sold to Mr Gathell, a Lichfield clergyman, who, on account of a dispute about the rating, pulled it down. He had already cut down the poet's tree, to save himself the trouble of showing it to visitors. Fortunately a cutting was planted by Garrick over the grave of Shakespeare's favourite grand-child Lady Barnard in Abington churchyard (near Northampton) and another is said to be at East Cliffe (Hastings), while the remains of the desecrated tree were sold in the shape of boxes, cups &c.

It's difficult to ascertain how much of the latter paragraph is true, but it remains a fascinating Victorian perspective on the well-worn story of Shakespeare.

A culinary theme continues further along the journey of the West Midland section of the Great Western Railway at Worcester. There's no indication that Mrs Beeton advocated the use of Worcestershire sauce, launched on unsuspecting British taste-buds in the 1830s. But it is the cornerstone of a British love affair with Indian food – albeit one with imperialist overtones – that has thrived ever since.

There is some confusion about the exact timeline of the sauce that is now a staple of the British dinner table, but there's consensus that

EDWARD ELGAR (1857-1934)

Worcester and its environs remained an inspiration to one of England's greatest composers. Edward Elgar was born 20 years after Victoria took the throne. His magnificent *Pomp and Circumstance* marches sound like a series of compositions from a man at the centre of British cultural life. With the first of the military marches also known as 'Land of Hope of Glory', his music is strongly associated with patriotism and imperialism.

Yet Elgar felt an outsider throughout his life and later deplored the use of his music to rally troops during the First World War, to fight for the British Establishment. He was a Catholic at a time when Britain was predominantly Protestant, although he had lost his faith by the time of his death. He lived in rural Worcestershire when the music world pivoted around London. And he was the son of a tradesman rather than a country gentleman, born in Lower Broadheath, Worcestershire, in a small house to a father who was a music dealer and piano tuner.

Elgar grew up with a hands-on mastery of music, quickly learning the piano, violin, cello, bassoon and trombone. Initial plans to work in a solicitor's office were abandoned in favour of a job as a music teacher. At 22 he became bandmaster at the local pauper's asylum, working for a superintendant who was convinced the sound of music would soothe some mental torment.

His output as a composer was at first limited and he only produced choral pieces and cantatas. He met his wife Caroline Alice when she became a pupil in piano accompaniment.

Her family were opposed to the relationship on the grounds of Elgar's class and faith. For her he wrote the popular 'Salut d'Amour' but sold the rights to it early on. Much later, he heard a busker play the tune outside the Queen's Hall in London and thought that the musician probably made more money from the piece than he ever had. When he asked the man if he knew its title, the violinist replied: 'Yes, it's "Sally, Damn her".'

His wife, who was nine years older than Elgar, devoted herself to his career, tidying his desk and maintaining a strict silence when he worked. For a while the couple lived in London, sure that Elgar would soon be fêted by the necessary musical impresarios. In fact the era was disastrously unproductive and they returned to the country, where Elgar found his greatest inspiration. It was spectacular scenery and gentle nature that stimulated his creativity. In

NOTES RETRIEVED AFTER HIS DEATH REVEAL THAT, FOR A JOURNEY TO LONDON, HE WOULD GET UP AT SIX AND WALK TO THE STATION AT MALVERN IN TIME FOR A SEVEN O'CLOCK TRAIN.

Sir Edward Elgar in his work room during his later years.

his remaining years he would take long walks and even longer cycle rides in search of musical revelation.

But Elgar knew he could not afford to sever links with the London music scene if his career as a composer was to flourish. As a result he used the train to visit London for day trips, keeping in touch with the musical trends that evolved there. The most important concerts took place at Crystal Palace.

Notes retrieved after his death reveal that, for a journey to London, he would get up at 6 and walk to the station at Malvern in time for a 7 o'clock train. By 11 a.m. he would have arrived at Paddington, and then he'd take the Underground to Crystal Palace via Victoria. Customarily, he listened to a rehearsal in the afternoon and a concert scheduled for tea-time so he could return home by the same route that evening.

In 1901 the first *Pomp and Circumstance* march was performed for the first time. It was, said Elgar, 'a tune that will knock 'em flat'. His prediction was spot on. Later, words with the title 'Land of Hope and Glory' were attached to the first march, although for Elgar the music became a wearying cliché with worryingly nationalistic overtones. Today *Pomp and Circumstance No. 1* is best known for its inevitable appearance at the London Proms and in graduation ceremonies across America.

Yet perhaps one of his most important contributions to today's musical world had yet to be made. After 1926 Elgar was able to record almost all his major works for the age of the gramophone, the first composer to do so. It provides a remarkable musical heritage, all the more valuable as Elgar's music had begun to go out of style even in his lifetime.

two chemists from Worcester, John Wheeley Lea and William Henry Perrins, concocted the first brew from a recipe brought back from India at the request of a local man who'd served there. The military type who provided it was brought in to sample the men's newly-made infusion – and spat it out immediately. It was, he declared, nothing like the spicy mix he had come to know and love in India.

Defeated by the endeavour, the chemists stowed the barrel containing the sauce in their cellar and only discovered it again much later. They decided to taste the sauce one more time before consigning it to a ditch, and found that it had matured into something altogether more palatable.

By 1837, the year Victoria came to the throne, Worcestershire sauce was being marketed, and soon it was popular worldwide. Locally it is better known as Worcester sauce. The recipe remained a closely guarded secret for years, but what is presumed to be original notes were discovered in a skip during the twentieth century and they throw partial light on it. In Victorian times Worcestershire sauce apparently contained cloves, salt, sugar, soy, fish, vinegar, essence of lemon, peppers, pickles and tamoraide – the Victorian spelling of tamarind.

Worcester wasn't famous for its sauce alone, however. Once the city was home to an army of glovemakers whose craftsmanship was celebrated worldwide. However, just as the sauce was coming into vogue, Worcester's glove trade was heading into a slow but certain decline.

British dominance in manufacturing faced the beginning of the end in 1826, when restrictions on foreign imports were lifted by the government as it embraced free trade. Initially, the law change wasn't disastrous. An estimated 30,000 people in Worcester were employed by 150 different glovemaking companies at the time, about half the glovemakers in Britain. But inevitably there followed death by a thousand cuts. The companies that survived had to modernise, and the outworkers in cottages spread around the Worcestershire countryside were usurped by factories.

In *Bradshaw's* there's a claim that, 40 years after the tariffs on imported gloves were lifted, Worcester still produced 'half a million pairs of leather and kid gloves annually, employing between one thousand and two thousand persons'. In fact, Fownes, one of the

country's leading glovemakers, didn't open its Worcester factory until 1887. But the line on the production chart was heading irrevocably downwards. Fownes survived until 1974, when the business transferred to Warminster in Wiltshire. But already Worcester's reputation for glove-making had long been consigned to history.

More than simply a fashion item, wearing gloves led to good health as they were a barrier to infection. Gloves also provided warmth in the days before efficient heating systems at home, in shops or on transport systems.

From Worcester, the line runs down to Malvern. Today's visitors to Malvern are usually keen to mimic Edward Elgar and stride out on the ancient granite hills which loom there. However, when Queen Victoria was a young woman the visitors were a different breed. Sickly, frail and optimistic that a newly fashioned water cure in Malvern would set them on the road to recovery, they arrived by carriage. Perhaps curiously, Malvern arrived late to the railway party despite its enviable reputation.

It is quite likely contaminated water may have been the source of numerous ailments at the time. London's water was notoriously noxious and other centres of urban population were distinguished by insanitary conditions.

In Malvern the spring water flowed clean and pure. That was not lost on one W. Addison, surgeon to the Duchess of Kent, Queen Victoria's mother. In 1828 the *Quarterly Journal of Science, Literature and Art* produced by the Royal Institution of Great Britain gave a warm reception to Addison's investigation into the health-giving qualities of Malvern water.

> *Mr Addison's work is scientific and ingenious; he attributes the many extraordinary recoveries which have occurred at Malvern partly to the salubrity of the air and partly to the purity of the water which from the analysis he has given of it seems to contain much less saline and earthy matter than any we are acquainted with and we think he has laboured with considerable success to prove that the continued use of a pure water may be a powerful means of removing or preventing many chronic disorders.*

AMONG THOSE WHO EXPERIENCED THE WATER CURE IN MALVERN WERE FLORENCE NIGHTINGALE, CHARLES DICKENS AND CHARLES DARWIN

With water cures something of a fashion in Europe, Malvern was soon on the radar of two doctors who had enduring faith in the hidden powers emanating from the filtered rainwater that bubbled up in the form of springs. Dr James Wilson and Dr James Gully were established in the town by 1842, a full 18 years before the railway arrived in Malvern, rigorously ensuring their patients exercised, ate properly, drank spring water and, more controversially, were douched in hot and cold water.

The regime was largely an improvement on prevailing lifestyles and the results garnered by the doctors were encouraging. Among those who experienced the water cure in Malvern were Florence Nightingale, Charles Dickens and Charles Darwin. To get there, they used carriages.

Bradshaw's guide speaks well of the cures:

> St Anne's and Holywell, springs much resorted to, are slightly tepid and sulphurated and useful, especially in glandular and skin complaints.

But it reserves its greatest praise for the surrounding scenery.

> The prospect from the hills embraces part of eight or nine counties, including the vales of the Severn and Evesham, or the Avon, the cathedrals of Worcester, Gloucester and Hereford, Tewkesbury Minster and the Welsh Hills &c and is the finest in the kingdom.

Water bottled in the Malvern Hills was taken to London's Great Exhibition in 1851 and presented to Queen Victoria. It provided the groundwork for the bottled water industry which is today worth about £1.4 billion in Britain.

In time the railway reached this corner of west England. The Worcester & Hereford Railway Act was passed in 1853 and, seven years later, the line from Worcester to Malvern was open for business. A year after that the railway tracks were laid beneath the Malvern Hills, extending the line to Hereford.

Today the station at Malvern is remarkable for its Victorian embellishments. It was designed by a local architect, Edmund Wallace Elmslie, apparently to the specifications of Lady Emily Foley, the lady of the Malvern manor.

Lady Foley was the daughter of a duke and for 54 years the widow of MP Edward Foley. Even by Victorian standards she was considered

Great Malvern Station, Worcestershire, England.

a harridan. It is said that when she dined alone at her home in Stoke Edith she was waited on by a butler and four footmen. When she visited tenant farmers and their families she expected a bow from the men and a low curtsey from the women she met. Habitually, no one entered church for Sunday services until she had taken her seat. Notwithstanding, her influence on the architecture in Malvern, both in the town and at the station – which she wanted to be better than any other except for the terminus – has meant a legacy of grandeur. Lady Emily died as the twentieth century dawned, aged 94.

Lady Emily Foley, c. 1840.

Going on from Malvern and Hereford the line swings across the border into Wales, where a rich green environment is soon eaten up by industry. Beyond Hereford on the West Midland main line is Abergavenny, about which *Bradshaw's* shares some compelling history. The guidebook reveals:

> Abergavenny became celebrated for its Welsh wigs, made of goats' hair, some of which sold at 40 guineas each. Physicians also used to send patients here to drink goats' whey.

Although it isn't specific about when the goat ruled in Abergavenny, the guide is presumably referring to Regency times when wigs were fashionable for men and women. As for Victorian Abergavenny, its outlook was much more industrial.

> Its present prosperity arises from its flannel weaving and the valuable coal and iron works at Clydach, Blaenavon &c in its neighbourhood – a state of things likely to be much increased by the Newport, Abergavenny and Hereford Railway, part of that important chain which unites South Wales to Liverpool and the North of England.

At the time this entry was written, the Newport, Abergavenny & Hereford Railway had been open for 13 years, having been sponsored by London & North Western Railway. In 1860 it merged with the

Oxford, Worcester & Wolverhampton Railway and the Worcester & Hereford Railway to form the West Midland Railway.

On the English side of the border, in the Forest of Dean, ancient rights laid down by law have for centuries given local men the right to begin mining what was once a rich coal seam. In effect, anyone born in the Forest who had been working as a miner for a year could start their own business. It was also their right to sell their mines to whomever they chose. Even by Victorian times many of these small mines had passed into the hands of bigger companies. Today, with the heyday of coal-mining well and truly at an end, only a redoubtable few continue. But evidence of the unique way of life that once existed there remains in the form of the tram rails built by miners for their own wagons.

By contrast, in nearby South Wales coal mines were proliferating. Alas for the local population, these were privately owned by people or companies that cared more for profit margins than for the men on their payrolls. Most of the 500 or more mines that peppered the landscape of South, Mid and West Wales were started during Victorian times, when coal was the principal fuel of steam engines on the railways, on ships and in factories. Life in the mines was at best unpleasant and at worst exceedingly dangerous.

At the Ferndale Colliery in the Rhondda, for example, 178 people died – including at least three aged 13 – in an accident on 8 November 1867. It happened just months after the opening of the pit. For weeks the bodies of the dead were being brought to the surface in a slow and painful recovery operation, most burnt beyond recognition. The two explosions that occurred were thought to have been caused by an accumulation of gas. Nineteen months later another 53 died in the same pit and the blast which killed them was also fuelled by gas.

Thirteen miles north of Cardiff in the village of Cilfynydd there were 290 deaths caused by an underground explosion on 23 June 1894, the most ever killed in a mine at the time. The youngest of the dead was 14; only 24 of the victims were aged 40 or above, and there were 25 who shared the surname of Jones. In a small, interwoven community, not a household was spared the grief of sudden and brutal loss. Of the 125 horses working underground at the time, only two survived. Nor were these isolated incidents. Between 1851 and 1920 there were 48 disasters in the South Wales coalfield, and 3,000 deaths.

AT THE FERNDALE COLLIERY IN THE RHONDDA, 178 PEOPLE DIED – INCLUDING AT LEAST THREE AGED 13 – IN AN ACCIDENT ON 8 NOVEMBER 1867

The life of a Welsh mining village during Victorian times was captured in the novel *How Green Was My Valley* by Richard Llewellyn, published in 1939. The author based the story on conversations he had with miners from the era.

Some advantages of the steam engine were brought to bear in coal-mining, in terms of pumping out water and winding up loads of coal. But largely working conditions were primitive and those that laboured in them included men, women and children.

In 1842 the Royal Commission report on conditions for women and children in mines caused concern in polite society, not least for its graphic illustrations. There was, the Commission said, 'cruel slaving revolting to humanity'. While eight-year-olds were commonly employed, it said, the starting age for mineworkers was often as low as five. There swiftly followed the Mines and Collieries Bill, prohibiting women, girls and boys under the age of 10 from working underground.

The Coal Mines Inspection Act of 1850 was an attempt to curtail the number of accidents, with inspectors appointed to check on the

A view of Ferndale Colliery (also known as Blaenllechau Colliery) and Tylorstown, Rhondda Valley, Glamorgan.

safety procedures in British mines. A decade later another law was passed, this time to enhance rules about safety and raise the age limit for boys working in mines from 10 to 12.

Doubtless the paperwork brought about some good effects, but lives were still lost in mining accidents every year, with many more men being injured underground. From 1872 Parliament insisted that pit managers had certificates to prove they were adequately trained in safety measures. Miners were also able to appoint inspectors among themselves, and the Mines Regulation Act of 1881 gave the go-ahead for parliamentary inquiries after accidents. Still, little could be done without the collaboration of pit owners.

No matter what the dangers, the coal industry snowballed in size and assumed extraordinary importance, as the appetite for coal appeared insatiable. What South Wales needed most was a transport link to a viable dockyard.

Cardiff seemed the obvious choice for such a dockyard. Given its size and significance today it is hard to imagine that the capital of Wales was, even at the end of the eighteenth century, just a humble shanty town with few prospects. No coal was exported from Cardiff as, everyone agreed, the operation would be too expensive to countenance.

In 1791 the Glamorganshire canal was built to bring iron ore from up-country mines, especially the Dowlais Ironworks at Merthyr Tydfil, to the coast at Cardiff. A sea lock was opened on the River Taff five years later. Yet still Cardiff was literally a backwater. The 1801 census numbers its population at just 1,870, making it only the 25th largest town in Wales at that time.

However, the world was on the cusp of great change as the age of the train began to unfold. For railways to succeed two commodities were needed in quantity: iron for rails and coal for fuel. And both were found in abundance in South Wales, which became a power house of the industrial revolution.

One man set about changing the face of Cardiff to greet a new industrial dawn. John Crichton-Stuart, 2nd Marquis of Bute and the premier entrepreneur of the age, sensed the potential of a port, and in 1839 Bute West Dock, the fruit of his investment, opened. For his

FOR RAILWAYS
TO SUCCEED TWO
COMMODITIES
WERE NEEDED IN
QUANTITY: IRON
FOR RAILS AND
COAL FOR FUEL

foresight he has been dubbed the creator of modern Cardiff. But still the city lacked some of the essentials of practical industry.

The missing connection was, of course, transport between the burgeoning coal and iron ore mines and the newly functioning outlet for exports at Cardiff. The Glamorganshire canal was choked with traffic ferrying some 100,000 tons of coal a year into Cardiff, a third of which was bound for London by ship. But the national thirst for coal was far from sated. The breach was filled by the Taff Vale Railway (TVR), proposed in 1836 by the ironworks' owners and built by Isambard Kingdom Brunel.

In a departure from his customary style, Brunel decided against broad gauge, believing the wagons transporting cargo like coal and minerals could never safely travel as fast as broad gauge allowed.

Coal ships tied up at Cardiff Docks.

The terrain was also hilly and thus more suited to narrower gauges.
The estimated cost of the TVR was not quite £191,000. With the
proposed route mostly shadowing a river valley there were no mighty
obstacles in its path but for one steep incline. At the beginning that
section was operated by stationary engines hauling the wagons by cable,
until a diversion made in 1864 allowed locomotives along the entire
route. In essence, loaded wagons from the coalfields headed downhill
to the docks.

The first stretch of the line between Cardiff and Abercynon opened
in October 1840 and the iron road reached Merthyr the following
year. In 1841 the first of numerous branch lines opened, linking the
main TVR at Pontypridd – then known as Newbridge – with Dinas.
Pontypridd became the beating heart of the line, with trains often
rumbling through its station at a rate of two a minute and a platform
that at one time was the longest in Britain. Its signal box was decked
with no fewer than 230 levers.

When the TVR was completed in 1841 it became possible to bring loaded wagons from Merthyr Tydfil to Cardiff within an hour. Now coal from Wales was sold on domestic and overseas markets, making the area's future seem assured. The number of daily dedicated passenger services was raised from two to three in 1844, and the following year prices for tickets in each of the three available classes were dropped by a shilling.

By the time of the 1851 census, Wales had become the first country registering more people employed in industry than in agriculture. But not everything was rosy among the railway operators, dock and mine owners. The TVR board felt the docks were slow to develop and sought a new outlet at Penarth. Meanwhile, the dock owners began backing other railway companies, although the TVR with its 124 miles of track remained the largest in the region (at its peak in 1897, it was carrying some 14 million tons of coal and coke, with its 216 locomotives covering some 2,800,000 miles a year). However, the TVR was limited in its scope, and not least by the short-sighted approach of its investors. Possessing only a single track, it soon became clogged with traffic much as the Glamorganshire canal had been before its arrival (the track was eventually doubled in 1857). The dock at Cardiff – which was incapacitated at times by the tide – was also often congested with cargo awaiting departure, even after the East Bute Dock was added in 1855.

Bradshaw's obviously believed the East Dock was an answer to the capacity crisis.

> The new Bute Docks made on a tract of wasteland by the Marquis of Bute who is lord of the manor are about one mile below the town, deep enough for ships, with a basin of one and a half acres and an entrance 45 ft wide. A ship canal 1,400 yards long, 67 yards wide, runs up to the town. The coal and iron of Merthyr Tydfil and the neighbourhood are the chief exports and the quantity almost doubles itself every two or three years.

Yet still, the amount of dock space was found to be lacking. In 1865 Penarth docks were built. The TVR leased the Penarth Harbour,

BY THE 1851 CENSUS, WALES HAD BECOME THE FIRST COUNTRY REGISTERING MORE PEOPLE EMPLOYED IN INDUSTRY THAN IN AGRICULTURE

Dock & Railway and the Penarth Extension Railway, operational from 1878, but capacity remained an issue.

Meanwhile, money was continually pumped into the Cardiff dock, with Roath basin opening in 1874, followed 13 years later by Roath Dock. Compelled to modernise to keep pace with demand, the dividends paid to investors in Cardiff's docks were marginal despite what were perceived to be high dock charges levied upon users.

Mine owners in the Rhondda saw opportunities for expansion being squandered by the limitations of the infrastructure so recently built. Raising their eyes to the horizon, their gaze fell upon a location beyond Cardiff which they thought might solve their problems.

Barry Island was so small as to be inconsequential. In 1841 the census recorded just 104 residents. Yet it was ideally placed by the sea to offer up new trade routes, breaking the monopoly enjoyed thus far by Cardiff. Despite heated objections from the high-powered group behind Cardiff's railway and docks, assent for Barry's rival scheme was given in 1884 at the second time of asking.

Members of the Barry Railway Company used joined-up thinking to open docks and dedicated track in 1889. Alongside its ship-filled dock was a repair yard, warehousing, cold stores, a flour mill and an ice factory. Almost immediately, vast quantities of coal once destined for Cardiff or Penarth were diverted into Barry. The financial impact on the TVR and its shareholders was colossal, with dividends reduced from a booming 15 per cent to 3 per cent in just two years.

The TVR responded by building another line that would connect Cardiff, Penarth and Barry along the coast. For its part the Barry Railway Company constructed a further direct line between Barry and Penarth. Other companies were keen for a slice of the industrial action, too. Coming late to the table were the Rhondda & Swansea Bay Railway, incorporated in 1882, and the Pontypridd, Caerphilly & Newport Railway, from 1884. As a result, that corner of South Wales became etched with railway lines in the same way as the north east of England.

In 1891 Barry's population had reached 765 and was rising fast. A decade later the figure stood at 27,000 (and within another 20 years the population figure for Barry, which by now spilled over into near

neighbourhoods, was 40,000). By the time of Victoria's death Barry was poised to overtake Cardiff as the largest docks operator in the region.

At the same time Barry Island laid down the foundations of its tourist trade. It became a favourite destination not only for coal but for the miners who hacked it out, easily accessible by railways which were extended in 1896 to take visitors beyond the docks to the island itself.

It was fortunate this alternative thread in the economy was developed, as the heady days of Barry Docks were already counting down. By the end of the First World War the British economy took on a different hue, not least because Germany paid reparations to Britain in the form of coal. Less was therefore needed from the Welsh coal mines.

One of the trades most severely affected by this was that of the coal trimmers employed at both Barry and Cardiff. It was their job to ensure a cargo of coal was evenly spread in a ship's hold. A load that shifted suddenly at sea could destabilise a ship, with disastrous consequences. The Cardiff, Barry and Penarth Coal Trimmers' Union was formed in 1888 to strike a fair deal for men who worked below deck wielding shovels in a grim and dangerous environment. Coal trimmers were eventually made obsolete by larger, self-trimming ships and the collapse of the coal industry.

However, other unions met with more lasting success despite a grim struggle at the outset. One such union was the Amalgamated Society of Railway Servants (ASRS), founded in Birmingham in August 1871, the same year the Trade Union Act gave groups like this one some status and protection in law.

With the hazards of railway work claiming hundreds of lives each year, there was a desire among the men for safer working conditions. Some railway companies like the Great Western Railway had a reputation for being paternalistic and provided outings, schooling and religious meetings for their staff. But care for the well-being of its workers stopped short of tolerating union activity. After guards working for the Great Western Railway formed a Railway Working Men's Provident Association in 1865, its leaders were sacked.

Profits were still the main motive for railway companies, which often compromised basic safety to save money. One parliamentary inquiry of the era discovered many men were exhausted, working 90 to 100 hours each week. Consequently, most employees felt themselves overworked and at risk.

WITH THE HAZARDS OF RAILWAY WORK CLAIMING HUNDREDS OF LIVES EACH YEAR, THERE WAS A DESIRE AMONG THE MEN FOR SAFER WORKING CONDITIONS

At the ASRS Charles Bassett-Vincent began organising railway workers, initially on an informal basis. He aired grievances by writing to newspapers and contacting the Trades Council. His aim was not to call for strikes – considered dangerously disloyal – but instead to enter into talks that would iron out disputes. (Bassett-Vincent went on to found the National Association of General Railway Clerks in 1897 and was its first general secretary.)

The new group was popular, given there was no real precedent for working men to follow at the time. Within a year some 17,000 men put their names to its register – only a small portion of the 250,000 who worked on railways nationwide, but it was a start. However, predictably, the new organisation was not only arguing with railway management but soon its members were arguing among themselves. Although it was aimed at everyone who worked in the railways there were sensitive demarcation lines recognised by certain sectors. Drivers and firemen, for example, refused to be grouped with other workers and formed their own Associated Society of Locomotive Engineers and Firemen in 1880.

By 1882 ASRS membership was pegged at 6,300, but the word continued to spread. The first meeting of the Merthyr branch of the

ABOVE: A steam train crosses the viaduct to Barry Island.

OVERLEAF: Workers at Cardiff Docks during the British Coal Strike.

ASRS was held on 15 July 1888. Richard Evans was elected chairman and the society decided on monthly meetings. Among others, the Merthyr branch represented workers on the Rhymney and Taff Vale railways.

The initial reluctance to strike was gradually eroded in the face of intransigence among railway company management. And one such action by the men of the TVR led to a major court case that shunted the British Labour Party to the political foreground.

In 1900 signalmen on the TVR went on strike, followed by the enginemen. The ASRS made the strike official, believing it was protected by the 1871 Act. Infuriated, the TVR, driven by its general manager Ammon Beasley, took out a legal injunction to stop the strike and sued the ASRS, claiming huge losses. At the end of lengthy proceedings the union was ordered to pay £23,000 in damages and £19,000 costs after a hearing in the House of Lords held in 1901.

The Lords' ruling rendered unions everywhere unable to take action against employers, no matter how legitimate the cause. Strikes were probably going to mean bankruptcy. Working men now looked for a new brand of representation that would give them a voice. The ASRS had been one of the founders of the Labour Representation Committee in 1900, which was renamed the British Labour Party six years later. In the meantime the newly elected Liberal Government introduced the Trades Disputes Act in 1906, which gave unions the right to call strikes without the threat of legal action being used against them.

At the heart of Welsh industry was Merthyr Tydfil, loud and proud. According to *Bradshaw's*:

It stands up the Taff, among the ragged and barren-looking hills in the north-east corner of Glamorganshire, the richest county in Wales for mineral wealth.

About a century ago the first iron works were established here, since which the extension has been amazingly rapid. Blast furnaces, forges and iron mills are scattered on all sides. Each iron furnace is about 55 ft high, containing 5,000 cubic feet; and capable of smelting 100 tons of pig iron

STRIKE - IDLE DOCK LABORERS, CARDIFF

weekly, and as there are upwards of 50, the annual quantity of metal may be tolerably estimated, but as great as that supply may seem it is scarcely equal to the demand created for it by railways.

Then there is an uncommon dose of heartfelt concern pouring forth from *Bradshaw's*.

Visitors should see the furnaces at night when the red glare of the flames produces an uncommonly striking effect.

Indeed the town is best seen at that time for by day it will be found dirty and irregularly built, without order or management, decent roads or footpaths, no supply of water and no public building of the least note, except barracks and a vast poor house lately finished in the shape of a cross on heaps of the rubbish accumulated from the pits and works. Cholera and fever are, of course, at home here in a scene which would shock even the most 'eminent defender of the filth'.

The rapid expansion of the town had not been accompanied by education, as the guidebook notes:

Out of 695 couples married in 1845 1,016 persons signed with marks...

We do hope that proper measures will be taken henceforth by those who draw enormous wealth from working these works to improve the condition of the people.

The guide implores ironworks owner Lady Charlotte Guest to become one of the 'Nightingale Sisterhood' in order to improve social conditions.

However, according to an obituary of Sir John Josiah Guest, Lady Guest's husband and the previous owner of Dowlais Ironworks, the couple had carried out ample amounts of charitable work. Minutes of the Institution of Civil Engineers after Guest's death in 1852 claim:

Although strict in enforcing subordination among the multitude of men in his employment, he was ever watchful for their interests, and sought their spiritual and temporal benefit in every way; founding places of worship, and establishing schools, whilst, during periods of mercantile depression and the visitation of disease, his charity was unbounded, and in these labours of love he was ably seconded by his wife, the Lady Charlotte Elizabeth Bertie, only sister of the Earl of Lindsey.

This estimable lady, whose literary powers are as well appreciated as her general talents and acquirements in branches of knowledge not usually presenting attractive features for ladies, appears to have felt, that on arriving among a dense population of hitherto ill-educated people, speaking a peculiar dialect, and isolated by their habits and manners, few of the inhabitants of Dowlais having ever travelled twenty miles from their homes, she was called to a task of no little

Factory smoke at Dowlais, South Wales.

The First Welsh International Rugby Match

Men who laboured hard during the week in heavy industry, living in deprived circumstances, increasingly sought recreation at the weekends. Rugby was poised to make its journey from being a public-school sport to a working-man's pastime.

The Welsh Rugby Union was formed after the nation was humbled in its first international, as sports historian Patrick Casey explains:

> The first international between England and Wales took place on 19 February 1881 at Blackheath.
>
> A game more noted for the chaotic organization of the Welsh side than anything else, it was Wales' first international. The players had never played together before.
>
> No formal invitations to play were sent out to the Welsh XV. Two of those expected to appear didn't turn up so bystanders, University undergraduates with tenuous Welsh links but who had travelled to London to see the match, had to be roped in to play for Wales.
>
> It also didn't help that the changing rooms were a local pub (The Princess of Wales, which remains to this day). Both teams had to walk the half a mile across the common to play. Rumour has it that the Welsh team needed some Dutch courage before the match so had been drinking heavily.
>
> The game was a farce. The Welsh were hopelessly outplayed and under modern scoring values lost 82–0.

> Richard Summers played in that match and said of the Welsh outfit: 'We played in ordinary, light walking boots with a bar of leather across the sole to help us swerve. Jerseys were fitted high at the neck with serge blue knickers fastened below the knee with four or five buttons. We changed at the Princess of Wales public house nearby.'

Richard Mullock is credited by many as the man behind a meeting that established the Welsh Rugby Football Union held soon afterwards. It became the Welsh Rugby Union in 1934.

'Collared', an engraving from Shearman's book on rugby, c. 1887.

and Germany. And by 1902 Britain was ranked third among steel-producing countries for production, and saw its export market diminishing by the year.

St David's was left off the railway map, with Haverfordwest being the nearest station. According to *Bradshaw's*:

> ...the road between Haverfordwest and St David's is the most execrable in the United Kingdom but replete with scenery magnificently grand.

A vintage portrait engraving print of Sir William Hamilton by Henry Hudson, c. 1788.

Roads had become something of a sore point in West Wales by Victorian times. In fact, it was not so much the roads but the tolls local people were forced to pay to use them. Farmers were scratching a living from a landscape that wasn't always forgiving. They needed lime to improve the soil and a ready access to market to sell their produce. Turnpike Trusts, established by Acts of Parliament, were intended to build roads and charge a small fee to users for their maintenance, but typically the roads were poorly maintained and the tolls were high. There were 11 Turnpike Trusts around Carmarthen alone, and sometimes farmers encountered several turnpikes on the same road, reducing their income in times of high taxation.

After a new turnpike was introduced on a road that linked farmers from West Wales to their local lime kiln in 1839, there was an uprising of an unusual kind. Men dressed as women, with blackened faces, turned up to smash the turnpike hut and began what became known as the 'Rebecca riots'.

No one knows for sure why these men assumed the identity of women. There was a long-standing custom in the area to put on women's clothes and darken faces for public parades. It was also symbolic of the world being upside-down. Some historians have linked it to a line in the Old Testament in which Rebecca is told, 'Let thy seed possess the gates of those which hate them'. A more down-to-earth explanation is that the leader of the first riot borrowed his garb from a woman called Rebecca.

In any event, the Rebecca riots escalated, and in 1842 a letter purporting to be from those involved warned: 'As for the constable and

A portrait of Lady Hamilton.

the policemen, Becca and her children pay no more attention to them than the grasshoppers which fly in the summer.'

On 26 May 1843 rioters went into Carmarthen to attack the workhouse – ostensibly built to give work to the poor but in reality akin to a jail. By now the authorities were gravely concerned. In July that year an officer insisted, 'Great numbers of discharged workmen from Merthyr and Dowlais have come into the county and are active in persuading the people to mischief'.

From folk hero status, Rebecca – who might well have been more than one man – and his colleagues began to spread fear in their communities as they took the law into their own hands. The death of an elderly woman turnpike-keeper turned the tide of public opinion against the rioters.

It was their good fortune that a reporter for *The Times*, T. C. Foster, had shone a light on their grievances. Shortly afterwards a Commission of Enquiry halved the tolls and the bizarre public protesting faded into history.

At the end of the line is Milford Haven. The arrival of the railway here in 1863 gave new life to a run-down town. At the town's inception some 70 years before it had been touched by celebrity and scandal. Its founder was the diplomat Sir William Hamilton, who was utilising land bequeathed to him on the death of his first wife. In 1791 he married for a second time, aged 60. His wife was 26-year-old blacksmith's daughter Emma Hart, a talented dancer and noted beauty. She was later considerably more famous as Lady Emma Hamilton, the mistress of British naval hero Lord Nelson. Nelson travelled with the Hamiltons, his presence tolerated and perhaps even encouraged by Sir William. They even visited Milford Haven together in 1802, when it was newly established as a whaling port with crews drawn from Nantucket. There were public celebrations to mark the occasion. Obligingly the Navy Board also established a dock there.

However, in 1810 the whalers returned to America, the same year Milford's bank collapsed. Four years later the Navy relocated to Pembroke and Milford was left in the doldrums. In 1874 Milford docks were under construction, laying the groundwork for the fishing industry which would dominate for decades. Only after the development of giant tankers in the 1950s did Milford become the focus of the oil transport industry.

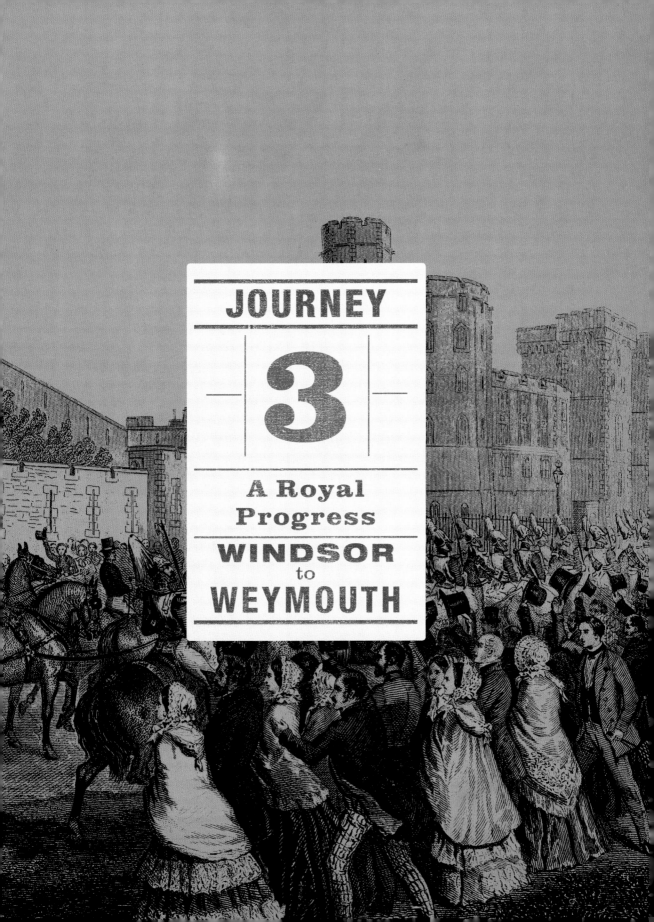

JOURNEY

3

A Royal Progress

WINDSOR
to
WEYMOUTH

Initially Queen Victoria was not a fan of railways. Although she was a child when the first railways began to operate, she still subscribed to the commonly held view that people could disintegrate and die under the pressure of excessive speed. However, her more scientifically minded husband, Prince Albert, had a more far-sighted view of the invention, although he was evidently a cautious passenger. He memorably uttered after one leisurely trip: 'Not quite so fast next time, Mr Conductor, if you please.'

After a delay brought about by concerns the railway would blight the castle, two stations were built in short order in Windsor by rival companies hoping to curry royal favour. Great Western Railways was laying tracks into Windsor from Slough while South Western Railway was heading in from neighbouring Datchet.

Both projects were running neck and neck until iron supports on a bridge between Windsor and Datchet wobbled, permitting Great Western Railway with its rock-solid Brunel bridge across the Thames to win the railway race. Windsor & Eton Central Station opened on 8 October 1849 and Queen Victoria made her first journey from it on 23 November. Within four weeks Windsor & Eton Riverside Station was in business, although its opening was a somewhat more downbeat occasion.

The fact that railways reached Windsor at all was a cause for celebration, as the authorities at nearby Eton College, founded by King Henry VI in 1440, were implacably opposed to any trains running in the vicinity, fearing they would be a distraction for students. At the time the college was an immensely powerful institution with plenty of friends in Parliament, where plans for new railways were agreed before they were built.

However, concerns that trains would provide a ready escape route to London for listless students, or become a target for stone-throwing scholars, proved unfounded. In fact, two Eton schoolboys became royal heroes one day after the Queen returned from a train trip.

On 2 March 1882 a disgruntled would-be poet, Roderick Maclean, fired a pistol at Victoria as her carriage was leaving Windsor railway station. Earlier on in her reign the Queen was not universally popular, after withdrawing from public life following the death of her husband. But by now she had been wooed back by politician Benjamin Disraeli and was more highly regarded than ever. Maclean's gripe was that

PREVIOUS PAGE: Queen Victoria and Prince Albert welcome Napoleon III and Empress Eugenie to Windsor Castle.

RIGHT: Roderick Maclean's attempt to assassinate Queen Victoria at Windsor Station.

OVERLEAF: Windsor Station, 1908.

THE ILLUSTRATED LONDON NEWS

REGISTERED AT THE GENERAL POST-OFFICE FOR TRANSMISSION ABROAD.

No. 2236.—VOL. LXXX.   SATURDAY, MARCH 11, 1882.   WITH TWO SUPPLEMENTS   SIXPENCE. BY POST, 6½D.

she had apparently not replied after he had sent her a poem. His shot missed and, while police hurried to the scene, two Eton schoolboys – Gordon Chesney Wilson and Leslie Murray Robertson – rained blows down on him with their umbrellas.

Tried for high treason, Maclean was found insane rather than guilty and was dispatched to Broadmoor asylum, where he died some 40 years later. For her part, Victoria was incensed that he could be considered not guilty when she was so obviously and deliberately put in the line of fire. Her ensuing wrath inspired a legal modification that thereafter permitted a verdict of guilty but insane.

The event was immortalised in verse by William McGonagall, acclaimed as the worst of British poets. He wrote:

> *Maclean aimed at her head;*
> *And he felt very angry*
> *Because he didn't shoot her dead.*
> *Maclean must be a madman,*
> *Which is obvious to be seen,*
> *Or else he wouldn't have tried to shoot*
> *Our most beloved Queen.*

Bradshaw's guide bubbles over in its praise of Windsor, claiming its scenery is remarkable for its

sylvan beauty and the weary citizen who desires to enjoy a summer holiday cannot do better than to procure an admission ticket to Windsor Castle from the printsellers Messrs Colnaghi, of Pall Mall, and then make his way to the Great Western Railway in time for an early train.

Within the next three hours he may see all the regal splendours of the palatial halls of Windsor and then, having refreshed the inward man at any of the hostelries which abound in that town, he may stroll forth into the country and contrast the quiet and enduring charms of nature with the more glittering productions of art with which wealth and power surround themselves.

The interior of the
Queen's railway carriage,
engraved by Jules David,
c. 1844.

It was from neighbouring Slough that Queen Victoria took her first
train ride on 13 June 1842 as she journeyed between Windsor Castle
and Buckingham Palace. Although she was nervous she was persuaded
to make the journey by Prince Albert, who had taken the trip from
Slough to Paddington for the first time some three years previously.

With scant notice, Great Western Railways prepared a royal
carriage. (It was in fact similar to a standard carriage but was liberally
decorated with flowers.) It was placed in the middle of seven carriages –
to protect the Queen if there was a shunt – and towed by the locomotive
Phlegethon. At the controls was locomotive designer Daniel Gooch, who
was later knighted for his work laying the first transatlantic telegraph
cable by ship, the *Great Eastern*. Alongside him stood Isambard
Kingdom Brunel and a royal footman, whose scarlet clothes were soon
covered in soot. The journey took 25 minutes. There was a red carpet
and a detachment of Royal Irish Hussars at Paddington to meet the
Queen, along with an army of GWR dignitaries.

The Queen was now converted to the benefits of rail travel, as a
letter written soon afterwards reveals: 'We arrived here [Buckingham

The Queen, a replica
of the royal train, at
Royal Windsor Station,
Windsor.

Palace] yesterday morning, having come by the railroad, from Windsor, in half an hour, free from dust and crowd and heat, and I am quite charmed with it.'

Eventually all the major railway companies produced a royal train, with sumptuous fittings, expressly for use by the royal family, and as the network expanded she was even able to reach her Scottish home, Balmoral, with greater ease. Nonetheless, Victoria applied strict rules to train travel, which were that the locomotive speed did not exceed 40 mph during the day and 30 mph at night, and that the train was stopped at mealtimes.

Of Slough there is not a word in *Bradshaw's* although today the station has a particularly quirky claim to fame in the shape of 'Station Jim', a dog that collected cash for the Great Western Railway Widows and Orphans Fund for two years from 1894. Brought to the station as a puppy, he was taught tricks and barked every time someone popped a coin in the collecting box he wore around his neck. He was credited with collecting more than £40, usually donated in pennies or halfpennies. After his sudden death he was stuffed and placed in a glass case on platform five with a collecting box so he could continue his work posthumously.

Inside the glass case there's an account from the nineteenth century about Station Jim's accomplishments:

> *He would sit up and beg or lie down and 'die', he could make a bow when asked or stand up on his hind legs. He would get up and sit in a chair and look quite at home with a pipe in his mouth and cap on his head. He would express his feelings in a very noisy manner when he heard any music … If a ladder was placed against the wall he would climb it. He would play leap frog with the boys; he would escort them off the station if told to do so but would never bite them.*

Slough Station was also pivotal in a sensational murder case that caught the imagination of Victorian England, not least for the involvement of a new communication method recently installed there. The murderer was John Tawell, apparently a model citizen and devout Quaker, and his victim was his one-time mistress, Sara Hart. Tawell's chosen method was poison, while the new technology in question was the electric telegraph, which went on to change Victorian communication beyond recognition.

Although Tawell appeared to be a pillar of the community he was in fact a convicted felon. Aged 30, and a husband and father, he was transported to Australia after being found with a forged bank bond. But his initial criminality was laced with charm. Soon he was given his freedom in Australia where he opened a successful drug store selling home-made remedies, proving he was more quack than Quaker. He also surrounded himself with adoring women, all of whom were taken aback when Mrs Tawell and her children arrived.

The couple eventually returned to England, where Mrs Tawell fell ill. Her husband employed Sara Hart to look after their child. Tawell and Hart promptly began an affair. When his wife died they lived together for a while but Tawell soon transferred his affections to another woman, a Quaker in nearby Berkhampstead. Despite his chequered past, the couple were married. However, disquiet among the Quaker community about his previous liaison persuaded him that Sara would have to be eliminated from his life.

SLOUGH STATION WAS ALSO PIVOTAL IN A SENSATIONAL MURDER CASE THAT CAUGHT THE IMAGINATION OF VICTORIAN ENGLAND

The offices of the Electric
and International
Telegraph Company,
in Bell Alley, Moorgate
Street, London, 1859.

On New Year's Day 1845 Tawell went to Sara's cottage in Slough and together they shared some ale. Unknown to her, he had poured prussic acid into her glass; the swift-acting toxin left her writhing in agony. A neighbour called the local doctor, who guessed Sara had been poisoned and could do nothing to save her. He did, however, persuade the railway station to send an alert using its newly installed electric telegraph.

At the time the new technology's use was tentative and the number of trained operators few. Fortunately, the far-sighted doctor and the quick-witted stationmaster valued its immediacy. The message sent from Slough read:

A murder has gust been committed at Salt Hill and the suspected murderer was seen to take a first class ticket to London by the train which left Slough at 742 he is in the garb of a kwaker with a great coat on which reaches nearly down to his feet he is in the last compartment of the second class compartment.

(The earliest telegraph kit did not have the letters Q, J or Z, or punctuation, among its keys.) Thanks to the telegraph message, police were waiting for Tawell at Paddington. He was followed and arrested the next day.

THE ELECTRIC TELEGRAPH

The commercial telegraph was patented by Sir William Fothergill Cooke and Charles Wheatstone in 1837. (Morse code was patented the same year in America although it was some time before the English telegraph and the American dot-dash signal system were united.) The inventors made liberal use of groundwork laid by Michael Faraday, who had linked electrical currents and magnetism and built the first solenoid that combined the potency of both.

Now, using the power of an electric current, magnetic needles could transmit messages in code over long distances. The telegraph was first used on the railway system to link Euston with Camden Town. On 9 April 1839 it was installed along the Great Western Railway between Paddington and West Drayton, and in 1843 it was finally extended to Slough.

Its potential for communication and railway signalling at the time was still largely unappreciated. However, soon the sending of telegrams would be an everyday occurrence for the Victorians, a first sortie into instant communication. Social and business networking was poised to spread around the globe, thanks to the electric telegraph, and by the time the 1866 *Bradshaw's Tourist Handbook* was published, the whereabouts of every telegraph station was included, a reflection of how important the technology had become.

Edison's electric telegraph system for railways, 1886.

Tawell believed his veneer of respectability put him beyond the law. 'You must be mistaken,' he told officers. 'My station in life places me above suspicion.' Soon he claimed Sara committed suicide expressly to implicate him. His wife and some elements of the Quaker community believed he was innocent. However, a London chemist testified at his trial, held at Aylesbury Assizes, that Tawell had bought prussic acid on the day of the murder. And a neighbour said Sara had been ill before following a visit by Tawell.

It was enough to convince the jury that Tawell was a murderer. He was found guilty and hanged at Aylesbury gaol on 28 March 1845 before a 2,000-strong crowd. Before his death he wrote a confession that finally persuaded his loyal wife that he was a killer.

The executioner failed to allow sufficient 'drop' on the rope to cleanly break Tawell's neck and instead he was slowly strangled by the noose. He was, as one newspaper of the day observed, 'the murderer who was hanged by the wires'.

In Slough the railways beckoned in the first commuter houses in the 1840s, built at Upton Park by James Bedborough, once a stone mason at Windsor Castle who later established himself as a builder, town councillor and one-time mayor of Windsor. He was clearly a man of vision and ambition, advertising the houses in terms of their proximity to Windsor Castle and the railway.

The new houses bordered parkland that was designed by noted gardener Joseph Paxton, who went on to find fame and a knighthood by designing the Crystal Palace in time for the Great Exhibition in 1851. He also made a fortune by joining the board of the Midland Railway Company.

Paxton became an MP but never forgot his humble roots. The son of a yeoman farmer, Paxton fared considerably better than Bedborough. Unfortunately, to buy the land in Slough and build the first 29 terraced houses and villas Bedborough steeped himself in debt, and when he died in 1860 there was no money available to settle the accounts. The tangled web apparently led to the suicide of two sons and left his family in financial ruin. He is the ancestor of television presenter Davina McCall.

The railway line between Maidenhead and Slough is distinguished by one of Brunel's most graceful bridges. To build it, he tore up the

Joseph Paxton
(1803–1865).

Brunel's railway bridge at Maidenhead, built in 1838.

rule books with characteristic flourish and produced the widest, flattest bridge in the world, opened in 1839. Nervous railway bosses who couldn't fathom the design principles insisted he left the wooden framework used during construction in place to help support the bridge. Cannily, Brunel lowered the framework a fraction so it appeared to anxious observers to be bearing a burden. Only when the timber skeleton was washed away in a storm did the apparent miracle of design become obvious.

A decade later the ripples of admiration for this achievement were still fanning outwards. In a county magazine, *Lipscomb's Buckinghamshire*, Brunel's triumph was once again heralded.

> *That this beautiful outline is wholly formed of insignificant little bricks, each course of which on this enormous span has not only to carry its own weight but its proportion of the road and the train. When he considers the strains to which these materials are exposed and remembers that they are subject to a pressure that must approach*

very nearly to the limit of cohesion he will sufficiently appreciate the
courage and the capacity which have approached so near to the verge of
possibility without transgressing its bounds.

Today the bridge still bears the weight of numerous trains, each ten times heavier than those Brunel would recognize. One of the land arches is known as 'the Sounding Arch' for its remarkable echo.

Isambard Kingdom Brunel (1806–1859) was a major figure in Britain's railway story, particularly on the westbound routes. He was the son of a French engineer, Marc Isambard Brunel, whose own sparkling career was dimmed only by a spell in debtors' prison.

After being educated in Paris, one of young Brunel's first projects was to work alongside his father on a tunnel that went underneath the Thames in London. While he was working there a tidal wave of water broke through the tunnel's defences and left him seriously injured and several workmen dead. As he convalesced he feared for a time that he would only be remembered for a part-built tunnel. He dreaded becoming a 'mediocre success', someone with only measured achievement in his chosen field.

However, opportunity arose even while Brunel's broken leg was still in plaster. There was a competition to find a design for the planned Clifton suspension bridge in Bristol and he submitted four entries. Judge Thomas Telford rejected all competition entries in favour of his own design, but the embarrassed organisers extricated themselves from Telford's plans and held a second competition, which Brunel won. He was still in his twenties, although the bridge wouldn't be built until after his death due to lack of funds.

In 1833 Brunel became chief engineer to the Great Western Railway, which had ambitions to snake into western England through all the major cities that side of the country. To get official permission for the project was no easy task and Brunel was at the forefront of its defence. Although it was thrown out by the House of Lords once, the company's proposal was given the go-ahead on its second presentation in 1835.

On 26 December 1835 Brunel wrote in his journal for the first time in two years:

When I last wrote in this book I was just emerging from obscurity.
I had been toiling most unprofitably at numerous things … what a

ABOVE: Isambard Kingdom Brunel (1806–1859).

OVERLEAF: The western entrance of Brunel's Box Tunnel, running under Box Hill between Bath and Chippenham.

change. The railway is now in progress, the finest work in England – a handsome salary – £2,000 a year – on excellent terms with my directors and all going smoothly, but what a fight we have had – and how near defeat – and what a ruinous defeat it would have been…

The bridge at Maidenhead and the one at Windsor were two in a string of remarkable engineering feats carried out as the line headed west. Another was the Box Tunnel between Bath and Chippenham, some two miles in length, that took almost six years to complete. Two gangs worked inwards from each side of the hill to meet in the middle at almost precisely the point that Brunel predicted – out by only one and a quarter inches.

Brunel was a hard worker who wasn't afraid of getting his hands dirty. However, he had little respect for money and many of the projects he was linked to were overspent. There's ample evidence that Brunel believed his own ideas to be the best, and that he was always the best man for the job. According to the memoirs of Daniel Gooch,

The last broad-gauge train leaving Paddington Station, 20 May 1892.

BRUNEL WAS A
HARD WORKER
WHO WASN'T
AFRAID OF
GETTING HIS
HANDS DIRTY

published before his death in 1889, 'One feature of Brunel's character … that gave him a great deal of extra and unnecessary work, was that he fancied that no one could do anything but himself.'

Brunel laid nearly 1,000 miles of track, nearly all of it broad gauge which measured 7 ft. His belief in broad gauge was not necessarily misplaced, as he correctly insisted it would take bigger trains at fast speeds for a more stable and comfortable journey. However, elsewhere in the country narrower gauges were better suited to the terrain, and they were invariably used in railways engineered by Robert Stephenson and his father George. The Stephensons, who did so much for locomotive development and track expansion, favoured a 'standard' gauge of just 4 ft 8½ in. Clearly the same train could not travel on both lines. Passengers whose journey spanned two different systems were compelled to change trains.

Brunel maintained that the Great Western Railway could operate in isolation. But the stark reality was that much more standard gauge track was laid in the early years of railway expansion. Eventually the government insisted on a national standard gauge and the standard it chose was the one favoured by the Stephensons. In 1846 the government made this standard gauge the norm.

For Brunel, the railways formed only part of his vision for extensive travel. Following a train journey he saw the traveller getting aboard a steamer and heading across the Atlantic to New York. He designed the *Great Western* paddle-wheel steamer in 1837, which operated a regular transatlantic service, the first ship of its kind to do so. There followed the *Great Britain* in 1843, the first big ship to use a screw propeller. His last ship was the *Great Eastern*, launched in 1858 after a series of delays. The largest ship ever built at the time, it had capacity for 4,000 passengers and stored sufficient coal to travel non-stop to Australia. But its construction was blighted by bad feeling between Brunel and his co-designer, John Scott Russell, and its first voyage was marred by an explosion below decks. Anxieties surrounding the ship may well have hastened Brunel's death, which came just a month before Robert Stephenson's in 1859.

The success of the *Great Eastern* as a passenger ship was blunted by the speed of smaller ships, which covered the same distances in shorter times. Nonetheless, it earned its place in history in 1863 by laying the first telegraph cable between England and America with Daniel Gooch at the helm.

Brunel's talents were not confined to pushing back the horizons for travellers, though. During the Crimean War in the 1850s he designed camp hospitals to the specifications of British nursing luminary Florence Nightingale, including lavatories and ventilator fans, and these prefabricated modules, put up under the supervision of 18 skilled men, were credited with cutting the number of hospital deaths thanks to this consideration for hygiene. Brunel also designed docks for Cardiff, Brentford and other ports. A noticeably short man, he favoured a stove-pipe hat to improve his physical bearing. His death at the age of 53 was almost certainly caused by overwork.

SEEING ABUNDANT POTENTIAL PALMER'S IDEAS WERE FAR MORE AMBITIOUS THAN ANYTHING THAT HAD GONE BEFORE

Beyond Maidenhead lies Reading, reached by the Great Western Railway in 1840, where the sweet smell of success came from a biscuit factory. And key to the prosperity of the factory was the web of railways that brought the product to tea tables up and down the country.

Huntley & Palmers began life as a small bakery. Joseph Huntley, the son of a headmaster, learned about the business of biscuits from his mother Hannah, who cooked them in the school oven and sold them at the school gates during his childhood. Much later, when he was 51, he moved to Reading and managed sales for his baker son Thomas. As Quakers the family believed in offering quality goods at a fair price. The biscuits were popular and business was good, although there were fewer than a dozen employees on the payroll.

After Joseph retired in 1838, another Quaker, George Palmer, paid £550 to become a partner in the business alongside Thomas. Seeing abundant potential, Palmer's ideas were far more ambitious than anything that had gone before.

He employed a network of salesmen who brought biscuits to new outlets up and down the country. A new factory opened in 1846, dramatically increasing production. Thanks to mechanisation, including automatic biscuit cutters and giant ovens through which biscuit dough was passed, production went up 500 per cent in five years. There was more expansion in the second half of the nineteenth century, incorporating new sites, and the army of employees increased accordingly.

The railways arrived in Reading in 1840 and Palmer had established all elements of the factory close to the railway lines.

Indeed, the factory had its own rails laid to link up the national network, at one point totalling some seven miles. For these lines there were even Huntley & Palmer locomotives, specially made to run on steam so pollution did not taint the biscuits.

The bosses considered themselves strict but fair. There was to be no swearing, no fighting, no drinking or smoking on company premises. Anyone caught contravening the rules was fined. However, all the money generated in this way was put into the Sick Fund, along with a compulsory donation made weekly by each worker. This money helped to finance those struck down by illness, years before state welfare was introduced. The partners regularly held parties for the staff, gave them paid holiday at Christmas, had wedding cakes baked for those getting married and paid for the funerals of those who died in service.

Advertisement, c. 1880, featuring a Victorian picnic, complete with Huntley and Palmers biscuits.

The atmosphere between the partners wasn't always harmonious, though. Thomas Huntley felt the business was growing too fast, too soon, while George Palmer felt he bore the lion's share of commercial responsibility.

In 1857, with 90 men now baking biscuits, Thomas Huntley died, leaving a son, Henry, who had no burning interest in the business. The Huntley and Palmer families parted company, with a sum of almost £34,000 being paid to the outgoing Henry Huntley. George Palmer's two brothers, William Isaac and Samuel, became partners instead.

By 1894 there were 5,000 people employed by the Huntley & Palmers factory working a 54-hour week, including unmarried women who were segregated from the men. (It would be another 50 years before the company agreed to employ married women.) Biscuit making was so key to the town that the prison was known locally as 'the biscuit factory' and the local football players were called 'the biscuit men'. Rows of red-brick houses sprang up around Reading to provide accommodation for the biscuit factory workers. Meanwhile, packets of biscuits in 400 varieties were being dispatched to 137 countries by 1904, with the first leg of their journey undertaken by rail. The shape of wholesale biscuit tins was even altered to better fit into railway carriages.

From Reading via a Great Western branch line the Victorian traveller heading south could reach Basingstoke – a 'straggling, ill-built town', according to *Bradshaw's* – to be united with the South Western main line. Basingstoke was for a while the end of the South Western line. It was finally linked with Winchester after four tunnels and a station were constructed and the line between London and Southampton was completed in 1840. Its first train took three hours to cover a distance of just under 80 miles between its terminus at Nine Elms and the end of the line at the south coast. Had the government been involved, the railway's destination would no doubt have been Portsmouth, where the Royal Navy had a large and important base, but the London & South Western Railway Company chose Southampton above its neighbour, although its dock facilities were modest.

From Basingstoke the line forges through some sparsely populated countryside before glancing off the western edge of the South Downs. On the face of it, Micheldever Station on the South Western line was

BY 1894
THERE WERE
5,000 PEOPLE
EMPLOYED BY
THE HUNTLEY
& PALMERS
FACTORY
WORKING A
54-HOUR WEEK

so insignificant it did not warrant a mention in Bradshaw's guide. Indeed, it is unlikely that *Bradshaw's* could have ever envisaged the reason for its fame. However, in 1895 Micheldever Station was the unlikely starting point of the first ever car journey in the UK.

The car was a Panhard-Levassor powered by a Daimler engine and it arrived by rail from France, where cars were a far more common sight, via Southampton docks. It was then transported to the Hampshire Station by rail. At the time it cost £200, which equates to about £14,500 in today's money. The purchaser was the Honourable Evelyn Ellis. He was accompanied on its first journey by engineer Frederick Simms, who wrote an article for the *Saturday Review* on the adventure.

We set forth at exactly 9.26 a.m. and made good progress on the well-made old London coaching road; it was delightful travelling on that fine summer morning. We were not without anxiety as to how the horses we might meet would behave towards their new rivals, but they took it very well and out of 133 horses we passed only two little ponies did not seem to appreciate the innovation. On our way we passed a great many vehicles of all kinds [i.e. horse-drawn], as well as cyclists. It was a very pleasing sensation to go along the delightful

LEFT: The Hon. Evelyn Ellis in his Panhard-Levassor, 1895.

OVERLEAF: *Bodmin*, a steam locomotive pulling on the Watercress Line.

roads towards Virginia Water at speeds varying from three to twenty miles per hour, and our iron horse behaved splendidly. There we took our luncheon and fed our engine with a little oil. Going down the steep hill leading to Windsor we passed through Datchet and arrived right in front of the entrance hall of Mr Ellis's house at Datchet at 5.40, thus completing our most enjoyable journey of 56 miles, the first ever made by a petroleum motor carriage in this country, in 5 hours 32 minutes, exclusive of stoppages and at an average speed of 9.84 mph.

The trip was more daring than it first appears. There were of course no petrol stations, so the oil they bought was from a chemist's shop. But Ellis and Simms were also flouting the law, which decreed motorised vehicles could only use the roads if a man walked in front waving a red flag. This law was repealed the following year. Still, on its early performance there was little to suggest that the motor car would have overwhelmed the train in terms of popularity and usage within a century.

It would be decades before road transport made it impact on industry in Britain. In the meantime, businesses that relied on getting produce to consumers in timely fashion were flourishing, as the railway network continued to expand.

The watercress business fell into this category, and its success contributed to an improvement in the general health of Victorian society. Watercress was favoured by rich and poor alike. Children would pluck bunches of the naturally occurring vitamin-rich plant to eat in the hand. Aristocrats enjoyed it as it garnished silver-service meals on porcelain plates. Its health benefits were immense, as it contains iron, calcium, sulphur and other nutrients.

Watercress was first farmed in Britain at the beginning of the nineteenth century. Hampshire soon became a centre of the trade as crops flourished in the chalky waters of its rivers. Before trains reached the county, stagecoaches were used to transport it to London. When the county was finally fractured by rail services, the one serving the heart of the industry was nicknamed 'the watercress line'. It was built between the existing stations at Alton and Winchester and was officially called the Mid-Hants Railway after it opened in 1865. The stations on the line were Itchen Abbas, Ropley and Alresford. Another station, Medstead and Four Marks, was opened three years later.

After willow flats or hampers filled with watercress were loaded onto the trains, they were taken to London and then across Britain for the watercress to be sold as a low-cost snack. Always a secondary line as far as the railway authorities were concerned, the Mid-Hants Railway nevertheless attracted interest for combating some severe gradients, ascending at its highest point to 652 ft (199 m) above sea level.

When the railway line linking Winchester and Southampton was built in 1838 by the London & South Western Railway, Winchester was its temporary terminus. Eventually tens of thousands of visitors used the train to wonder at the ancient glories in the Roman city. *Bradshaw's* describes how one of the first organs made in England was installed in Winchester's cathedral in the year 951. 'It was a ponderous thing containing 400 pipes blown by 24 pairs of bellows.' In 1854 the organ was replaced by one that had thrilled visitors to the Great Exhibition three years earlier, with 5,500 pipes.

At first, Winchester was the only major centre of population on the London to Southampton line, with Basingstoke a minor market town. The railway's arrival altered the destiny of one hamlet along its route, transforming it into a major industrial hub.

Although Eastley had existed for a long time, it was so remote that the station built there was called Bishopstoke Junction in order that passengers might better recognise their whereabouts. Early on, the railway company built cottages there to house staff, and it assumed greater importance when it was linked by a branch line to Portsmouth. From 1852 it was the site of a cheese market and even had a dedicated siding for cheese transport.

A programme of house building finally united two parishes, Barton and Eastley. From 1868 the combined parish was called Eastleigh at the suggestion of a local author, Charlotte Yonge, who donated £500 for the building of a parish church. Growth accelerated still more after 1891 when the London & South Western Railway opted to switch its carriage and wagon works from Nine Elms – previously the company's London terminus – to Eastleigh and, later, its locomotive works. The site wasn't picked for its proximity to coal deposits or iron ore mining works but for its unexpectedly strategic position on the company network.

By the end of the Victorian era Eastleigh was known as a railway town, with some 2,600 people in the pay of the railway company. It

was also a passing point for military traffic during the Boer War, all funnelled overseas through Southampton. Much later, commentator John Arlott said: 'The very name "Eastleigh" means railways … Eastleigh has a heart – a huge fiery, steam-pulsed, hammer-beating heart.'

While the British love affair with railways continued, the economy of Eastleigh was assured. But, like other towns, it was at risk when passenger numbers declined. Eastleigh has been comparatively lucky, with some locomotive work still continuing today in the town, although on a much-reduced scale.

Queen Victoria became well acquainted with the railways of southern Britain, and especially those of the L&SWR, as she made regular trips to Osborne House on the Isle of Wight, apparently her favourite royal residence. Her patronage of the island in turn led to a major boost in its tourism.

Today a visitor on the boat trip from Southampton would feel hemmed in by the commercial dockyards and colossal container ships that line the water's edge. For Queen Victoria the view would have been very different. According to *Bradshaw's*, Southampton was

> 79 miles from London by the South West Railway, on a point at the head of a fine inlet called Southampton Water into which the [rivers] Test and Itchin run.
>
> When the mudbanks are covered at high tide its inlet is a fine sheet of water seven miles long and one or two broad, and exactly the spot for a sail with groves along the shores, especially in the west, in which the nightingales are heard all night long.

When Queen Victoria disembarked from the ferry she might well have fancied a spot of lunch, and the prestigious yacht club at Cowes was the perfect destination. There was one problem: the club only allowed men inside its doors. The single-sex ruling would not be relaxed even for the Queen of England. However, the club was obviously keen to garner royal custom so a conservatory was built leading from the club

PREVIOUS PAGE: Visiting Winchester Cathedral.

LEFT: The yacht *America* won the sailing match at Cowes for the Club Cup – the race was renamed 'The America's Cup' in her honour.

but, as far as etiquette was concerned, not a part of it, and here the Queen was welcome.

Queen Victoria and Prince Albert bought Osborne House in 1845 for £28,000. They didn't want a palace – they had several of those already – but a family home that would be a refuge from the demands of public life for themselves and their children.

The house they bought was grand but unexceptional. Prince Albert set about redesigning the building and favoured Italian architecture that he had seen on his travels prior to marriage. He collaborated with Thomas Cubitt, an eminent builder whose company had been responsible for many of London's most prestigious and stylish neighbourhoods. The effect of their plans was startling and sympathetic. The attention to detail extended to the interior, to the luxurious fixtures and fittings bearing Victoria and Albert's monograms, carefully chosen by the royal couple to complement their island home.

Osborne House gave the royal family an opportunity to enjoy a brand of domesticity, albeit one that was very much sheltered from the stresses of everyday life. In 17 years Victoria gave birth to nine children: Victoria, Edward, Alice, Alfred, Helena, Louise, Arthur, Leopold and Beatrice. It was in many ways a remarkable feat as Victoria was ambivalent about

the young. 'I don't dislike babies,' she once insisted, 'though I think very young ones rather disgusting.' Included in the grounds of Osborne House was a chalet known as the Swiss Cottage, where the couple's brood were educated. Beyond the tutoring that many children of the era came to expect, Prince Albert insisted they learned how to grow vegetables and, further, to sell and cook them.

When Albert died after contracting typhoid in 1861 at the age of just 42, Victoria turned her room at Osborne into a shrine dedicated to him. There was a portrait of her husband set up by her bed so it was the first thing she saw every morning. His pocket watch, regularly wound, was kept in a pouch at the bed head. And when Victoria herself died at Osborne House in 1901 after suffering a stroke, the pattern was repeated, her son Edward ordering metal gates to be fitted in the corridors so her room would not be disturbed for 50 years. It wasn't until 1954 that Queen Victoria's great-great-granddaughter Queen Elizabeth II consented to the gates being opened.

Queen Victoria's body was taken from the south coast to London for the funeral service. Afterwards her coffin was taken back to Windsor by train for burial.

ABOVE: Osborne House, Queen Victoria's home on the Isle of Wight.

OVERLEAF: Alum Bay, Isle of Wight.

AFTER IT BECAME
THE FOCUS OF
ROYAL FAVOUR,
THE ISLE OF
WIGHT ENJOYED
SOMETHING
OF A HEYDAY
AS TOURISTS
FLOCKED THERE

After it became the focus of royal favour, the Isle of Wight enjoyed something of a heyday as tourists flocked there. Among the attractions were the variously coloured sands of Alum Bay. The colours, which form naturally in the cliffs, were used either to create decorative strata in glass jars or, more intriguingly, to make pictures.

Sand art was pioneered by German painter Benjamin Zobel in the eighteenth century when he was a court artist at Windsor Castle. Before his tenure, the royals were amused by pictures made from sand which were, by their nature, temporary. However, using gum Arabic and white lead, Zobel found himself able to stick the sand to a board to create more lasting images, calling the results of his technique 'marmotinto'. During Victorian times this style of art enjoyed remarkable popularity, particularly on the Isle of Wight where visitors collected the coloured sand from the cliff face.

With rail travel the Victorians could indulge their curiosity as never before. They had a weakness for freakiness and it was this fancy for the strange, shocking and downright extraordinary that brought fame to Joseph Merrick as the Elephant Man (and to any number of excessively tall, short, fat, thin, physically tormented or unusually hirsute people). Previously their curiosity was confined to sensational pamphlets or dependent on visiting circuses or neighbourhood 'penny gaffs', informal venues that hosted travelling shows. However, thanks to an ever-extending network of trains, the upper- and middle-class Victorians now travelled to marvel before novelties and oddities at work and play. For those who became spectacles the dubious reward of celebrity was rarely matched with fortune.

Beyond the New Forest on the south coast lies Bournemouth, described by *Bradshaw's* as

a fashionable modern watering-place and winter residence ... It is situated in a beautiful sheltered spot in the chine of low chalk cliffs and is much resorted to by invalids for its health situation and quiet retirement.

Some of Bournemouth's health-giving qualities were attributed to the great number of pine trees planted by the town's first landowners in the early nineteenth century. There is evidence of this in street names that still exist today, including Pine Walk, which was originally called Invalids' Walk by the Victorians.

Settlement didn't start in earnest until Queen Victoria acceded to the throne, so Bournemouth became a truly Victorian town. The town's first hotel, the Royal Bath, opened on the day of the Queen's coronation: 28 June 1838. Among the notable visitors to have stayed there are Prime Ministers John Russell, Benjamin Disraeli and William Gladstone, Empress Eugenie, the wife of Napoleon III, and other foreign royalty.

Given the town's glorious reputation for good health, the train, when it finally arrived in Bournemouth, led to an influx that more than doubled its population in a decade. Still, Bournemouth was slow out of the blocks. An extension to a branch line serving Ringwood and Christchurch arrived in 1870. In 1874 Bournemouth West Station was opened for the Somerset & Dorset Joint Railway, although passengers were compelled to change at Wimborne. Two years after that it was linked to Poole by rail. Only in the 1880s did the improved railway system begin to have an impact on visitor numbers. By the time Victoria died Bournemouth encompassed some of its surrounding villages and had a population of 59,000. It also had by then a library, a symphony orchestra, a hospital and a pier.

For the Victorian visitor guided by *Bradshaw's*, making a choice between Bournemouth and its near neighbour Weymouth was not difficult. Bournemouth is dismissed in little more than a line. Weymouth, on the other hand, is given almost ceaseless praise for being 'striking', 'picturesque' and 'delightful'.

No place can be more salubrious than Weymouth. The air is so pure and mild, that the town is not only frequented during the summer but has been selected by many opulent families as a permanent residence; and the advantages which it possesses in the excellence of its bay, the beauty of its scenery and the healthfulness of its climate, have contributed to

Points of interest included a regatta, a theatre, assembly rooms, a castle
and pleasure boats. Yet most went to bathe in the crisply chill waters off
the Dorset coast. To enter the water, swimmers climbed into a bathing
machine, divested themselves of clothes and were towed into the water
either by horse- or manpower. At a certain depth they could modestly
plunge into the water away from prying eyes. The machine was left in
place until the dip was finished so bathers could return to shore the same
way, after waving a flag to attract the attention of the machine driver.

When bathing became fashionable in Victorian times the first
swimmers were men and they went into the water naked. Costumes
became compulsory for all by the 1860s, not least to spare the blushes
of women swimmers, and by the 1880s swimsuits had become suitably
large and robust so that women were unafraid to be seen in them.
The era of bathing machines was at an end. But when *Bradshaw's*
guide was written there were still two decades to go before swimmers
strolled unaccompanied into the sea from the shore.

The water is generally very calm and transparent.
The sands are smooth, firm and level and so gradual is the descent towards the sea that, at the distance of 100 yards, the water is not more than two
feet deep. Bathing machines of the usual number
and variety are in constant attendance and on the
South Parade is an establishment of hot salt-water
baths furnished with dressing rooms and every
requisite accommodation.

Weymouth was also at the end of the Somerset, Wiltshire & Weymouth
Railway, planned from 1845 but not completed until 1857. This was a
delightful holiday line edging down from Bristol and Bath and prized
by the Great Western Railway, which took over the line, for its cross-
Channel port.

Bradshaw's discusses the merits of Portland, linked to the coast
by a ridge of shingle called Chesil Beach, in terms of a day trip from

PREVIOUS PAGE: A view of Bournemouth from the West Cliff.

LEFT: Queen Victoria's bathing machine on the Osborne House estate.

Weymouth. It fails to note the impact of industry on the peninsula which sets it apart from resorts around it. Portland was among the forerunners of the rail age with the Merchant Railway, built in 1826 with a unique 4 ft 6 in gauge. It's not lodged into the history of railways because, with innovation coming thick and fast, its owners failed to keep pace with the changes.

The Dorset line launched in the wake of the pioneering Stockton to Darlington railway on which George Stephenson's *Locomotion* had towed cargo and passengers. Already industrial tracks and waggonways were relatively common sights. And thanks to the Industrial Revolution, the makers of the Merchant Railway could lay iron rails rather than wooden ones. This reduced friction and allowed for longer, smoother journeys.

THE SNAKE-CATCHER OF THE NEW FOREST

One man who capitalised on the vogue for quirky tourism was Harry 'Brusher' Mills, the famous snake-catcher of the New Forest. This charismatic countryman was happy to share the secrets of his success with hordes of visitors who descended on the Brockenhurst station after it opened for just a few pennies.

Places like the New Forest were populated with snakes to a far greater extent than now, including poisonous adders. Using his bare hands, Mills caught snakes, killed them and made up snake-bite antidote from their body parts. He even laid claim to a cure for rheumatism from the cooked-up bodies of New Forest adders. Dead snakes were also transported back to London by train to feed animals at London Zoo.

With a forked grey beard, Mills cut an eccentric figure. Whatever the weather he wore two coats over a waistcoat and gaiters. His snake-catching kit included sacks, a pronged stick and a sharp knife. He used this to make a deep cut in his own flesh if he ever suffered a snake bite, before applying a home-made ointment. It's thought his snake tally eventually numbered something around 30,000, including some 4,000 adders.

Although he was hampered by a cleft palate it never stopped him from chatting with visitors. They were welcomed to his hand-built hut for a cup of tea, brewed on a wood fire, served in tins without milk but laced with sugar and stirred by a homemade spoon.

An ancient law governing the New Forest would have given him 'squatters' rights' where he lived if his hut had not been burned down one night, apparently by vandals. Stories abound about Mills, who was known to clear a path to the bar through a crowded pub by casually tossing a live snake on to the floor.

HIS SNAKE-CATCHING KIT INCLUDED SACKS, A PRONGED STICK AND A SHARP KNIFE

Still he was clearly held in fond regard by locals, not least for establishing the New Forest as a must-see tourist attraction. After his death a collection among friends and drinking partners raised sufficient money for a marble memorial in the churchyard at Brockenhurst. It bears the following inscription:

His pursuit and the primitive way in which he lived, caused him to be an object of interest to many He died suddenly July 1st 1905 aged 65 years.

WITH
CHARACTERISTIC
VISION, THE
VICTORIANS SAW
THAT PORTLAND
HAD POTENTIAL
AS THE LARGEST
DEEP-WATER
HARBOUR IN
EUROPE

Perhaps because it was built on a one in seven incline – from the quarry at the hill top to the port below – the Merchant Railway failed to graduate to locomotive traffic like other early railways. Instead it depended on either horsepower or chains and wire hawsers to haul its wagons. As a consequence it stayed isolated on the end of the Portland peninsula, unable to expand in the same way as other railway lines. Nonetheless, the Merchant Railway remained in service until the start of the Second World War.

Its freight was soft, grey Portland stone, quarried for centuries and already apparent in St Paul's Cathedral and Buckingham Palace. With the Merchant Railway, however, some very tricky transport issues were resolved for the industry. With stone from the quarries now dispatched quickly to the port side and winched aboard cargo ships, thanks to the railway the market for Portland stone was dramatically expanded.

Meanwhile, an ambitious Victorian plan for Portland would keep quarrymen busy for decades. Portland was already a frequently used harbour for shipping but it was known for its treacherous waters. With a near-perpetual meeting of tides, the offshore Portland Race was a hazard that hampered the progress of the port.

With characteristic vision, the Victorians saw that Portland had potential as the largest deep-water harbour in Europe, key for a country that invested as heavily in its navy as Great Britain. Several breakwaters were needed to create a refuge from the elements. Portland not only had a suitable seafront but an abundance of breakwater stone. With plenty of convicts held in the nearby Portland prison, thanks to a tough national legal code, there was also a labour force that would oblige in the mammoth building project.

Prince Albert laid the first stone in 1848, signalling the start of a quarter-century-long project. An estimated 5,731,376 tons of stone were taken from Portland quarries out to sea. (Subsequently there was still sufficient to provide a tombstone for every Commonwealth grave in the two world wars and for the Cenotaph in Whitehall.) It was tough and treacherous work for the convicts, with one estimate claiming that a dozen were killed for every year it was under construction. However, locomotives operating on broad-gauge track built for the purpose, in addition to the Merchant Railway, made the labouring inestimably easier.

In 1858, a full decade after the breakwater project began, writer Charles Dickens wrote about what he saw when he visited the site in his own magazine, *Household Words*.

Up the hill to the right run the inclines; the heavy four-wagon trains rattle down them and flit by us, each with 'Prince Albert' or 'Prince Alfred' puffing away behind and dashing them off rapidly to the far end of the cage…

A good railed passage is provided, leading between two of the five broad-gauge roads which run to the end of the inner breakwater abreast over open rafters. The large blocks of heaped stone, which at first underlie the rafters, soon become dashed with surf and then give way entirely to the sea, which, if the day be at all fresh, will give the visitor a sprinkling. Six hundred yards from the shore the inner breakwater ends in a noble bastion-like head rising with smooth, round sides some 30 ft above the waves. A space of four hundred feet separates this head from its partner, the precisely similar work at the end of the outer breakwater…

It is a scene of bustle. Here, we pass a gang of men preparing timber for the shores and brackets that support the road-pieces; there, we see a man running along the narrow footway of the workmen – a single plank laid on each side of the rails – as much at ease as if a false step would not tumble him thirty feet down into the sea or worse upon the rugged rubbly heap; which, now emerging from the waves, indicates what the nature of this outer arm is hereafter to be…

Every two or three minutes comes rumbling behind us a train with its four loaded wagons, each wagon averaging 12 tons in weight. An ordinary load consists of a large block in the centre, some two or three feet in diameter, around which are heaped fragments of smaller sizes, the whole rising to a considerable height in the wagon. It is a fine thing to watch the tipping of the rubble through the open rafters of the cage. Every wagon has a dropping floor, slanting downwards from back to front, but with its iron-work lighter and less massive in front than behind. It is so contrived that a brakesman, with a few blows of his hammer, knocks away the check and sets the floor free to drop … A puff or two of the engine brings each wagon in succession over the required spot and, unless the large stone should become jammed, the whole load is tipped and the empty train is on its way back in less than a minute.

The jamming, when it happens, is an awkward business, and men are sometimes at work for hours with picks and crowbars before some obstinate mass will slip between the iron sides. Such accidents are almost always the result of careless packing on the part of the convicts at the top of the inclines, the process being, indeed, one that demands not a little art and skill.

ABOVE: The Verne, Portland, Dorset.

OVERLEAF: Her Majesty's Prison, Portland, on Portland Bill in Dorset.

Convicts were also employed in another major undertaking, as the limestone landscape encasing Portland was forever altered by the building of Verne Citadel. This impressive fortress, made once again from Portland stone, initially housed prisoners building the breakwaters. It was later given over to the army and could accommodate 700 men in peacetime, and at least double that in times of war. It was ideally placed to guard the new Portland harbour that opened in 1872. (Two further breakwaters were added in the early twentieth century.)

The effect of all this on native Portlanders can only be guessed. Novelist Thomas Hardy alluded to Portland in his 1897 work *The Well-Beloved* as the Isle of Slingers for the residents' accuracy at throwing stones, a skill honed to keep strangers at bay. Incomers were referred to by local people as 'kimberlins', and no one was permitted to use the word 'rabbit' for fear of invoking a quarry collapse in the same way as rabbit burrows were wont to do.

However, a liking for eighteenth-century life did nothing to stop Portland being dragged into the twentieth century. The creation of the harbour led to trials of self-propelled torpedoes, a new weapon created by British engineer Robert Whitehead in 1866. In Britain the concept of stealthy torpedoes was considered unsporting in the late nineteenth century, so Whitehead manufactured torpedoes overseas for a worldwide market. But ultimately Britain, like every other country, needed an arsenal incorporating every conceivable weapon as the largely peaceful Victorian age gave way to periods of unprecedented global conflict.

As international tensions increased the Admiralty Board quietly told him they would only purchase weapons made in Britain. The venue for Whitehead's new factory was obvious: Portland was already a tried and trusted environment as far as he was concerned. It often hosted Royal Navy ships and there was plenty of space available for a factory on the harbour shore. Thus Britain's first torpedo manufacturer opened at Ferry Bridge in the parish of Wyke Regis, providing new job opportunities for local people.

Even in 1914 torpedoes were viewed with suspicion, with the military 'old school' regarding them in the same way Queen Victoria first saw trains. That year's *Naval Review* revealed the continuing caution when it stated:

> *Until lately it was a generally accepted maxim that the torpedo could not play any part in a fleet action until one side had established a definite superiority in gun-fire and that then its function was merely to complete, in the shortest possible time, the work begun by the guns.*
>
> *The introduction of the long range torpedo has changed these conditions entirely and rather suddenly. Its range approaches equality and its effective range may in some circumstances prove superior to that of the gun; it is quite conceivable that some future fleet actions may commence with torpedo fire.*

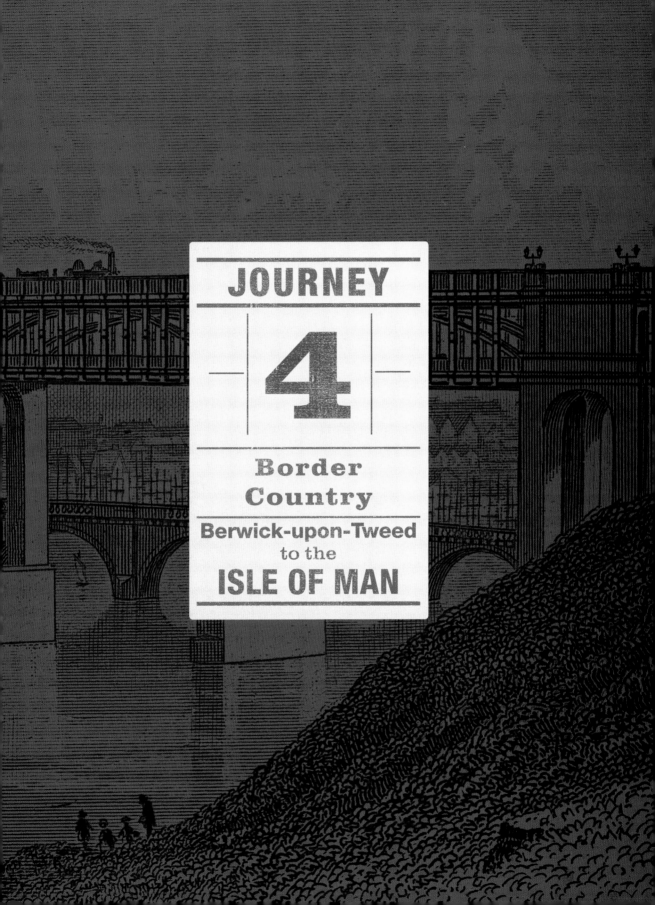

JOURNEY

4

Border Country

Berwick-upon-Tweed
to the
ISLE OF MAN

Railways arrived hand in glove with immense and spectacular bridges that became enduring monuments to the triumph that was British engineering. One of the most striking is the Royal Border Bridge, built by Robert Stephenson in 1850, one of 110 bridges needed for the newly constructed York, Newcastle & Berwick line. It has 28 arches – 15 over land and 13 over water – made from brick, clad with stone. A steam-driven pile-driver pioneered by engineer James Nasmyth in 1845 forced girders into the dense gravel on the floor of the River Tweed to a depth of some 36 feet to ensure the foundations were secure.

Stephenson made such a good job of building the bridge that it didn't need serious repairs until the 1990s. And although it didn't precisely mark the England–Scotland border, as its name implied, Queen Victoria cannot but have been impressed when she officially opened the bridge in August 1850.

But Stephenson had good reason for making this bridge soundly. He was the engineer behind the ill-fated bridge over the River Dee that had collapsed under the weight of a train in 1847, with the loss of five lives. The reason for this catastrophe is still not entirely certain. The disaster happened within a few hours of ballast being laid around the rails by way of fire prevention, following a blaze in Uxbridge, London, which had caused a bridge built by Isambard Kingdom Brunel to crumple. Some believed the ballast brought extra weight to bear on the bridge. Others thought the ballast may have caused the train to derail. Doubts were also raised over the dovetailed cast-iron girders that had been used on the Dee crossing to hold up the Chester to Holyhead railway line. Beforehand there had been warnings issued about the possible hazards of using cast and wrought iron in bridges.

Stephenson was accused of negligence during a later investigation by the Railway Inspectorate, formed in 1840 to safeguard passengers. He was also quizzed closely by a subsequent Royal Commission. He felt the engineering failure keenly. However, most engineers of the day had no wish to see an accomplished man like Stephenson publicly made a scapegoat. Many agreed that virtually all engineers of the era were guilty of being short-sighted about the viability of cast-iron girders.

It is a tribute to his strength of character, and a sign of the bold times, that Stephenson's career did not end in tatters with that

PREVIOUS PAGE: The High Level Bridge at Newcastle, designed by Robert Stephenson.

RIGHT: *The Illustrated London News* reports on the Dee Bridge disaster.

OVERLEAF: Stephenson's Royal Border Bridge at Berwick-upon-Tweed.

THE LATE RAILWAY ACCIDENT, AT CHESTER.

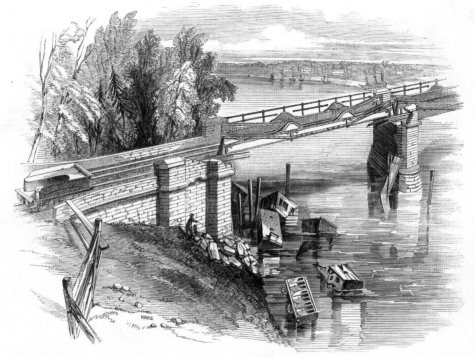

SCENE OF THE LATE RAILWAY ACCIDENT, AT CHESTER.—DILAPIDATED SPAN OF THE DEE BRIDGE.

In fulfilment of our engagement, we this week present our readers with Illustrations descriptive of the late lamentable accident at the Dee Bridge, on the Chester and Holyhead Railway.

The general view is taken from the high ground on the Saltney side, looking down upon the dilapidated span of the Bridge, and showing the space left open between the piers by the fall of the girder and road-way. The bent ends of the overhanging rails are shown for the purpose of marking more clearly the late track; the rails, as well as every other part of the ruin having been removed from the verge of the opening before we visited the spot.

The Bridge crosses the river at an angle of about 48°, is constructed with three spans—skewed to the same angle—of 100 feet each; each span being sustained by four trussed girders, one on each side, and two in the middle, making the two roadways independent of each other; on the inside of the bottom flange of each pair of girders, shoes are cast, having a doun-tail socket, into which

wrought-iron ties are fitted to secure the girders from springing outwards at the bottom, a tendency to which is occasioned by the weight of the road-way and the oscillating pressure of the passing trains. Between these, and resting upon the same flange, are strong timber bearers or joists, upon which a flooring of four-inch planks is laid; on this the longitudinal sleepers are fitted, carrying the rails and check-rails, the latter being continued twenty-six feet beyond the span of the Bridge each way. Between each pair of girders near twenty tons of ballast had been recently laid, and we were informed by a gentleman on whom we can rely, that the unfortunate train in question was the first that had attempted to cross the Bridge after the ballast was so deposited.

Having heard much about the deflection of the girders when a train passed over, we watched them carefully on the occasion of two goods trains coming up, and could not perceive any more than a slight vibration, certainly nothing like a deflection of *inches*; they were unaccompanied by engine and tender. We have

given this brief and general description, with the view of making the following details—more immediately referring to the melancholy catastrophe—clear and intelligible to the general reader.

By the evidence given on the inquest, the public are already aware that the same facts are adduced in support of widely differing opinions; and—as it is our object rather to furnish the material for others to judge from, than to volunteer an opinion of our own—we shall proceed to state the facts as they existed on our visiting the spot.

Fig. 1 is a side elevation of the broken girder, showing the exact form and position of the fractures. A is the Saltney end. From B to the fracture C, the girder is represented in its perfect state (except the rails which are indicated at

the opposite end, and shown entire in the general view), with the truss or tension plates, D, which run through, and are secured at A and B to the plates E. F F are enlarged transverse sections, and G G are plans of flange, showing the fracture, H. At the end I, is a section of masonry, showing the bearing of girder.

Fig. 2, is an elevation of the inside of the parapet, commencing from the end of the fallen girder, and extending 36 feet toward the Saltney end; the fractures and abrasions are carefully marked; as, on this piece of shattered wall, arguments of a very varied character are founded. J shows the end of the girder; K, where the tender first struck the wall; L L L, marks of abrasion, made by the screws and other slight projections on the side of the tender, several of which are broken off, and others much ground down.

The train consisted of the engine and tender, following which the carriages were arranged—1st. One first-class. 2nd. One second class (with break and guard-box); 3rd. One second. 4th. Luggage-van; 5th. Second-class.

One opinion, having the weight of high authority, is, that the tender, by some means, got off the rails whilst upon the Bridge, and struck the girder at I, which, instantly giving way, the train fell through, the connection between the first-class carriage and the tender being broken in the fall; whilst the latter, having received additional impulse from the engineer turning on the steam just at this point, cleared the Bridge, struck and grazed the wall as before-named, running, still off the rails, a distance of seventy feet, to where it now lies. The engine had parted from the tender, and continued on the rails, having sustained scarcely the slightest injury.

Another opinion attributes the accident to some radical defect in the material or construction of the girder. Evidence having been given that the deflection had amounted to from four to six inches during the passage of a heavy train, it is inferred that on this occasion the girder gave way first at C, and that the piece I, was "jumped" out by the fall.

It was at this point that the engineer states he felt the sinking, and turned the steam full on; the sudden jerk from which gave an impetus to the tender, and enabled it to reach the Saltney side. The way in which it got off the line, before it reached the end of the check rails, is thus accounted for:—

ELEVATION OF GIRDER.

The tender has six wheels: the curvature of the sinking rails would throw two or four of them out of bearing, where the slightest impediment or impulse, at either side, would make it change position on the line; and that this occurred just before striking K, and that the coupling at a was broken by the sudden elevation of the fore part, and consequent bending down of the screw to the tug of the engine.

The evidence of the boy went to show that the carriage had nearly all crossed the Bridge, before the entire floor and rails gave way, and that the last carriage ran back, dragging the others, which had become disengaged from the tender, into the river ; and it does appear that the first-class carriage struck the parapet at K, from whence portions of the plate glass and window frame were projected, and were found, and seen by us, on the 5th June, lying on the coping stone, as marked in the large drawing at X. From this, it would appear that a portion of the carriage was *outside* the parapet at the time it struck, which would make it very unlikely that any of the carriages had actually reached the Saltney side in comparative safety.

Another opinion is that the masonry was defective, and that the girders had not sufficient bearing ; but, on examination, no deficiency was apparent in either respect. Others, that the tender struck the end of the girder, A, and dislodged it from its bearings, from whence it fell into the river, and got broke by the fall. But there is no appearance on the coping of its having been driven off in that way the stone being perfectly free from any marks of the girder having slid outward.

There appears no very clear mode of accounting for the tender leaving the line where the check-rails were fixed, except by supposing a curve in the rails ; and, if a curve did occur, it must have been produced by something having sunk or given way.

The conduct of the engineer on the trying occasion is deserving of all praise; and there is a satisfaction in knowing that all that presence of mind and courage could do, was done at the *moment*, and done well.

Whilst we regret the absence from Chester of Mr. Lee, the Engineer to the line, and Mr. Munt, of the Chester and Holyhead Railway, to whom we were directed for information, we gladly acknowledge the readiness with which those gentlemen who were on the spot, and connected with the Railway, furnished us with some of the foregoing facts; and, if we have omitted any points which to them seemed important, it is only because we wished to avoid implying censure on any parties.

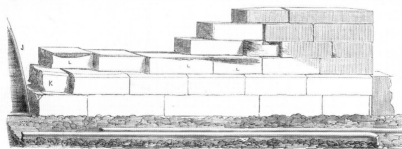

PARAPET OF THE BRIDGE.

calamity. In fact it continued with a pace that matched one of his own locomotives. The Newcastle to Berwick line bears Stephenson's stamp elsewhere too.

In Newcastle the High Level Bridge was opened a year before the one at Berwick, and is equally treasured today. Running 100 feet above the waters of the Tyne, it was neatly dual purpose with a road running underneath the rail bridge. Bridging the river it also linked two communities that had been hitherto kept separate. Newcastle's elegantly curved railway station was also influenced by Stephenson. However, it is perhaps worth noting that his projects helped to obliterate ancient castles in both Berwick and Newcastle.

Stephenson was already an immensely important figure in the north east before the advent of the Royal Border Bridge. His name was over the door of the family engineering works in Newcastle where locomotives were made, an early sign of the faith that his father George invested in him.

George Stephenson died two years before the opening of the Royal Border Bridge, but he had been a huge influence on Robert and no doubt a steadying one after the Dee Bridge collapse. To Robert he bequeathed a singular belief that the future lay with locomotives no matter what technical hitches lay in the way. George was a cow-herder turned coal-picker who didn't learn to read and write until he was in his late teens. But he became one of the most famous engineers ever known, credited with levering Britain into the modern age.

His fascination for the early steam-powered engines led him to dismantle and reassemble several models at Killingworth Colliery, to discover how they worked, and he eventually became the colliery's engine-wright. To earn extra cash he was also a watch repairer, and he devised a new safety lamp for miners as well.

By 1814 he had built his first locomotive and soon he persuaded pit managers to let him build an eight-mile track from Hetton Colliery to the coast, to transport coal. He worked with his brother, also called Robert, on this project, and when it was opened in 1822 locomotives pulling eight wagons at a time, each holding more than two and a half tons of coal, used the line along its flatter portions. The Hetton railway ran uphill and, for these steeper inclines, a stationary engine was used to move the coal. For the first time in pit history no animals were needed for hauling coal.

This early line convinced George Stephenson of the need for cuttings and tunnels, to keep a line as flat as possible. With future projects father and son generally collaborated to bring their work to fruition. In fact, there's speculation that George depended on the expertise of his son to pull off the most ambitious projects attached to his name. Certainly, George was more of a broad-brushstroke individual, whose time cultivating rich and powerful acquaintances had as much to do with his success as the nuts and bolts of the steam engine. By the end of his career he was perhaps more polished at marketing than mechanics, an entrepreneur with interests in railway companies, locomotive manufacturers and coal, iron and lime mines.

At the insistence of his father, Robert Stephenson had enjoyed the benefits of an education. But his first job in 1819 was as an apprentice in a colliery and he was always aware of the plight of ordinary people, even while he rubbed shoulders with the wealthy and powerful. His reputation was for even-handed treatment of fellow engineers and navvies alike. 'The true and full effect of railways would not take place,' he insisted 'until they were made so cheap in their fares that a poor man could not afford to walk.'

He joined his father George in surveying the proposed route for the Stockton to Darlington railway after it was authorised in 1821. Following a spell at Edinburgh University, he joined the team building it. On its opening in 1825, the Stockton & Darlington was the first purpose-built locomotive-driven railway in Britain capable of carrying passengers and freight. It was from the outset a highly successful venture, meeting local needs and running at a profit for investors.

In 1824 Robert's health declined and he went to live abroad for three years, spending time establishing a rail network in South America. When he returned to the UK there were numerous projects that clamoured for his attention. After the success of the Stockton & Darlington Railway the indications were all good for a link between Manchester and Liverpool. Already plans were in place for this, although belligerent landowners and protective canal operators did their best to stymie the scheme. The necessary parliamentary bill was passed in 1826 and construction of the tracks, the bridges and viaducts needed for the 35-mile route got underway. All that was then needed was to persuade the board of the Liverpool & Manchester Railway that locomotives were the better option for pulling trains at a time when

Robert Stephenson
(1803–1859).

The opening of the
Stockton & Darlington
Railway, 27 September
1825.

the most obvious choice still seemed to be horses, although stationary engines using hauling equipment were also closely considered.

To nail the debate, trials between the different options were organized at Rainhill in 1829 and the *Rocket*, built by George and Robert Stephenson, was triumphant after achieving an impressive speed of 30 mph. There were other engineers competing that day – Timothy Hackworth, John Braithwaite, John Ericsson – but history is written by the winners and other locomotive builders from that day to this were eclipsed by the success of the Stephensons.

When the line was opened a year later, their glory was marred by the death of William Huskisson, at the time the most prominent victim of a railway accident. He was the local MP and a former president of the Board of Trade when he was mowed down by the *Rocket*, with engineer Josiah Locke at the wheel. Sympathy has to go to Huskisson, who wandered on to the tracks at a time when the danger from trains was barely broadcast.

Robert Stephenson's first major solo project was the London to Birmingham railway, which received the necessary go-ahead in September 1833. Although there were some serious difficulties in its construction, not least building a tunnel at Kilsby, south of Rugby, after the good folks of Northampton resisted the railway's arrival. (The tunnel also fitted better with Stephenson's policy of flat lines as there was an incline at Northampton.) The line was opened in stages from 1837. The first train to travel between London and Birmingham on 17 September 1838 took four and a half hours. At its Birmingham terminus, Curzon Street, a passenger could link to the Grand Junction Railway and head onward to Manchester and Liverpool.

After that, Stephenson's services were in demand across Britain and the world. A keen yachtsman, Robert had little time to bob about on the waves thanks to the weight of work. At one point his name was associated with 160 different projects from 60 separate railway companies. He became a Conservative MP, president of the Institution of Mechanical Engineers for five years and later president of the Institution of Civil Engineers. He was showered with honours from countries across the globe but declined a knighthood.

Although he often spoke and acted in opposition to Brunel, the two men were friends. This friendship, like his one with engineer George Bidder, was rooted in a mutual fascination for mechanical ingenuity and a sense of being in the first wave of railway engineers who would leave an indelible mark on Britain.

Speaking to friends in Newcastle in 1850, Robert declared:

It seems to me but as yesterday that I was engaged as an assistant in laying out the Stockton and Darlington Railway. Since then, the Liverpool and Manchester, and a hundred other great works have sprung into existence. As I look back upon these stupendous undertakings, accomplished in so short a time, it seems as though we had realized in our generation the fabled powers of the magician's wand. Hills have been cut down and valleys filled up; and when these simple expedients have not sufficed, high and magnificent viaducts have been raised, and, if mountains stood in the way, tunnels of unexampled magnitude have pierced them through, bearing their triumphant attestation to the indomitable energy of the nation, and the unrivalled skill of our artisans.

On his death Queen Victoria gave permission for the funeral cortège to go through Hyde Park on its way to Westminster Abbey, where he was

THE FIRST TRAIN TO TRAVEL BETWEEN LONDON AND BIRMINGHAM ON 17 SEPTEMBER 1838 TOOK FOUR AND A HALF HOURS

A ventilation shaft on the Kilsby Tunnel, designed by Robert Stephenson.

buried, and the route was lined with thousands of mourners keen to pay respects to a man who had done so much to change the landscape.

It's only possible to imagine the sense of awe that might have filled the fishermen of the Tweed who watched as the Royal Border Bridge rose brick by brick to the lofty heights of its eventual splendour. *Bradshaw's* gives some insight into what life was like in Berwick 150 years ago, when the railways took salmon produced in the vicinity to London, packed in ice.

> **The salmon fisheries in the Tweed, once worth about £15,000 a year, have declined to £4,000. About Christmas the people here eat kippered salmon and plum pudding ... Much whisky is exported.**

Charting the journey to the next stop, Alnwick, *Bradshaw's* refers to 'that courageous heroine Grace Darling', an icon of the Victorian age lauded for her courage in helping to rescue passengers from a shipwreck off the Farne Islands.

Continuing down the line, using the Morpeth junction it was possible to join the Newcastle & Carlisle Railway, the first east-to-west railway link, completed in 1839. A branch line from it leading to Alston was in business from 1852. It was on the Newcastle & Carlisle Railway that a small but enormously significant leap was taken in railway administration, thanks to the foresight of one man.

For some time railway tickets took the same shape as stagecoach tickets had before them. They were nothing more than scraps of paper, only sometimes bearing scrawled details of the journey purchased.

Two tickets issued by the Great Western Railway (GWR) in 1864 and 1865.

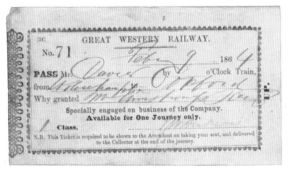

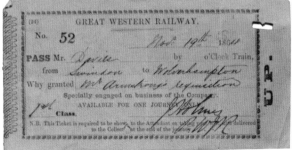

GRACE DARLING (1815-1842)

Grace Darling was the seventh child of the Longstone lighthouse keeper, who spotted the shadowy outline of the four-year-old steamship *Forfarshire* before dawn on 7 September 1838. The ship had been sailing between Hull and Dundee with a cargo of cloth, soap and engineering equipment as well as 60 passengers and crew when it was driven onto rocks. A dozen survivors were left clinging to a rock off the Farne Islands greasy with pounding waves after the ship broke in two.

Grace Darling's heroic rescue of 7 September 1838.

Recognising their plight, 22-year-old Grace and her father William oared their own open boat a mile through rough seas to reach the rock, where a woman, her two children and nine men were stranded. Although they were still being gripped by their mother, the children were already dead. Grace and her father persuaded the woman to return in the boat with an injured man and three others. William, helped by two survivors, then set off a second time to rescue the remaining survivors. The bodies of the two children and a man were recovered by the Sunderland lifeboat later that day.

———

After word of the daring rescue spread, Grace Darling's life was turned upside-down as she became the object of national adoration. Artists painted her portrait; poets, including William Wordsworth, dedicated verses to her. There were Grace Darling chocolates produced by Cadbury's, and she was even offered a role in a circus.

———

At Longstone lighthouse letters containing high praise, gifts and money – including a £50 donation from Queen Victoria – turned up daily. More significantly, she and her father received gold medals from the Royal Humane Society and silver gallantry medals from the National Institution for the Preservation of Life from Shipwreck, the forerunner of the Royal National Lifeboat Institution. (At the time only gentlemen received gold medals. Those of lesser birth received reduced honours and sometimes only money.)

———

Although she didn't relish the public spotlight, she only had to endure it for a short time. Grace died of tuberculosis in 1842.

Thomas Edmondson ushered in a new age when he invented a railway ticket that could be punched by a station guard and bore a serial number. Before joining the Newcastle & Carlisle Railway in 1836 as stationmaster at Milton (later called Brompton) Edmondson had been a cabinet maker, and he still possessed some of the tools of his trade. In spare moments he began to make machinery that could produce cardboard tickets for train trips. His first efforts were comparatively rudimentary. The ticket number had to be filled in by hand and the mechanics of the validation stamp left railway staff in fear for their fingers. Still, Edmondson could clearly see a future for better ticketing.

When he received scant support from railway management, he changed jobs and began working for the Manchester & Leeds Railway Company when it opened in 1839 with an enhanced salary as chief booking clerk. However, he still sought to perfect the apparatus so it could produce fully printed tickets with ease. After he teamed up with mechanical engineer William Muir, Edmondson finally left his job at the railways and achieved his ambition. He patented the design – no mean feat for those days when the system was weighted with bureaucracy – and charged railway companies 10 shillings per year per mile for its use. His invention and its application to the new fashion of train travel made him a rich man.

The railways didn't make everybody rich, though. In the mid-1840s a rampant railway mania gripped the country and ended with many people suffering grievous financial losses. It was more than simple economics that led to ruin for many.

Although new railway lines needed parliamentary approval they were built by private companies that had to raise funds for the necessary building work. At a glance, the provision of railways seemed like a sure-fire way of making money, and railway schemes became a popular choice for investors. After all, railways were welcomed as a swift alternative to uncomfortable and sometimes dangerous coach travel. They enabled existing and new businesses to function. Despite a slow start, railways had won the hearts and minds of the British public by the 1840s and financial advisors of the day were impressed enough to funnel all the customers they had into railway investment. For the first time, entrepreneurs who alighted on railways as a means to make

money could not only find investors among the aristocracy but also in
the burgeoning ranks of the middle classes. But there was no national
strategy in place to create a sound, sensible railway system, nor were
there safeguards at hand if things went wrong.

For a while everything went according to the railway companies'
plans. Nationally the economy appeared to be booming, and rates
of interest were favourable to investors. Lots of companies offered
enticing deals. People only had to produce 10 per cent of some
investments in hard cash while the rest was 'on a promise'.

Meanwhile, the business of railway building was indisputably
expanding at an immense rate. In 1844 just 805 miles of line were given
government approval. The following year the figure was 2,700 miles. At
the planning end of countless schemes, Brunel was something of a lone
voice when he made his objections to railway mania known in a letter:

*I am really sick of hearing proposals made. I wish it were at an end.
I prefer engineering very much to projecting, of which I keep as clear as
I can … I wish I could suggest a plan that would greatly diminish the
number of projects; it would suit my interests and those of my clients
perfectly if all railways were stopped for several years to come.*

The Scottish historian
Thomas Carlyle (1795–
1881).

Generally, the interest of the public was not waning; indeed, it was
sharpened by the prospect of making quick, clean money. Most
investors, however, failed to ask the right questions. There were
schemes for railways that went to places no one wanted to go. Others
were planned for inhospitable terrain that would be costly to bridge.
Many plans were poorly costed, and in numerous cases there was
sharp practice among some businessmen who had an eye for a fast
buck. In general, the promises made in newspaper advertisements
about the proposed benefits of railway investment were at best
optimistic and at worse downright fraudulent.

Landowners didn't help, either. Believing railway construction to
be a golden goose, they demanded high prices before giving up land for
track beds. Railway companies were also obliged by law to fence every
foot of line they laid. As a consequence it was much more expensive to
build railways in Britain than anywhere else in the world.

Inevitably, with so much of the promised capital amounting
to no more than a fiction, there was an economic implosion that
left numerous first-time investors out of pocket. The historian and
commentator Thomas Carlyle explained it like this:

*Then railways bubbled. New ones were advertised, fifty a month,
and all went to a premium. High and low scrambled for the shares,
even when the projected line was to run from the town of Nought
to the village of Nothing across a goose common. The flame spread,
fanned by prospectus and advertisement, two mines of glowing
fiction, compared with which the legitimate article is a mere tissue of
understatements.*

There was one final, optimistic rush in 1845, as solicitors sought to
bring new plans to their local clerk of the peace by 30 November, so
they could be included in the next parliamentary session. No fewer
than 879 plans missed this deadline, causing considerable panic among

their investors. But it was worse still for those who gained approval and began spending money that was promised, fraudulently or otherwise, only to find the company purse all but empty.

As the juggernaut driven by railway investment juddered to a halt after 1846 there were some benefits to the long-term security of train travel. Small companies that failed in the face of unchecked business chicanery were amalgamated with larger ones, making better sense of long-distance railway journeys for the train-travelling public. One early example of this was the Midland Railway, formed in May 1844 out of numerous lines proliferating around Birmingham and Derby. In 1848 the London & Birmingham, Grand Junction and Liverpool & Manchester companies came together to form the London & North Western Railway. One useful spin-off that followed was a limit on the number of stations. Instead of towns getting numerous railway stations to serve different companies – at one stage Swansea boasted no fewer than six termini – just one or two were built.

George Hudson invested his inheritance in railways and eventually controlled over 1,000 miles of track.

But there were a string of disaster stories, with many people left destitute. Those who borrowed to furnish railway companies with an initial stake were particularly hard hit. John Francis, who wrote two volumes on *The History of the English Railway*, published in 1851, was emotional on the topic: 'It reached every hearth, it saddened every heart in the metropolis. Entire families were ruined. There was scarcely an important town in England but what beheld some wretched suicide. Daughters delicately nurtured went out to seek their bread. Sons were recalled from academies. Households were separated . . .'

George Hudson was one of Britain's prominent businessmen whose bloated speculation lit the fuse of railway mania. When the bubble popped he was left in chronic debt and shamed by his risky business practices. However, in Sunderland, where he was the MP, York and Whitby he was held in an unshakeable affection, having brought the railway and all its advantages to those places.

Hudson was the son of a farmer, born just outside York at the turn of the nineteenth century. He moved to York to work in a drapery business, becoming a partner after marrying the daughter of his boss. His ambition heightened considerably with an inheritance of some £30,000 from a distant relative in 1827. He indulged himself in the two abiding passions of his life: railways and politics. During his tenure as Lord Mayor of York he invested in the North Midland Railway.

MIDLAND RAILWAY.

GEO. H. TURNER. GENERAL MANAGER. DERBY.

A poster produced for
the Midland Railway to
promote their rail routes,
c. 1900.

He saw to it that a planned route for London dropped by his home city, and the profits rolled in with ease. In 1833 he formed his own railway company, the York & North Midland Railway, to link other Yorkshire populations. He raised some £446,000 in capital and the line was finished by the middle of 1839.

His next aim was to lay a line between York and Newcastle that would, he realised, be an important part of an east coast line to link London with Scotland. To win official permission for the work to take place, he distributed some £3,000 in bribes.

By 1844, through his various railway companies, he controlled an estimated 1,000 miles of track, and the chaos that was engulfing some railway companies seemed to be passing him by. Observers tagged him 'the Railway King' and for a while it must have seemed his star would never fade. He became Conservative MP for Sunderland in the 1845 election and used his newly won position to fight against a proposal by William Gladstone for partial state ownership of railways, as the first victims of railway mania began falling by the wayside. If he wasn't enhancing his own business, he spent time sabotaging the chances of rivals.

One of his close friends was the Duke of Wellington, both hero and villain to the British public and a man who wielded considerable power in and out of Parliament. Wellington had become Prime Minister in 1828 but painfully misunderstood the political process. (After his first cabinet meeting he remarked: 'An extraordinary affair. I gave them their orders and they wanted to stay and discuss them.') Wellington – who ring-fenced his home against railway development – harboured reservations about the railways after witnessing the death of William Huskisson at the opening of the Liverpool & Manchester Railway in 1830. He was also concerned that the railways offered travel opportunities to ordinary people – something which earned his hearty disapproval.

As late as January 1846 the *Standard* newspaper lauded Hudson's work. 'Two hundred thousand well-paid labourers, representing as heads of families, nearly one million men, women and children, all feast through the bold enterprise of one man. Let us hear what man or class of man ever before did so much for the population of a country.'

But it was at about this time that his friendship with railway godfather George Stephenson petered out, with the engineer concerned

**TO WIN OFFICIAL
PERMISSION
FOR THE
WORK TO TAKE
PLACE, HUDSON
DISTRIBUTED
SOME £3,000
IN BRIBES**

about many of Hudson's business methods. And Stephenson's suspicions were justified. As the shakedown sparked by rail mania continued Hudson found himself in difficulty.

It was a desire to spike the guns of a rival business that made him take over the Eastern Counties Railway in 1846. To do so, Hudson trebled the dividends of shareholders, illegally dipping into company capital to do so. In short, he was guilty of embezzlement. Although it was a widely used device in business it drew unwelcome scrutiny to his business dealings. Soon the fact that he used inside information to massage share prices, that he'd lied to shareholders about the viability of his various businesses, and that he had sold land he didn't own to the Newcastle & Berwick Railway came to light.

The Times reflected public enmity towards Hudson and his role in the railway mania in 1848, saying:

> *It was a system without rules, without order, without even a definite morality. Mr Hudson, having a faculty for amalgamation and being so successful, found himself in the enjoyment of a great railway despotism, in which he had to do everything out of his own head and among lesser problems to discover the ethics of railway speculation and management.*

Hudson was compelled to resign as chairman of all the railway companies in his portfolio. Although he remained an MP until 1859 he could not shake off the odour of corruption, nor would he pay back shareholders' money they had lost through his dubious dealings. As a result he was imprisoned in York Castle in 1865 for debt. His friends clubbed together to settle his liabilities and as a result he was behind bars for only 16 months. Five years later he died, having both fuelled railway mania and fallen foul of it.

It wasn't the end of railway mania, which returned to haunt industrialists including Sir Samuel Morton Peto, who built widely in eastern England, in 1866. By this time, though, the network of lines around the UK was looking more like a finished article than ever before, with major cities linked one to another – although, incredibly, it was set to double from its 1860 size before railway construction came to an end. (One enduring argument put forward by business rivals against the construction of the Great Central Line, which came

Bradshaw's railway map of Great Britain and Ireland, 1901, showing the huge expansion in railway construction from 1860 onwards.

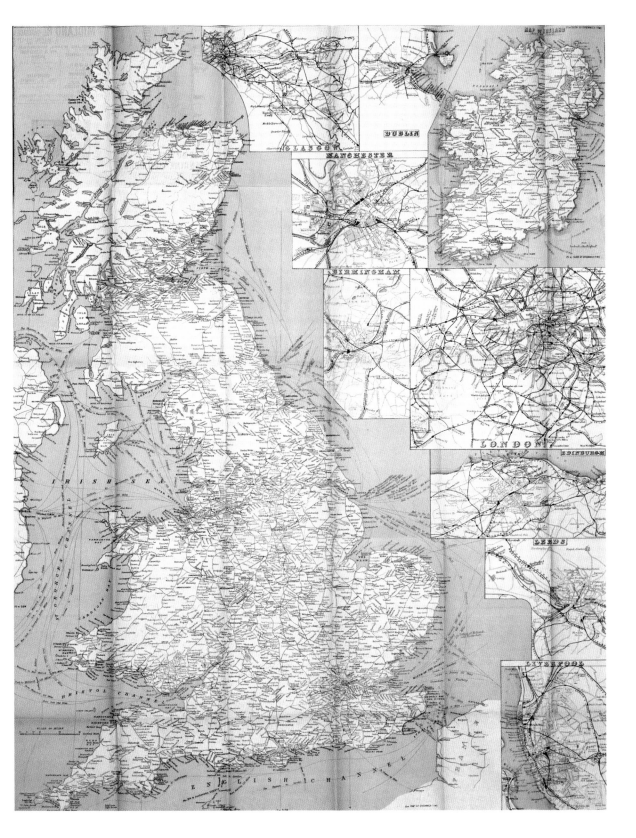

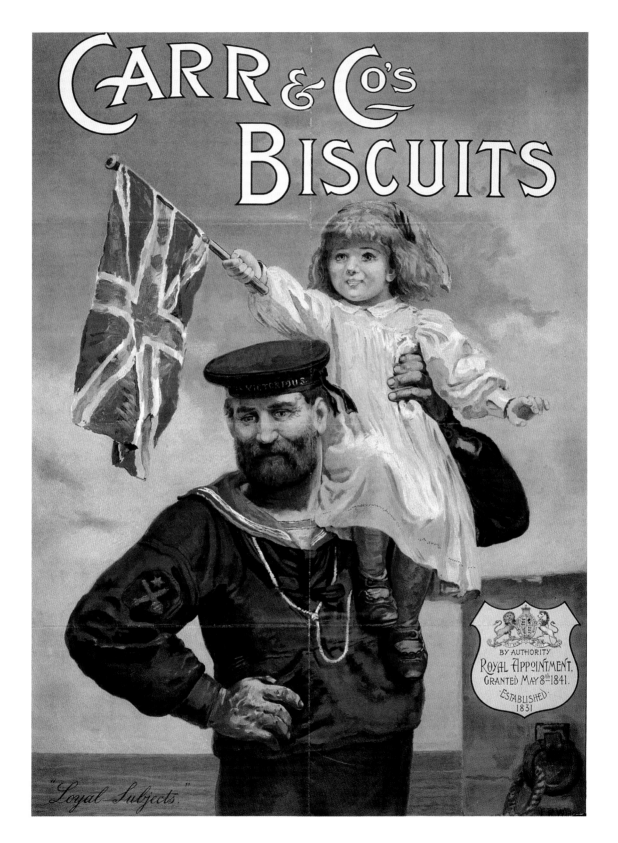

NO FEWER THAN
SEVEN DIFFERENT
COMPANIES RAN
THEIR ENGINES
INTO CARLISLE'S
CITADEL STATION

into the newly built Marylebone Station in London via Nottingham, Leicester and Rugby in the 1890s, was that there were plenty of rail services already doing the same job.)

So much for the north east, where early episodes of railway history were wrought. Across the neck of the country in a landscape marked by Hadrian's Wall, the railway ploughed through heather and bracken to link two centres of population. At the Carlisle end of the Newcastle to Carlisle line there is, concedes *Bradshaw's*, a cathedral, a port and an eight-sided brick chimney 305 feet high. But the guide's most vivid description is for the biscuit factory Carr & Co, opened by Jonathan Dodgson Carr in 1837, the year Victoria came to the throne. The bread and biscuits Carr's made were so well regarded the firm received a royal warrant from the Queen in 1842. *Bradshaw's* concurs, saying:

> [Carlisle] is also celebrated for its manufacture of fancy biscuits, which are produced in a most complete state, all by machinery and to an extent that would certainly astonish visitors ... if curiosity should induce the tourist to make a visit to the manufactory of this noted firm, we do not hesitate to say that it would be found highly interesting. If any prejudice exist against the free use of fancy biscuits, it will at once be removed on an inspection of the works and the process of production, even from the minds of the most fastidious – the most scrupulous cleanliness being observable throughout the whole works.

LEFT: A poster advertising Carr's biscuits.

OVERLEAF: The iron and steel works at Barrow c. 1880. A print from *Great Industries of Great Britain Volume I*, published by Cassell, Petter and Galpin c. 1880.

What the guide fails to note is the extensive railway workings in the city. At one time no fewer than seven different companies ran their engines into Carlisle's Citadel Station, and its marshalling yard was one of the biggest in Europe.

The next stage of the journey runs from Carlisle down to Barrow-in-Furness. The rump of land beneath Barrow was kept remote from the rest of the country, not least because of the racing waters that filled Morecambe Bay to the south. But railway accessibility from Carlisle

changed all that. Thanks to Victorian technology this previously isolated region became the home of cutting-edge industry. In the early decades of the eighteenth century there was small-scale trade in iron ore, richly deposited around the region.

The Furness Railway, distinguished by marine blue and white livery, was originally a secluded line built in 1846 in response to this limited industry. Locomotive no. 3, built in 1843 and called *Old Coppernob*, used to ply this route. Yet the Furness Railway emerged as the most famous line in the area, although the coast-hugging Maryport & Carlisle Railway was completed by 1845 while the Whitehaven Junction Railway was in operation two years later. Also in 1847, a spur was laid inland from Workington to form the short-lived Cockermouth & Workington Railway. In 1865 the tracks were re-aligned and a new station built for the Cockermouth, Keswick & Penrith Railway.

A relentless campaign to keep the railways out of the Lake District hindered progress but did not stop railway expansion. Opposition was

From 1907 to 1941 the famous Furness Railway steam locomotive *Old Coppernob* was preserved in a special glass case outside the station – it is now in the National Railway Museum at York.

largely founded in a belief that ordinary people would not be able to appreciate the beauty of the lakes and would probably wilfully ruin the place. Poet Laureate William Wordsworth was a key figure in the anti-train lobby before his death in 1850. When a railway link between Kendal and Windermere was proposed he wrote a poem opposing it, with the first line: 'Is then no nook of English ground secure from rash assault?' Although construction was postponed the line was eventually built, albeit with a modified route.

A later pamphlet directed at railway companies addressed the perceived difficulties of bringing working people to the Lake District.

> …can't you teach them to save enough out of their year's wages to pay for a chaise and pony for a day, to drive Missis and the Baby that pleasant twenty miles, stopping when they like, to unpack the basket on a mossy bank? If they can't enjoy the scenery that way, they can't any way; and all that your railroad company can do for them is only to open taverns and skittle grounds round Grasmere, which will soon, then, be nothing but a pool of drainage, with a beach of broken gingerbeer bottles; and their minds will be no more improved by contemplating the scenery of such a lake than of Blackpool.

Writer John Ruskin – whose father-in-law was a victim of railway mania – took up the baton from Wordsworth and declared:

> I have said I take no selfish interest in this resistance to the railroad. But I do take an unselfish one. It is precisely because I passionately wish to improve the minds of the populace, and because I am spending my own mind, strength, and fortune, wholly on that object, that I don't want to let them see Helvellyn while they are drunk.

Indeed, the Buttermere & Braithwaite line, proposed in 1882, fell through after orchestrated opposition. But some tendrils of tracks made their way into the Lake District from Furness Railway territory. Mostly the trains helped local communities make the most of their natural resources. Ruskin's ire for railways was raised when the Furness Railway built a line in close proximity to Furness Abbey in 1864.

For a description of the industry in 'prosperous' Whitehaven in 1866, there's no need to look further than *Bradshaw's*:

POET LAUREATE WILLIAM WORDSWORTH WAS A KEY FIGURE IN THE ANTI-TRAIN LOBBY BEFORE HIS DEATH IN 1850

The coal measures form a thin strip round the coast past Workington and Maryport. The mines are worked by deep shafts a quarter of a mile down, close to the edge of the sea, under which they run more than two miles, the dip of the beds being as much as one ft in ten. Some of them are eight and ten ft thick with good coal. When raised the 'black diamonds' are turned into the wagons which descend the tram road by their own weight to the quay and drag up the empty ones; here they are dropped through the wooden lurries into the vessel's hold.

A Furness Railway No. 20 steam engine at the recreation of Rowley Station, Beamish Museum, County Durham.

The Furness Railway had many success stories but one failure. It seemed to be the perfect way to bring tourists to Seascale, a small coastal settlement that seemed packed with potential. The railway's general manager, James Ramsden, earmarked the place for development as a resort in 1879, believing it a perfect location from which to explore the Lake District, and he encouraged a Liverpool architect, Edward Kemp, to draw up plans for a hotel, villas and seaside promenades that would befit a prestigious Victorian holiday destination. Although some notable dwellings were built, the momentum faltered and Seascale never rivalled places like Southport or Scarborough.

Bradshaw's was sensitive to the changing landscape in the area and notes of Furness that: 'Iron is now forged in this vicinity where the stag, wolf and wild boar were formerly hunted.' Industry hastened in after 1850 when speculator Henry Schneider discovered a large new source of iron ore. Applying the vision that distinguished many Victorian businessmen, he went about exploiting this resource using the railways.

He became one of the movers and shakers behind the railway, which not only served the numerous iron ore mines that were by now in operation in Lindal but also the blue slate mines at Kirby. The railway headed for the port at Roa Island, from where ships had access to other British ports and the rest of the world. There were a series of extensions and branch lines until the area was webbed with lines and Barrow, Whitehaven, Workington and Maryport became prominent harbours.

BARROW AND SHIPBUILDING

In a natural progression, a new generation of industrialists sought to make ships in Barrow out of the steel that was readily at hand. (With opportunities abounding in the 1870s it was said that there were more aristocrats per head of population in Barrow than anywhere else in Britain.) Despite taking immense pride in the Royal Navy, Britain lagged behind the French as shipbuilding moved from the use of wood through iron cladding to steel.

For several decades the Royal Navy was content to assert itself by numerical superiority alone. However, the end of the nineteenth century saw an escalating arms race, primarily between Britain and Germany. Britain could no longer rely on having plenty of ships to win supremacy at sea if they weren't modern and powerful.

Barrow began building naval ships at the behest of the Admiralty in 1877, and within a

A railway being used to feed the blast furnaces at the Barrow Haematite Iron and Steel Company, 1890.

decade had branched out into submarine construction. But the Royal Navy was not the shipyard's only customer. The first submarines – built to the specification of Swedish industrialist and arms dealer Thorsten Nordenfelt – were sold to Turkey and Russia. By 1888, reflecting its international role, the shipyard was renamed the Naval Construction and Armaments Company.

BY 1897 SHIPBUILDING WAS A BIGGER EMPLOYER THAN BOTH THE RAILWAY AND THE STEELWORKS.

Still its expansion was not complete. The company was bought by Vickers in 1897, after which it claimed to be 'the only shipbuilder capable of designing, building, engineering and arming its own vessels'. Four years later it was the Barrow shipbuilders who got to work, in secrecy, on the first five submarines ordered by the Royal Navy, using a blueprint from Irish-American John P. Holland. The first submarine was consequently generally known as Holland 1. By 1897 shipbuilding was a bigger employer than both the railway and the steelworks.

The effect on the area in five short decades was immense. Midway through the nineteenth century the population of Barrow was a mere 700. By 1865 the number had grown to 10,000 and by 1881 it stood at 47,000.

The success of initial iron-based industrial ventures fired the imagination of Schneider and Ramsden. There was more profit to be had in smelting the iron ore on the peninsula in Barrow to make steel. British industrialist Henry Bessemer discovered a cheap way to convert pig iron into steel and established steel works in his home town of Sheffield. When the patent restrictions on his method ran out in 1870 it was adopted by others, including Schneider and Ramsden. Consequently the largest steel works in the world sprang up in this somewhat unlikely corner of the country.

There is a thought-provoking footnote linked to the railway lines around the Furness peninsula. On 22 September 1892 a steam engine towing a goods train was stopped just beyond Lindal passenger station when driver Thomas Postlethwaite felt the ground beneath him start to shake. He leapt off before the engine lurched forward as the ground beneath the tracks began to yawn. Fortunately no one else was in the immediate area.

A gang of recovery workers soon uncoupled the wagons and they were pushed back to the safety of the station. Retrieving the 35-ton engine was a more difficult prospect. The best plan seemed to be to dig away an incline on which tracks could be laid, then the engine could be hauled to safety. But as the digging began the earth rumbled again, this time swallowing the engine entirely. No one knows how far into the Parkside mine workings beneath the railway the engine sank, although it was never seen again after its final descent. Inside the cab Postlethwaite's jacket containing his long-service gold watch remains to this day.

The railway shadowed the coastline around Morecambe Bay, striding across two significant stretches of water, until it reached Carnforth. The line between Carnforth and Whitehaven was opened in 1857, offering links to the Lake District via the Kent Viaduct. When it was built in 1857 a new technique was employed by engineer Sir James Brunlees. The supports were tubular cast-iron piles with large discs at their bases, jetted into place through the shifting sands of the River Kent and filled with concrete. A similar viaduct was built on the same lines at Leven. The single-track Kent Viaduct was completed at a cost of little more than £15,000. In 1863 the Furness Railway Company

OVERLEAF: **A view from Arnside Knott over the Kent Viaduct to Whitbarrow and the Lakeland fells.**

widened the viaduct so it could accommodate twin tracks. However, its ironwork deteriorated with comparative speed and by 1915 the weakened piles were encased in concrete and brickwork. Engineer Brunlees was also behind the Mersey railway and piers at Southport, Llandudno and Southend.

Initially, Carnforth was a small station opened in 1846 on the Lancaster & Carlisle line. A decade later it was transformed into a busy junction when the Furness and Midland tracks met there. The station was sufficiently important to be rebuilt entirely in 1880 at a cost of £40,000. And it was at this new station that Prime Minister William Gladstone was publicly humbled by Queen Victoria, to his intense indignation. Gladstone had been staying at Holker Hall with the Duke of Devonshire in February 1885 when news broke about the fall of Khartoum.

Sudan was a thorny subject for government and monarch. Gladstone believed it was an unnecessary conflict at the time, while

Carnforth Railway Station was later used as a location for the film *Brief Encounter*.

staunch imperialists – like the Queen – believed control of overseas dominions was pivotal. General Gordon had been dispatched to Khartoum to organise a withdrawal of forces. Instead he upped the defences and prepared for a siege. Vastly outnumbered by desert fighters, Khartoum was eventually breached and the defenders slaughtered. Against the specific orders of their leader, triumphant warriors paraded Gordon's head on a pole. The relief force eventually sent by Gladstone arrived two days later.

As Gladstone arrived at Carnforth for a hurried journey back to London, the stationmaster handed him a stinging telegram from Queen Victoria: 'These [sic] news from Khartoum are frightful and to think that all this might have been prevented and many precious lives saved by earlier action is too fearful.'

Even to the unpolitical eye of the stationmaster, the Queen's fury was evident. But Gladstone was also cross as the proper code that normally accompanied official missives like this had been dropped, and the split between Prime Minister and Queen was now obvious to all. Both the Queen and Gordon were popular figures. The débâcle at Khartoum was one of the major reasons that Gladstone lost the election later that year.

In railway terms, Carnforth was always overshadowed by its southerly neighbour, Lancaster, a historic city once isolated by the coast in the west and miles of inhospitable terrain to the east. Lancaster became a regional centre for justice and punishment.

The railway ran from Lancaster to Heysham, where the ferry to the Isle of Man set sail in the summer months. In the 1850s this rocky, self-governed island set between Scotland, England and Ireland became popular with tourists, not least thanks to pioneering travel agent Thomas Cook.

It was once claimed that Thomas Cook & Son ranked with the Roman Catholic Church and the Prussian Army in terms of efficiency in the Victorian age. His extraordinary powers of administration were matched by a fervent desire to see travel available to all. 'Railway travelling is travelling for the millions,' he declared in 1854. For him, trains breached the class divide as never before, with passengers including 'a mourning countess and a marriage party – a weeping widow and a laughing bride – a gray head and an infant of days'.

'RAILWAY TRAVELLING IS TRAVELLING FOR THE MILLIONS'

A portrait of Thomas Cook (1808–1892).

He hit on the idea of chartering a train in 1841 on the 15-mile walk between his home in Harborough and the temperance meeting he attended in Leicester. After negotiations with the Midland Counties Railway Company he could offer cut-rate fares to fellow Temperance Society members for a scheduled meeting. Accordingly, 570 set off in third-class open carriages, or 'tubs' as he called them, between Leicester and Loughborough, to be met by a brass band.

Cook had fond memories of this first outing:

The people crowded the streets, filled windows, covered the housetops and cheered us all along the line, with the heartiest welcome. All went off in the best style and in perfect safety we returned to Leicester; and thus was struck the keynote of my excursions, and the social idea grew upon me.

Initially he satisfied himself with organising this type of trip, until in the summer of 1845 he arranged an excursion to the seaside at Liverpool. Its administration wasn't easy as passengers would encounter four different railway companies en route. There were hotels and restaurants to consider. Nonetheless, after the trip was offered to the general public it proved so popular that all 350 tickets were gone within a week.

Cook's next target was Scotland, where large swathes of land were as yet untouched by track. Here he learned that steamer connections were as reliable as trains and equally as popular. However, it was London's Great Exhibition in 1851 that secured his future as a travel agent. There was grave concern among some of the exhibition organisers that thousands would be excluded from it as they lived too far away, could not afford the entrance fee or did not have the wherewithal to work out the journey.

They approached Thomas Cook with a view to organising cost-cutting excursions from the Midlands. For his part, Cook was delighted to play a role in peopling the Exhibition, which he thought would bringing a 'harmonising and ennobling influence', and he threw himself into finding cheap accommodation. He encouraged men in factories around the Midlands to begin Exhibition clubs, saving a small amount each week to cover the cost of the trip. He even launched a newspaper, *The Excursionist and Exhibition Advertiser*, to generate interest.

VICTORIAN CRIME AND PUNISHMENT

The Victorian public had specific mores, and concern for law and order was among them. A fresh look at crime and criminals in the era inspired some radical changes in punishment, nowhere more apparent than at Lancaster.

The era of the Bloody Code – when a man could be hanged for any one of 200 different offences – was over. Transportation to Australia was also off the agenda after 1852, following complaints from Sydney about this booming country becoming a dumping ground for British villains. Instead came the age of incarceration. And before a prison-building programme could be got underway, Lancaster Castle, bleak and comfortless, filled the breach.

The castle's medieval cells were used as a men's jail from 1794. Thirty years later a women's prison was added to the castle, which followed the principles of the Panopticon advocated by Jeremy Bentham in the late eighteenth century. In it, single cells radiated out from the guards' post and were under constant surveillance. (It was a design that found greater favour in America than Britain.)

Until 1835 all major trials in the county were held at Lancaster and the court there was known as 'the hanging court' for giving the death sentence more often than anywhere else outside London. After that date Manchester became the busiest court and condemned prisoners were hung at Salford and Strangeways gaols.

But by Victorian times the number of capital sentences nationwide was falling, with only murderers and traitors given the death penalty. Between 1836 and 1840 the number of people hanged was just 10 per cent of that in Georgian times. Provincial executioners were no longer required, and a single hangman travelled across the country, using the burgeoning rail service to reach his destinations.

Only eight men were hanged at Lancaster during Victoria's reign, each to the sound of the mournful toll of the prison bell. The first of those was Richard Pedder on 3 September 1853, the last man to be hanged in Lancaster on a 'short drop', which usually resulted in a slow death by strangulation and was national hangman William Calcraft's favoured method.

Calcraft's successor, William Marwood, brought a measure of science to the business of killing by calculating the length of rope needed for a swift death by a broken neck. He also replaced the slip knot with a metal ring to speed the grisly event. Marwood was duly succeeded by James Berry in 1884, a religious man who became deeply opposed to capital punishment after becoming convinced he had killed innocent men.

Only occasionally did the hangman tread the platform at Lancaster station, opened in 1846. In 1862 Walker Moore cheated the hangman of a day's pay when he drowned himself in the prison cistern on the morning his execution was scheduled. Three years later, Stephen Burke became the last man to be publicly hanged at Lancaster. Five more men died at the State's behest in Lancaster gaol before the Edwardian age. The last man to die there was Thomas Rawcliffe, who was hanged in 1910.

Lancaster Castle.

Although hangings were less frequent in Victorian times, the daily drudgery for prisoners was numbing. In common with other prisons, Lancaster gaol used treadmills for those prisoners sentenced to hard labour. There were two inside the prison, one used to power calico looms that made material for prison uniforms and a second to draw water from a well.

The treadmill, also known as 'the shin scraper', was developed by Sir William Cubitt and was in use at Lancaster from 1822. Cubitt also helped to build the South Eastern and Great Northern railways and he was a key designer for the 1851 Great Exhibition. For the psychologically damning treadmill, however, he is less fondly remembered.

Prisoners trod the wheels for 10 hours a day, averaging 96 steps a minute. For five minutes in every 20 they were permitted to rest on a nearby stool. Between each prisoner on the drum of the wheel was a partition to prevent talking. The rule of silence in prisons at the time was held in high esteem by the Victorians as a way of giving convicts the time to reflect on their crime. Attempts at communication were swiftly punished. Religious services, held regularly in gaols, were enthusiastically attended and prisoners sang lustily, eager to hear the sound of their own voices and those of others.

Reformers, including Quaker Elizabeth Fry, were unsure about the new trend. She insisted: 'In some respects I think there is more cruelty in our gaols than I have ever before seen.' Much later, Charles Dickens wrote: 'I hold this slow and daily tampering with the mysteries of the brain to be immeasurably worse than any torture of the body.'

But the overriding concern was not rehabilitation but punishment. When Sir Edmund Du Cane took over responsibilities for prisons in 1865 he promised a concerned Victorian society 'hard bed, hard board and hard labour' for those behind bars. It would be years before free association was allowed between British prisoners.

An Isle of Man Railway steam train at Douglas Station.

By now other railway companies were catching on to Cook's ideas, and he found himself undercut by several. Undaunted, he matched their prices and vowed to learn some hard commercial lessons. Ultimately, an estimated 165,000 people visited the Exhibition on Cook's tours, some 3 per cent of the total number of visitors.

It was only a matter of a few years before Thomas Cook's business expanded to involve the Isle of Man. For the Victorians there was plenty to recommend the island, from its bracing climate to its stunning scenery. Bradshaw's guide gives some indication as to why people were drawn to the island. Barren and blowy, the slate and heath landscape is, the guidebook says, 'like a beggar's tattered coat'.

> These healthy breezes, with the short, springy turf, reconcile the pedestrian to the wild, desolate character of the scenery only enlivened by a few small sheep and occasionally the skulking sheep-stealer. The view from the summit of the mountains embraces the island and the sea in which it is set, as far as the shores of England, Wales, Scotland and Ireland if the air is sufficiently clear.

There's a word of warning too for those so taken with the island that they are tempted to move there.

> Strangers before becoming residents should make themselves well acquainted with the Manx laws, they being totally unlike those of England, Ireland, Wales or Scotland. Arrests for debt can be made even for a shilling on this island and execution follows instanter.

Bradshaw's was right to point out that the Isle of Man enjoys its own jurisdiction. However, the implied threat that many were killed by capital punishment was mistaken. The last person to be hanged there was John Kewish Junior, who was hanged on 1 August 1872 after being convicted of murdering his father. Before that no one had died on a gallows there for three decades.

Kewish lived with his parents and sister at the time his father was found dead. Police believed a pitchfork was used as a weapon. At his first trial Kewish denied the charge of murder and the jury could not agree on a verdict. After the jury foreman fell ill, the jury was dismissed and another trial was ordered. This time Kewish's advocates insisted he was not guilty by reason of insanity. It was, thought the jury, tantamount to an admission of guilt. After considerations lasting only an hour, the jury duly found him guilty and he was sentenced to death.

Under Manx law, Queen Victoria was required to indicate whether or not she wished the sentence to be commuted to life imprisonment, and she became reluctantly embroiled in the case. In Britain she was kept at arm's length from capital cases, only called on to dispense mercy on the recommendation of government ministers. On the face of it, Kewish had killed an older man for personal gain. There were few grounds for clemency, and the Queen was advised to give his hanging the go-ahead. So unhappy was she with her role in the affair that she insisted the law be changed so that she never again had to decide whether a subject lived or died.

After executioner William Calcraft made his way to the island, Kewish was hanged behind closed doors at Castle Rushen in Castletown. Although the Isle of Man did not abolish the death

UNDER MANX LAW, QUEEN VICTORIA WAS REQUIRED TO INDICATE WHETHER OR NOT SHE WISHED KEWISH'S SENTENCE TO BE COMMUTED TO LIFE IMPRISONMENT

penalty until 1993, no one else since suffered the same fate there, with all death sentences being commuted to life imprisonment.

Early transport enthusiasts were intrigued by the island's travel options, which ranged from the curious to the workaday. By 1874 there was a steam train service running on a 3-foot gauge that covered some 50 miles of the island in three separate lines. Almost immediately there were extensions to it, but a decline in the mining industry left parts of the line in the doldrums. Competition from the electric railways was also an issue. However, the service continued to run in a truncated form.

Meanwhile another entirely industrial railway was at work on the island, with a diminutive 19-inch gauge. It was laid in the Great Laxey Mine, once a centre of lead and zinc exploitation. In the middle of the 1870s the Great Laxey Mine was one of the richest in Britain. It possesses the world's largest working water wheel, in grand testament to its previous significance. It wasn't until 1877 that ponies used for hauling wagons out of the mine were replaced by two small steam locomotives, endearingly named Ant and Bee, built in Poole, Dorset. An electric railway was also opened on the island in 1893, with its owners deciding the rough terrain between the Manx capital, Douglas, and Ramsey to the north would be best combated by a double track and electric power.

At the turn of the century railway companies were experiencing financial hardship that often led to company collapses and business takeovers. The Isle of Man Tramways and Electric Power Company was no exception, and it failed in 1900 while still a juvenile. Fortunately another company stepped in to save the services, which by now had gone beyond a mere tourist attraction into being a welcome and necessary part of island transport, albeit one that could boast glorious coastal and countryside views. The Manx Electric Railway remains in service with trams that run on rails and are attached to overhead wires.

The dust had long settled on railway mania when the Snaefell mountain railway was opened in 1895. A narrow-gauge railway powered by electricity, it still runs from the former mine site at Laxey to the mountain top. Its target customer was always the holidaymaker.

To combat the gradients the mountain railway used a braking system created by John Barraclough Fell. He helped to build the

IN THE MIDDLE
OF THE 1870S THE
GREAT LAXEY
MINE WAS ONE
OF THE RICHEST
IN BRITAIN

Furness & Whitehaven Railway before moving to Italy in the 1850s.
The Fell Centre Rail System incorporated a third rail which was
gripped by added drive wheels on the locomotive. There was also
a special brake van to slow the progress of the train when it was
heading downhill. His design was patented in 1863 and he continued
experiments in England before the system was used on an Alpine
railway in 1867. It was a particularly welcome development while
tunnelling – the other option for mountain railways – remained a
slow process.

His son, G. Noble Fell, brought the system to Snaefell where it is
still visible today. It seems he was overcautious with the railway coping
independently with the gradients. Nonetheless, the central rail was
kept in case of emergency braking, another visible testament to great
Victorian technology.

JOURNEY

5

Bradshaw's Ireland

Dublin to BELFAST

As in mainland Britain, the late nineteenth century brought railway fever to Ireland. For Victorian travellers arriving by ferry at Kingstown (now Dún Laoghaire) the chance to explore a country so rich in myth and mystery must have been truly mouthwatering. Certainly George Bradshaw thought so in his 1866 *Descriptive Railway Handbook of Great Britain and Ireland*, telling readers:

> **The entrance into the bay of Dublin unfolds one of the finest land and sea prospects ever beheld. On the right is the rugged hill of Howth, with its rocky bays, wanting only a volcano to render the surrounding scenery a fac-simile of the beautiful bay of Naples; whilst, nearer to the eye, at the extremity of a white line of masonry just fringing the sea, the light-house presents its alabaster front. On the left are the town of Dalkey with its romantic rocks, mutilated castles, Martello towers, elegant villas and the picturesque town of Dunleary, whilst behind is seen a line of parks and plantations, above which the mountains of Wicklow ascend with the greatest majesty.**

By 1866 Ireland had amassed a rail network of around 1,000 miles, driving an economic boost which 20 years previously, at the height of the Great Famine, would have been hard to envisage. Many rural towns had become accessible to tourists and trades-folk, and the east coast line between Dublin and Belfast, via Drogheda and Dundalk, opened up the great Victorian cities of Dublin and Belfast to commuters.

From Belfast it was soon possible to reach the dramatic Antrim coast and the historic port of Derry, aka Londonderry, with comparative ease. A tourist travelling from, say, Dublin to Derry could take in some of the marvels of nineteenth-century engineering, such as the Boyne and Craigmore Viaducts, while experiencing some of the unexplained, weird, wonderful and plain bizarre sights of rural Ireland.

Before following one of Bradshaw's Irish journeys, it's worth romping briefly through the country's railway history to consider how

its great designers and entrepreneurs ensured the future of steam travel, despite formidable economic, bureaucratic and geographical barriers.

The first track opened to the public in 1834 and ran for some six miles from Kingstown into the heart of Dublin. It was designed to provide an affordable mass-transportation system for commuters, and its success, just ten years after England's first railway, helped concentrate the minds of investors and financiers on the potential for new lines across Ireland.

The main instigator of the Dublin & Kingstown Railway was a leading Dublin stockbroker, James Pim, who became convinced of its viability by virtue of his own daily commute from Monkstown, above Kingstown harbour, into the city. Pim made the journey on a road teeming with horse-drawn carriages (the surface could be a mudbath in winter and a lung-busting dustbowl in summer) and reasoned that a reliable rail link would be a welcome alternative. Like many of the English railway promoters he was a Quaker, and believed strongly that a proportion of his wealth should drive progress for the public good. His connections with Quaker entrepreneurs in key ports such as Dublin, London, Bristol, Liverpool and Cardiff provided the contacts to make it happen.

The proposed railway was part funded through a £75,000 loan from the British government's Board of Works. However, the Parliamentary Bill underpinning the project ensured that financial risk was placed squarely on the shoulders of the private sponsors, the 'Gentlemen, Merchants, Traders, Freeholders and others of Dublin … subscribers to an intended Company to be called The Dublin and Kingstown Railway Company'. Together these financiers put up £100,000 on the understanding that their personal assets would be forfeited in the event of bankruptcy.

Surveys commissioned by the directors showed there were 70,000 road journeys made per month between Kingstown and the Irish capital. Of these, 48,000 were by various types of horse-drawn carriage, 6,000 by horse, and the remainder in an eclectic selection of farm carts, gigs and 'jingles'. Averaged out per day, this translated to 2,300 journeys – a level of demand the Dublin & Kingstown Railway calculated would generate around £30,000 worth of income on operating costs of £10,000. The railway would run seven return journeys per day with regular stops en route and with enough carriages

to accommodate 300 people. Moreover, the new port of Kingstown was expected to create plenty of extra business through freight, mail and cross-channel tourism, a prospect seized upon in one early promotional notice:

> *The railway with its trains of carriages in rapid motion, will form a novel and not uninteresting foreground … Kingstown will become a resort to which all classes will be attracted by the opportunity for the enjoyment of healthy exercise amidst a pure atmosphere and romantic surroundings.*

Of course, for the government the new line meant much more than an easy ride for commuters, a jolly day out for trippers and a profit-generator for business. The War Department understood very well that the railway could move troops quickly through Kingstown and on to Dublin in the event of an armed Irish rebellion similar to the uprising that had occurred in 1798. Its strategic importance was further heightened by fears that the French might try to invade Ireland as a stepping stone to attacking England.

In addition to Pim, the D&KR's key movers and shakers included James Perry, a financier with experience of canal construction, engineer Thomas Bergin, who was appointed general manager, and the Irish-born engineer Charles Vignoles, whose appointment was demanded by the Board of Trade to ensure taxpayers' cash was spent wisely. But above all the company needed a hands-on, experienced contractor who could drive the project forward and prove that steam was the future. In William Dargan they found the very man. Not for nothing would he be hailed as Ireland's 'King of the Railways'.

Born in 1799, Dargan was the son of a tenant farmer from rural Carlow. His natural aptitude for mathematics, a sound English education and good family contacts helped him begin a career as a back-office junior with a Dublin surveying company. Later he travelled back across the Irish Sea to work on George Stephenson's plans for the *Rocket* and was soon hired to help on Thomas Telford's London-to-Holyhead rail link. In 1820 he started surveying for another Telford project – the road to Holyhead, Anglesey. After this Dargan returned to Ireland, set up on his own account and completed various small engineering projects before making his name through the construction

RIGHT: **Travelling on the Downpatrick Heritage Steam Railway.**

ABOVE: **William Dargan (1799–1867).**

of the Dublin-to-Howth road, an important arterial route north of the capital, and the hugely impressive Ulster Canal link between Belfast and Lough Erne. But railways had become his passion, and he seized the chance to submit a tender for the D&KR project.

By now Dargan had carved out an enviable reputation as an entrepreneur of vision. He became popular with his workforce because he paid by results (a scheme that was much more lucrative for the labourers than the miserable day-rates offered by some construction companies) and made sure wages arrived punctually. His navvies told other workers of his reputation for fairness, with the result that Dargan had access to a reliable, able and willing labour force, making him well placed to meet the huge demand for track expansion which lay ahead.

It's hard to overstate the colossal task, in man hours, which faced the early railway labourers who weren't working under Dargan's enlightened management. Initially hours were long and pay poor, a state of affairs which led to simmering resentment and ultimately, in June 1833, a riot. Some of the 2,000 navvies employed on the D&KR clashed with police and the entire site ground to a halt until Dargan persuaded Pim and Bergin to introduce his piecework system of remuneration. Typically, this meant paying a man by the number of spoil-filled wheelbarrows he shifted.

Industrial action was by no means the only thorny issue. Negotiating land purchases with wealthy estate owners was a management horror story, given that the incumbents held the cards. In later years George Bradshaw's readers bound for Dublin would admire the superb Italianate Bridge above the line at Blackrock and, nearby, an elegant folly on the shore which appeared to be a bathing hut modelled on an ancient Greek temple. Both were built by the D&KR at the behest of landowners – but hardly willingly.

The problem for the railway was that hearings before an Irish Land Jury to decide fair compensation were slow and cripplingly expensive. Achieving a swift out-of-court settlement was therefore preferable, but this meant kowtowing to the landowners and to two in particular – Baron Cloncurry and the Reverend Lees. Cloncurry, an eccentric Irish nationalist who had served time for his anti-government activities, squeezed £3,000 out of the D&KR, plus an additional bridge across the line, built 'in the best Italianate style', so that he could walk his dogs down to a private bathing area. He also required

A coloured drawing of
the steam locomotive
Hibernia, 1834.

a granite bathing hut modelled on a Greek 'pleasure-dome for men'. Lees's demands were limited to cash but he also forced a hard bargain, winning an exorbitant £7,500 in compensation.

Construction work finally started in 1833 and the service was launched, half an hour late, at 9.30 a.m. on 17 December 1834, when the Manchester-built locomotive *Hibernia*, pulling packed carriages, steamed out of Dublin for the 19½-minute ride to Kingstown Harbour. Historically, this truly was a great train journey, as the *Dublin Evening Post* reported the following day:

> *This splendid work was yesterday opened to the public for the regular transmission of passengers to and from Kingstown, and the intermediate stage at the Black-rock. Notwithstanding the early hour at which the first train started, half-past nine o'clock, the carriages were filled by a very fashionable concourse of persons, and the greatest eagerness was manifested to witness the first operations of the work. Up to a quarter past five the line of road from Merrion to Salthill was thronged with spectators, who loudly cheered each train that passed them.*

A view of Killiney Bay, Co. Dublin, looking towards Bray Head.

The reporter is mildly critical of the railway's method of boarding passengers – 'much confusion was occasioned at starting up by the want of proper arrangement' – but praised precautions taken to prevent accidents. These included a team of line marshals and mandatory slow starts for the engines. 'Although there could not have been less than from three to four thousand persons upon the railway during the day, we are happy to state that these very necessary precautions were attended with the desired effect.'

However, according to *The Times* of Monday 22 December, those travelling on the train were at substantially greater risk than those watching from trackside:

All the machinery works well as yet, except in one particular: the springs are not sufficiently elastic to prevent sudden shocks when the carriages stop. Three or four gentlemen had one occasion to-day [sic] their heads knocked against each other and the carriage doors and severe contusions were the consequence. A county of Kildare gentleman's head was laid open. The majority had, however, hard Irish heads, and did not mind a few knocks.

Health and safety laws were rather less rigorous in those days, and *The Times* correspondent cheerily concludes: 'The weather is delightful for December, and a few broken heads does not throw much damp on a scene of Irish amusement where everything else goes well.'

The success of the D&KR led to demands for a line extension south-east, and in 1844 Dargan obliged with the Dalkey Railway. Among the guests at this opening ceremony was Isambard Kingdom Brunel, arguably the greatest of all Victorian engineers, who took the opportunity to reveal an ambitious new venture to the D&KR Board. Brunel explained that he was planning a new line across South Wales, servicing a sea ferry between Fishguard in Pembrokeshire, South Wales and Rosslare, the closest port to Wexford in Ireland's far south-east. Logically, he needed a rail link from Wexford to Dublin. Would the Board consider a joint venture to achieve this? The proposal was duly agreed and the Waterford, Wexford, Wicklow & Dublin Railway was born. Work on the route began at various locations in 1847 but construction progressed

agonisingly slowly due to geological problems around Bray Head.
It wasn't until 1854 that the stretch from Dalkey to Bray was finished,
while the Wicklow section didn't open until the following year.

The boost to Bray's economy was a game-changer for locals.
Suddenly it was possible for people to live in the town yet commute
daily to Dublin; within 20 years of the line's opening in 1854 the
area's population rose from 4,151 to 6,504. Railway trippers would
pour down from the city or Kingstown ferry, perhaps conscious of
Bradshaw's exhortations:

> The stranger would do well to make this place his
> headquarters for a few days, being most beauti-
> fully situated, and in the very heart of scenery the
> most attractive. In the town are the remains of a
> castle (now used as a barrack) and a race course.
> There is also a pretty lake and a river abounding
> with trout. Close at hand is Kilruddy *[sic]*, near the
> Sugar Loaf, seat of the Earl of Meath. Bray Head
> is within twenty minutes walk of the station and
> is well worth a visit. Its excellent winding path,
> cut in the cliff, affords the tourist a magnificent
> view, embracing the Hill of Howth, Dalkey Island
> and Killiney Bay, with the railroad below, and the
> ocean washing the base of the 'head'.

The prosperity being bestowed on previously isolated towns was not
lost on the rest of Ireland (although this sentiment faded as people
became more cynical about the railway investment 'bubble'). In 1852
half the electorate of Cashel, Co. Tipperary, pledged to support *any*
prospective Member of Parliament – irrespective of his politics – who
could provide a rail link to the town. It seems the public took the view
that establishing a railway was not that hard. Back in Bray, Dargan and
Brunel would have begged to differ.

Scenic it may have been (and still is) but the geology and geography
governing their next section of track, south past Bray Head, was the
stuff of nightmares for an engineer. There are competing theories as
to why they persisted with a coastal line rather than a simpler, inland
route to Wicklow. Some say it was to tempt tourists with the glorious

IN 1852 HALF
THE ELECTORATE
OF CASHEL …
PLEDGED TO
SUPPORT *ANY*
PROSPECTIVE
MEMBER OF
PARLIAMENT
… WHO COULD
PROVIDE A RAIL
LINK TO THE
TOWN

RIGHT: A geological map
of Ireland, drawn and
engraved by John Emslie,
c. 1855.

OVERLEAF: The accident at
Bray Head in 1867.

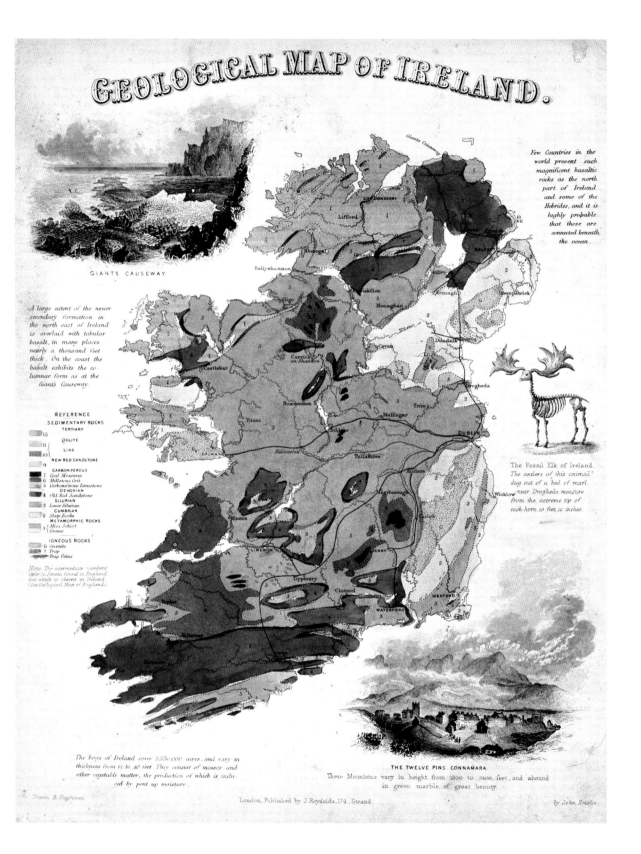

GEOLOGICAL MAP OF IRELAND.

GIANTS CAUSEWAY

Few Countries in the world present such magnificent basaltic rocks as the north part of Ireland and some of the Hebrides, and it is highly probable that these are connected beneath the ocean.

A large extent of the newer secondary formation in the north east of Ireland is overlaid with tabular basalt, in many places nearly a thousand feet thick. On the coast the basalt exhibits the columnar form as at the Giants Causeway.

REFERENCE
SEDIMENTARY ROCKS
TERTIARY
15
11 OOLITE
10 LIAS
9 NEW RED SANDSTONE
CARBONIFEROUS
7 Coal Measures
6 Millstone Grit
5 Carboniferous Limestone
DEVONIAN
4 Old Red Sandstone
SILURIAN
3 Lower Silurian
CUMBRIAN
2 Slate Rocks
METAMORPHIC ROCKS
Mica Schist
1 Gneiss
IGNEOUS ROCKS
G Granite
T Trap
Trap Veins

Note. The intermediate numbers refer to Strata found in England, but which is absent in Ireland (see Geological Map of England.)

The bogs of Ireland cover 2,830,000 acres, and vary in thickness from 12 to 40 feet. They consist of mosses and other vegetable matter, the production of which is induced by pent up moisture.

The Fossil Elk of Ireland. The antlers of this animal dug out of a bed of marl near Drogheda measure from the extreme tip of each horn 10 feet, 10 inches.

THE TWELVE PINS, CONNAMARA.
These Mountains vary in height from 1800 to 2400 feet, and abound in green marble of great beauty.

Drawn & Engraved

London, Published by J. Reynolds, 174, Strand

by John Emslie

cliff views; others claim Lord Meath donated land around Bray Head to ensure the vista from his Kilruddery estate wasn't spoiled. No doubt there was also a part of Brunel and Dargan which simply relished the challenge; critics of the new line often claimed that 'Bray Head would never be conquered' by the railway.

As it turned out the naysayers would be proved wrong, though at times it was a close-run thing. The rock on these cliffs is Cambrian and the vertical strata can easily collapse when disturbed. This made tunnelling tricky while the erosive effects of the waves and wind on the foundations produced regular landslips. Brunel's experience of constructing the Thames tunnel and Bristol's Clifton Suspension Bridge proved invaluable as work slowly progressed down three separate tunnels. But long after the line was finished four new tunnels had to be bored – the last in 1917. Each saw the track pushed further and further back from the sea (today's travellers can still see the old entrances) and a profit-sapping £40,000 was spent on sea defences inside ten years.

At one point a rock fall forced the line to be moved 10 feet. The bridging of a ravine with a 300-ft-long, 75-ft-high wooden viaduct was severely delayed when the first structure was destroyed by heavy seas. And such was the unstable nature of the cliffs that trains traversing a ledge 70 feet above the waves needed protection from rock falls; roofs were bolted into the cliff face above the track.

Against this background accidents were almost inevitable, and on 23 April 1865 a first-class carriage of the Dublin train jumped the rails in the middle of a viaduct. The engine halted but then, remarkably, pulled the carriage to safety. Less fortunate were two passengers who, two years later, lost their lives as an engine, tender and three carriages crashed through the side of a bridge and plunged 30 feet into a ravine.

Yet the Victorian can-do approach to engineering eventually triumphed. The line to Wicklow opened in 1855 and reached the copper mines at Avoca via a majestic five-arch viaduct in July 1863. From here the track was quickly extended towards Arklow and Enniscorthy, finally reaching Wexford in 1872. Brunel and Dargan had fulfilled their dream of opening the south to the rail revolution – albeit with a legacy of high maintenance.

Of course Dargan did not confine himself to contracts south of Dublin. By 1853 he had already constructed around 600 miles of track, including sections of what would become the Great Southern & Western Railway, the Midland Great Western Railway and the Great Northern Railway. The latter was itself the result of mergers between three founding companies: the Dublin & Drogheda Railway, the Ulster Railway and the Dublin & Belfast Junction Railway.

The success of the Dublin & Kingstown Railway's partnership with Brunel in the south-east could have been a useful business model for these emerging operators. The reality was very different. Each had their own plans, their own routes, their own trains and, especially, their own track gauges. There was no Regulator galvanising the various Boards into considering the necessity for national services in which trains from one company could run on the tracks of another.

This problem might never have arisen if Thomas Drummond, Under-Secretary of State for Ireland from 1835 to 1840 and a mainspring of the Irish Railway Commission, had had his way. In 1837 Drummond headed the Commission and tried to argue for a greater degree of state control in the industry's development. But his ideas were anathema to the private enterprise lobby and the result was industrial brinkmanship on a grand scale.

In Belfast many factory owners had made their fortunes from the Industrial Revolution and knew how steam technology had transformed their linen mills. They began pushing for their own rail link, and in 1836 an Act of Parliament approved the founding of the Ulster Railway Company. Its aim was to establish a line south from Belfast, via Lisburn, Lurgan and Portadown, to Armagh, thus providing the population of the Lagan Valley (seen as an untapped labour source) speedy access to the textile mills.

Construction began in 1837 with George Stephenson as Ulster Railway's consulting engineer. In fact Stephenson spent only a few days in Belfast and it was William Dargan who took on the bulk of the work. He monitored the work in his personal coach – fitted out as a mobile operations HQ – and again charmed the 3,000-strong workforce with piecework bonuses linked to the speed of advance. Within two years the line was open between Belfast and Lisburn, with return fares fixed at a shilling for first class and sixpence for second.

While the Ulster Railway pressed on to Armagh, the Dublin financiers behind the successful Dublin & Kingstown Railway were busy preparing their own plans for a direct link between Ireland's two great cities. They formed the Dublin & Drogheda Railway Company and unveiled a route which headed straight up the east coast. The Dubliners saw no reason to divert inland to Armagh – it was not in their commercial interests to deliver passengers to the Ulster Railway – but their Belfast rivals treated their proposal with disdain, claiming it would reduce overall demand, and therefore the profitability of both lines. The linen merchants also genuinely feared that the hills between Dundalk and Newry would prove too costly an engineering challenge.

Deadlock followed. The 1838 Railway Commission preferred the inland route via Armagh, but wrangling continued, leading to a two-year delay for the D&DR. The latter eventually appointed William Dargan as its main contractor with Professor John MacNeill, first

PREVIOUS PAGE: A locomotive on the Downpatrick Heritage Railway.

BELOW: A locomotive from the Irish Railway collection at the Ulster Folk and Transport Museum.

professor of engineering at Trinity College Dublin, as consultant. And so was seeded the genesis of a new problem.

MacNeill advised a gauge of 5 ft 2 in, arguing that this would make the track cheaper to build. However, the 1838 Commission had already recommended 6 ft 2 in and the Ulster Railway had dutifully followed that guideline. To further complicate matters, the D&KR had mirrored George Stephenson's *Rocket* with a 4 ft 8½ in gauge. It seemed Ireland was destined for the same compatibility problem as had bedevilled the early rail industry across the water. It was left to the Board of Trade to sort things out.

The Board appointed a well-respected arbiter, Major-General Sir Charles Pasley, the Inspector-General of Railways and a former head of the School of Military Engineering, Woolwich. Pasley quickly ruled out Brunel's suggestion of a 7 ft gauge and then considered the Stephensons' advice that a compromise should be struck somewhere between 5 ft and 5 ft 6 in. Pasley presumably saw little reason to prolong the debate. He chose 5 ft 3 in, one of those rare imperial lengths which can be converted precisely to a metric round figure: 1,600 mm.

This caused few problems for the Dubliners as the Dublin & Drogheda Railway was still at an early stage of construction. But the Ulster Railway faced a £20,000 bill to replace its original gauge, and in 1843 successfully argued to the Board of Trade that other companies should pay it compensation. A clause covering this appeared in several Railway Acts from 1850 onwards. To minimise disruption the Ulster Railway built a 5 ft 3 in line alongside its redundant 6 ft 2 in original, and completed a full switchover in September 1847. Incidentally, the Dublin & Kingstown wasn't changed until 1857, no doubt because at £38,000 the cost was not easily recouped. Interestingly the 'Irish Gauge' is now only found in three Australian states – Victoria, New South Wales and South Australia – and Brazil.

In 1844 the D&DR completed its track to Drogheda. Four years later, the UR reached Armagh. Around 56 miles of glorious, green Irish countryside lay between the two, with the result that a new player entered the game – the Dublin & Belfast Junction Railway. This was incorporated by an 1845 Act of Parliament with the declared intention of extending the D&DR line from Drogheda to the key UR station at Portadown, north-east of Armagh. And once more William Dargan got the lion's share of the contract.

THE 'IRISH GAUGE' IS NOW ONLY FOUND IN THREE AUSTRALIAN STATES – VICTORIA, NEW SOUTH WALES AND SOUTH AUSTRALIA – AND BRAZIL

Work started at numerous locations along the proposed route but Dargan took personal charge of the section south of Portadown across the difficult marshland area towards Mullaghglass and Goraghwood. The Newry Valley was his next major challenge; the quarter-mile-long Craigmore Viaduct was needed to span the River Camlough and connect to the important coastal town of Dundalk. But a still more complex engineering project lay ahead – the bridging of the River Boyne further south at Drogheda. Dargan used designs by John MacNeill for both the Craigmore and Boyne Viaducts, though not without some controversy. When they were completed in 1849 and 1855 respectively these bridges ranked among the wonders of the railway world and were landmark attractions for Victorian tourists.

With the Dublin to Belfast link finally complete there was a new impetus for railway entrepreneurs to build connecting branch lines. From Belfast this allowed Bradshaw's late Victorian travellers to embark on a series of rambling detours, and our route takes in a couple of these – the Belfast & County Down Railway south-east to Downpatrick, supposedly the site of St Patrick's grave, and the Carrickfergus & Larne Railway north to Whitehead and the extraordinary Gobbins Path. But the main route continues on north-west, along the old Belfast & Northern Counties line, via Ballymena and Coleraine to Londonderry.

With the end of the Great Famine in 1849, and with track construction proceeding apace, William Dargan decided it was time to relaunch Ireland as a new industrial powerhouse. Inspired by London's Great Exhibition of 1851, he kick-started plans for the 1853 Dublin Exhibition by depositing £30,000 with various organising committees, and later by advancing a further £70,000 in loans and guarantees. Dargan lost around £20,000 on the venture, but achieved his aim. More than 100,000 people attended the exhibition, including Queen Victoria, Prince Albert and the Prince of Wales, and there were claims that 1 million visitors were attracted to Dublin that year. On 29 August 1853 the Queen visited Dargan and his wife, Jane, at their Mount Annville house where, according to the *Illustrated London News* of 10 September, she offered Dargan a baronetcy in recognition of his contribution to the railways. He politely declined.

Dargan's final years were devoted to extending Dublin's rail link south to Wexford. He also dabbled in the tourism business, building

OVERLEAF: **Sackville Street and O'Connell Bridge,** Dublin.

THE RAILWAYS AND THE GREAT FAMINE

The fact that Ireland built such a vast railway network at a time when the country was suffering appalling deprivations from the Great Famine of 1845–9 is a tribute to the indomitable Irish spirit. But from another perspective it also heightens the atrocious failure of government, in both Westminster and Dublin Castle, to grasp the disaster of genocidal proportions that was unfolding. This is not a book about the Famine but it is worth highlighting what the shiny new Irish railways did, and did not do, for their starving people.

Historians differ over the exact number who died – statisticians put the figure anywhere between 775,000 and 1.5 million – but whatever the numbers the human tragedy is beyond the imagination of most Westerners today. Thousands queued on the streets at soup kitchens, the sick and painfully thin besieged rural hospitals – 'skeletal armies', as the Irish historian Robert Foster described them – while in the far west of the country entire families walled themselves into cabins and cottages to await death. Irrespective of who was to blame, the Great Famine remains perhaps the most shameful peacetime event in recent British history.

The irony, of course, is that the railways offered the greatest potential for mass transport of food which Ireland had ever seen. Instead, they became the conduit for a mass exodus. Some 1.5 million people are thought to have emigrated during the Famine years, and although the government did provide some food relief, political leaders saw the railways more as a means of providing extra employment, allowing labourers to feed their families, than a food distribution network. Certainly the great campaigner for Catholic emancipation and Lord Mayor of Dublin, Daniel O'Connell, pressurised the companies into hiring extra labour, and there is evidence that Dargan took on more men than he strictly needed to in the worst-affected areas.

IRRESPECTIVE OF BLAME THE GREAT FAMINE REMAINS PERHAPS THE MOST SHAMEFUL PEACETIME EVENT IN RECENT BRITISH HISTORY

and running the Royal Marine Hotel at Kingstown. Presumably this magnificent landmark building, which opened in 1865, didn't quite hit Bradshaw's deadline for the 1866 *Descriptive Guide* – he mentions only Rathbone's Hotel as a berth for weary ferry travellers – but it soon developed a reputation for luxury and extravagant cuisine. When Queen Victoria visited Ireland on 4 April 1900 she apparently headed straight off the boat and into the Royal Marine Hotel for a 16-course breakfast.

Sadly, Dargan was seriously injured falling from a horse in 1866. He never fully recovered, his financial affairs unravelled and he ended direct involvement in his railway projects. He died on 7 February 1867 and was buried in Dublin's Glasnevin cemetery. In 2004 a new cable bridge for the Dublin Light Railway was named Dargan Bridge in his honour.

There seems little doubt that the coming of the railways made a huge contribution to Dublin's prosperity. Bradshaw notes:

> **The appearance of Dublin is very much improved of late years. Streets have been widened, new squares skilfully laid out, and many public monuments freed from buildings which concealed their beauties.**

He is captivated by the view from Carlisle Bridge, the ship-cluttered Liffey, the Bank – 'the most perfect building in Dublin'– and a dozen or more public edifices which would no doubt interest the architecturally literate rail traveller. However, the one attraction which really did inspire the masses to take to the rails gets only a passing reference, alongside the Phoenix Park Barracks: Dublin Zoo.

The Victorian public loved zoos, and railway managers realised that here was an excellent opportunity to fill trains on high days and holidays. Walsh's train timetable was advertising Dublin Zoo in 1848 (although with a 6d standard entry fee it was still an expensive day out) and Penny Sundays were introduced to attract working-class families. Still, it wasn't until the Dublin Exhibition that zoo visitor numbers really took off, and 120,000 passed through the gates that year. In 1855 the zoo acquired its first pair of lions; they bred for the first time in 1857 and soon the lions of Dublin, particularly a superb specimen

Tylers' BOOTS ARE THE BEST

HATCH ST

named Charlie, became a world-famous attraction – so much so, it was claimed that the lions pushed up railway share prices.

It says as much in a colourful newspaper report on the visit to Dublin in 1878 by General Ulysses S. Grant, the renowned commander of the Union forces during the American Civil War and former President. It was filed with the minutes of the Royal Zoological Society of Ireland in December that year.

General Grant (former US President) visited the Zoo and was observed to smile. This remarkable event occurred during his visit to the Zoo … Secretary [the Rev. Professor Samuel Haughton] exhibited his tigers, jaguar, pumas, leopards and even the new lioness … the general neither spoke nor smiled at any of their performances and at length stood impassive, lighting a fresh cigar opposite the cage of the celebrated lion 'Charlie' the gem of the collection.

Hereupon the secretary, changing his manner of deferential courtesy, which he had hitherto maintained, into one of more familiarity, said: 'General, that lion's name is Charlie, he is three inches higher in the shoulder than his grandfather, who came from South Africa. I have reared ninety-six of that old lion's children and grandchildren in these gardens and I reckon Charlie is the biggest of them. I am now going to tell you something which you will not, perhaps, believe: that lion was the cause of the shares of the South Western Railway rising 2 per cent in the open market. When it became known in the United States how large that lion had grown, the Transatlantic passengers all commenced landing at Queenstown [Co. Cork] instead of proceeding to Liverpool by sea. They now travel by the GSW line from Queenstown to Dublin and on arrival drive out to the gardens to see the big lion. Comfortable seats are provided for them in the lion house where they sit for hours smoking silently and admiring the proportions of the vast brute.'

⤺

With Bray, Kingstown and Dublin disappearing into the distance, the route heads due north, along the old Dublin & Drogheda Railway via the fishing port of Balbriggan. Bradshaw has little to say of Balbriggan, presumably calculating that readers will find limited interest beyond the 35-ft-tall lighthouse and 600-ft-long pier. There's a brief mention for the

BALBRIGGAN WINKLES WERE MUCH IN DEMAND AND SOLD IN BULK AS FAR AWAY AS LONDON'S BILLINGSGATE MARKET

local industries – stocking, linen, tanning, muslin and embroidering trades – but nothing of the railway's important links with the local fishing industry.

The old lighthouse at the entrance to the harbour at Balbriggan, Co. Dublin.

It was a truly symbiotic relationship. The fleet's catch provided regular freight business and during the herring season between October and January so many boats based themselves at Balbriggan that it was said you could walk across the harbour without getting wet. The local kipper factory flourished, as did the trade in winkles – a favourite Victorian delicacy. Winkles were gathered in sacks at the harbour and then hauled up the hill to be weighed at the station. Once the sacks contained a couple of tons of shellfish they would be loaded onto the next train and transported to market. Balbriggan winkles were much in demand and sold in bulk as far away as London's Billingsgate market.

The railway played one other, unintentional role in supporting fishermen. As trains crossed the viaduct alongside the harbour, drivers were instructed to give a loud blast on the whistle. This helped guide boats back to harbour in fog or at night, and was a practice which continued right up to the 1950s, when new navigational equipment became available.

From Balbriggan Bradshaw's traveller passed through what the guide describes as an 'undulating, rich and highly cultivated plain'. While the countryside is agreeable enough, Bradshaw is scathing about the living standards of the poor, warning readers:

> The farms are often very extensive but the farm houses, except when they belong to large proprietors, are in general wretched huts; and the houses of the humbler classes are nothing more than mud hovels.

Thankfully his mood brightens when he crosses the River Boyne, perhaps because it offers an opportunity to enlighten readers on one of modern Ireland's bloodiest and most significant events, the 1690 Battle of the Boyne, which effectively ensured Protestant dominance of Irish public life for generations to come. From Bradshaw's point of view this location demands the retelling of Irish history's most withering put-down.

The battle was fought between the deposed Catholic monarch King James II (James VII of Scotland) and his son-in-law and successor, the Protestant ruler of the Netherlands, William of Orange (William III). James was the last Catholic to rule the combined British kingdoms but was distrusted by Protestant leaders as being too pro-Pope and (possibly even worse) pro-French. They invited William to claim the throne, and in 1688 his invasion forced James to flee to France.

The following year James landed in Ireland with the intention of reclaiming his birthright. But his inexperience as a commander shackled his mainly Irish Catholic army, who, though mostly raw recruits, were by no means destined for defeat. Many of his soldiers were furious at James's lack of personal leadership (he stood on a hill out of the way, in contrast to William, who led his troops from the front) and Irish commanders were aghast when the order came to retreat from the banks of the Boyne. James, with a small escort, was first to head for safety – earning the Gaelic nickname *Seamus an Chaca* (James the

British cavalry charge through the waters of the Boyne at the Battle of the Boyne, 1690.

Shit) – and his French cavalry proved similarly keen to disengage. While many Irishmen regrouped to fight on for another year, James rapidly headed south, first to Dublin, then to Duncannon harbour, bound for exile in France.

In his description of the battle and aftermath, Bradshaw writes:

'Change leaders', said the beaten Irish, 'and we will fight the battle over again' but their despicable sovereign made off as fast as he could to Dublin where he met the Duchess of Tyrconnel. 'Your countrymen run well, madam,' he said. 'Not quite so well as Your Majesty,' said the lady, 'for I see you have won the race.'

For the Victorian traveller to Drogheda there was obviously little tangible evidence of the battlefield, although Bradshaw recommends a carriage drive through King William's Glen to get a flavour. But in terms of hard-core sightseeing the Boyne Viaduct must have more than made up for this. Quite apart from the technical achievement, the bridge was both a masterpiece of design and the final link in the Dublin–Belfast rail link. It said to the world that Ireland was in the fast lane of industrial development.

Work didn't begin on the viaduct until 1850, delayed by the continuing shadow of the Famine and a protracted dispute over the design calculations. The 98-ft-high bridge had 15 stone arches bearing 1,760 feet of track; its 226-ft-long central iron truss stood on piers sunk 30 feet into a morass of alluvial clay, tons of which had to be removed by chain bucket. With such a massive commitment in terms of labour and materials it was essential that planning drawings were error-free.

Professor John MacNeill (now consultant engineer to the Dublin & Belfast Junction Railway) had handed in his specifications but the

The Dublin and Belfast Viaduct across the Boyne near Drogheda.

company's chief engineer, James Barton, questioned the load-bearing calculations and it was left to the Department of Engineering at Trinity College to adjudicate. No doubt choosing words carefully, the Department backed Barton and recommended a strengthening of the latticework, which was then the longest stretch in the world. It was redesigned so that two locomotives and carriages, with a combined weight of 1,000 tons, could pass simultaneously on the central point of the viaduct. While such an occurrence was deemed unlikely in the extreme, Board of Trade railway inspectors were known to have a fearsome reputation for strict safety margins. Ultimately this was not misplaced; the Armagh Rail Disaster (see below) was a classic example of the tensions between company profits and the interests of passengers.

When the Boyne Viaduct opened for business many rail travellers were entirely unconvinced by its stability, even though tests proved the structure was accurate to one third of an inch – an extraordinary achievement. It was a view no doubt encouraged by carriage drivers who had made a good living ferrying Dublin and Belfast-bound passengers across the river via a road bridge. Public concern was heightened at the 1855 opening by the sight of wooden scaffolding (used for construction rather than load-bearing) still cloaking the sides of the new bridge.

These fears soon passed and the viaduct was hailed by many as a wonder of the industrial age. Yet its completion was never a cause for wild celebration. The famine years were not yet over and the railway was seen by some critics as an instrument of an uncaring government. There were even reports of starving farmworkers in the far south-west attacking railway employees.

Understandably, Bradshaw makes no mention of this and from Drogheda escorts his readers north through the 'inexpressibly beautiful' countryside of the Boyne, the rural stations of Beauparc and Navan and on to Kells, Co. Louth, an important centre of Irish Bronze Age architecture and culture.

One of the smallest counties in Ireland, it abounds in those rude vestiges of antiquity which consist of earth-works, chiefly designed for sepulchral purposes, or acting as places of defensive habitation. Cromlechs, and other relics of anti-Christian ages,

THE BOYNE VIADUCT WAS BOTH A MASTERPIECE OF DESIGN AND THE FINAL LINK IN THE DUBLIN–BELFAST RAIL LINK

although much lessened in number within the last century, are still numerous, and in some instances extremely curious.

Among the most curious is the Proleek Dolmen, a short carriage drive from the railway, which stands in the grounds of the Ballymascanlon House Hotel (built in the 1860s). The two upright or 'portal' stones mark the doorway to a 4,000-year-old burial chamber. They support a 40-ton capstone known as 'the Giant's Load' on the basis that only a giant could have placed it there (the giant concerned was apparently Parrah Boug MacShagean, from Scotland). This was all good stuff for a Victorian public fascinated by mystical matters. According to local folklore, anyone throwing onto the capstone a stone which stayed in place would be married within the year. Giant or no giant, it had to be good for the tourist trade.

From Louth, the journey north continues through the seaport of Dundalk and on to Newry, where the guide notes that a yew tree in the grounds of a thirteenth-century monastery was planted by Ireland's foremost patron saint, St Patrick. By Bradshaw's time Newry had become an important railway hub, providing both a service to Belfast via Portadown and a link between Armagh to the north-west and the seaside town of Warrenpoint to the south-east. It was along this latter stretch of track, 2½ miles out from Armagh, that a tragic combination of circumstances led to the deaths of 80 people and changed the operation of railways across Europe forever.

On 12 June 1889 a special excursion train, booked by Armagh's Methodist Church Sunday School, set out on the 24-mile day trip to Warrenpoint. Organisers had planned for 800 people and the engine house at Dundalk calculated that 13 carriages would be required, pulled by a four-coupled locomotive (i.e. with two pairs of driving wheels). In the event they sent two extra carriages with instructions to driver Thomas McGrath that these should not be used. Neither McGrath nor his Dundalk managers were familiar with the steep, steady climb for the first few miles of track south-east of Armagh. The locomotive concerned, engine 86, was probably underpowered – even for 13 coaches.

Saint Patrick, the patron saint of Ireland.

Unfortunately, many more than 800 passengers turned up to join the Warrenpoint Special that day, and the Armagh stationmaster, John Foster, began issuing tickets for all 15 carriages. Evidence at the subsequent accident inquiry was confusing and contradictory; McGrath claimed he'd opposed the increase while Foster insisted the argument was over his own request for still more coaches. According to McGrath the stationmaster told him ten minutes before departure: 'Any driver that comes here does not grumble about taking an excursion train with him.' McGrath claimed that he had replied: 'Why did you not send proper word to Dundalk, and I should have a proper six-wheeled coupled engine.'

The railway's chief clerk, a Mr Elliott, who was accompanying the excursion, suggested a solution: the scheduled train following 15 minutes behind could assist the Special up the climb. Either that, or some carriages could be left behind for the later service. However, McGrath was reluctant to do this, and at 10.20 a.m. he set off with 940 people crammed into 15 carriages.

Initially it seemed the decision might be vindicated. There had been no rain to turn the rails slippery, and at full throttle the locomotive made good progress. But then at Derry's Crossing, some 700 yards from the Dobbin's Bridge summit, the train began losing momentum. It halted just 200 yards short of the top.

To stop the train rolling back McGrath applied what were known as 'continuous brakes'. These relied on a vacuum produced by the engine; if power was lost the brakes were released. It was not a system recommended by the Board of Trade, which preferred a fail-safe arrangement in which a vacuum held the brakes *off* while the engine was running. These so-called 'automatic continuous brakes' slammed on immediately in the event of engine failure.

With the Special stationary, guards in the two brake vans at the front and rear of the train applied their handbrakes. Some stones were used to wedge or 'scotch' carriage wheels (ineffectively, as it turned out) and the chief clerk ordered the crew to divide the train, taking on only the front five carriages to the next station at Hamilton Bawn. The engine could then return to collect the remaining ten carriages.

From the moment the fifth and sixth carriages were slackened and decoupled the continuous brakes came off the entire rear section of the train. As Thomas McGrath attempted to move away he rolled

TO STOP THE TRAIN ROLLING BACK MCGRATH APPLIED WHAT WERE KNOWN AS 'CONTINUOUS BRAKES'

back slightly, striking the sixth carriage. This was enough to crush the makeshift stone wedges and produce sufficient momentum for the ten rear carriages to overcome the sole remaining handbrake. Inexorably the Special began rolling back – a runaway train heading straight for the 10.35 scheduled service steaming out of Armagh. It was the railwayman's worst nightmare. McGrath and his crew reversed the front section of the train and tried pursuing the carriages in an attempt to re-couple them, an act of desperation doomed from the outset.

Paddy Murphy, the driver of the 10.35 service, spotted the carriages heading towards him when they were still 500 yards away. He managed to cut his own speed to 5 mph but by now the freewheeling carriages were travelling at 40 mph. It must have been a dreadful sight, with passengers flinging themselves from the running boards and children thrown from the windows. In the inevitable collision carriages 13, 14 and 15 were obliterated, 80 people died (including 20 under the age of 15) and at least 170 were injured. Murphy survived but he never drove a train again.

Wreckage litters the hillside after the Armagh Rail Disaster on 12 June 1889.

The subsequent inquiry cast a very public spotlight on the murkier corners of the railway industry. The inspector's findings were many and varied but the upshot was a realisation that passenger safety was not a top priority, that track and signalling procedures were unacceptable, and that many railwaymen worked way above their allotted hours. In Ireland it was discovered that only one engine and six carriages were equipped with automatic continuous brakes.

Within two months of the Armagh Disaster – and despite intensive lobbying from rail companies pleading poverty – Parliament enacted the Regulation of Railways Act 1889. This made automatic continuous brakes compulsory on all passenger railways, introduced a block system of signalling (which prevented a train from entering a track area until it was confirmed clear) and required the interlocking of points and signals (to prevent false signals). Out of the tragedy emerged a determination to learn – a heartening example of Parliament placing people before profit. Hasty it may have been, but the 1889 Act ushered in the modern era of rail safety.

In Bradshaw's day Belfast was in the midst of an unprecedented era of prosperity driven by its high-tech textile industry, a fast-expanding port and the shipyards. While Dublin was the seat of government, it was Belfast which set the pace of Ireland's economy. Nowhere is this clearer than in the census figures; in 1841 Belfast's population was 70,447, compared with Dublin's 232,726. Yet within half a century Belfast was the larger city, the 1891 census recording a population of 276,114 compared with 269,716 for its southern rival.

Bradshaw gives a nod to this expansion, noting that customs duties at the port rose from £3,700 in 1805 to more than £360,000 in 1846.

Since 1839 very great improvements have been made in the harbour, a deep channel having been cut right up to the town, so that large vessels drawing 16 or 18 feet water ... are now able to discharge cargo at the new quays, which with splendid docks etc, have cost the corporation half a million of money.

Harland & Wolff's South Yard, Belfast

The contractor responsible for digging out that harbour silt was the
ubiquitous 'King of the Railways' himself, William Dargan. The docks
were now perfect for new shipbuilding ventures, and in 1858 Edward
Harland, manager of a small yard on Queen's Island, bought out his
employers and installed a colleague, Gustav Wolff, as his partner.
Harland & Wolff went on to become arguably the biggest name in the
industry (they built the White Star liners *Titanic*, *Olympic*, *Britannic* and
Oceanic) and Harland knew from the start that the company's fortunes
were inextricably linked to the railways. He lobbied for track to be
laid straight to the quayside, giving his own yard and rivals such as
McIlwaine & Coll easy access to imported heavy components while
ensuring speedy docking for the big textile factories such as Irish Linen
Mills, Blackstaff Falls Flax, Emersons, Greeves, New Northern and
Springfield. In time Harland & Wolff branched out into designing
railway locomotive engines using the labour skills and equipment it
already used for shipbuilding.

ABOVE: **Harland and
Wolff's shipbuilding yard
in Belfast.**

OVERLEAF: **Queen's
University, Belfast.**

Bradshaw is rather underwhelmed by Belfast city centre, remarking that:

> The tall chimnies [sic] and factories for spinning linen and cotton yarn are the most conspicuous buildings; none of the churches are worth remark; in fact Belfast is a modern town, scarcely going back beyond the last century.

While undeniably true, this dismissal of the city's architecture is not entirely fair. The architect Sir Charles Lanyon produced some outstanding work in the mid-nineteenth century. His great landmark structures include the main red-brick building at Queen's University (1849), the innovative Crumlin Road Gaol and Courthouse (1850), the imposing Italian Renaissance-style Customs House (1857) with its carved statues of Neptune, Mercury and Britannia, and The Abbey at Whiteabbey – a grand country residence built for a local MP but later acquired by Lanyon himself. But for the Victorian tourist, perhaps Lanyon's most celebrated achievement was the Palm House in Belfast's Botanic Gardens.

Established in 1828, these gardens became, and remain, a much-loved green oasis in the heart of the city. The Palm House, completed in 1852, was a particular favourite of the Victorians because its 'stove wing' utilised new hothouse technology to nurture some of the world's most exotic tropical plants. This elegant structure rises to a 46-ft-high elliptical dome and is one of the earliest examples of a curved iron glasshouse.

Early rail travellers to Belfast would have been familiar with the Railway Tavern in Great Victoria Street as a refreshment stop. However, this pub's glory days emerged only after it was taken over by Michael Flanagan in 1885, who renovated it as a fashionable 'gin palace' and renamed it the Crown Liquor Saloon. Gin palaces date from the mid-eighteenth century when gin, supposedly a medicine, was sold by chemists as a 'quick nip' on the spot or to take away. These gin-shop counters were designed for speedy service and later became a model for the traditional pub bar. By the 1820s they had become large and outrageously decorated licensed establishments, often illuminated by gaslight.

Though thought to be a vulgar haunt of the lower classes, gin palaces were massively popular; Charles Dickens described them as 'perfectly dazzling' in one of his literary sketches. In the case of the Crown Liquor Saloon, the wonderful tiling, woodwork and stained-glass windows are largely thanks to Flanagan's legendary charm – he talked Italian craftsmen engaged on the city's newly built churches into moonlighting after hours in his pub. Today customers sitting in the pub's discreet 'snug' bars can still see the bells used to summon drinks and the gunmetal plates conveniently sited for smokers to strike matches.

The extension of the Belfast & County Down railway to Downpatrick in 1859 should have allowed Bradshaw to wax lyrical on the town's ancient association with St Patrick. Ireland's foremost patron saint is reputed to be buried there, but Bradshaw notes only that Down Cathedral 'contains the tomb of Lord Kehany; the window at the east end is worth notice'. Whereas Kehany was a minor aristocrat, Patrick is reputed to have converted Ireland to Christianity in the fifth century. His hagiographies claim he could pass through locked doors, turn night into day and transform his followers into deer to protect them from enemies. Later legends tell how he banished all the snakes from Ireland.

Restoration of the original fourteenth-century Down Cathedral was completed in 1826, but the inscribed chunk of Mourne granite marking Patrick's grave wasn't placed in the grounds until 1900. Perhaps this is why Bradshaw overlooked the saint whose feast day on 17 March has since become a truly worldwide celebration.

While Downpatrick was a popular site with visitors it was the Antrim coast north of Belfast which saw an explosion in late Victorian rail tourism. This was great news for the Belfast & Northern Counties Railway and its chief engineer, Berkeley Deane Wise, in particular. Wise, who had cut his teeth on the railways as an assistant to Dargan and Brunel back on the Bray Head line, designed more than a dozen stations and hotels for his employers, the most famous of which is the mock-Tudor station at Portrush. This was built to help cope with unprecedented summer traffic to the north-west coast and still stands today.

RIGHT: **At the Downpatrick Heritage Steam Railway.**

OVERLEAF: **Gobbins Path, the walk Wise constructed along the magnificent Gobbins cliffs.**

Wise was also in the business of creating tourist attractions to drum up passenger numbers. His Gobbins Path at Whitehead, reached via the Carrickfergus & Larne rail line north of Belfast, comprised a remarkable series of tunnels, walkways and tubular bridges which stretched for two miles along spectacular cliffs. This pushed all the right buttons for the Victorians, combining a bracing seaside walk, wonderful sea views and breathtaking engineering. One advertisement held in the archives of Whiteabbey Presbyterian Church reads: 'New cliff path along the Gobbins Cliff, with its ravines, bore caves, natural aquariums etc, has no parallel in Europe as a marine cliff walk.'

Luring tourists to Antrim helped make the BNCR Ireland's most profitable railway, and Wise, backed by his general manager Edward Cotton, was given a free rein to pursue his ideas. As well as tea rooms, bandstands and golf courses, these included the Promenade in Whitehead, constructed using railway sleepers and set above a man-made beach, and the Blackhead Path (The Gobbins' 'sister-path') which stretched 1¼ miles out to Blackhead promontory. Among Wise's most celebrated tourist 'honey-pots' was a walk alongside the waterfalls at Glenariff, one of the nine Glens of Antrim, which included cantilevered cliff paths and picturesque natural shelters. Tourists ferried by carriage from the Parkmore narrow-gauge railway station could refresh themselves in a tea room below the Ess-na-Larach waterfall. This also offered budding landscape photographers a fully equipped darkroom.

The Gobbins was to prove almost as popular as the Giant's Causeway, near Coleraine to the north-west, another destination which boosted BNCR railway traffic out of Belfast. Sightseers heading to this dramatic volcanic rock formation near Bushmills would travel via Ballymena to Portrush Station near Coleraine before crossing Eglinton Street to board the Giant's Causeway, Portrush & Bush Valley Railway and Tramway. This was a revolutionary 3-ft-gauge electric railway partly powered by a hydro-electric turbine station at Walkmill Falls, Bushmills.

The line was fully open by July 1897 but suffered a setback eight years later when a cyclist was fatally electrocuted after touching the live conductor rail. A later inquiry established that voltage on the electrical feed varied between 290 and 360 volts and the company was compelled to agree a voltage reduction which restricted the number of services.

An overhead conductor rail was installed, with mixed results, and it wasn't until 1907 that a reliable voltage of 550V was established.

Of the Causeway itself Bradshaw is suitably impressed, urging readers to head for the Causeway Inn and walk to Dunseverick Beach before taking a boat back, preferably with a guide (fee two shillings and sixpence). The advantage of this plan was that 'the succession of pillars and stratifications of the rocks along this remarkable coast are now fully visible'.

The final leg of the route goes west from Coleraine to Londonderry, or Derry as many prefer to call it. A few miles south of the railway lies Dungiven Castle from where the music to 'Londonderry Air', better known as 'Danny Boy', is said to originate. It is claimed the composer of this haunting melody (whose identity is lost in the mists of time) wrote it to mark the passing of the great Irish chieftain Cooeyna Gall O'Cahan, last of the O'Cahan chiefs, for whom Dungiven was the ancestral home. The music would have been played by Irish fiddlers in the nineteenth century but became internationally famous only after the Victorian era when the English lyricist Frederic Weatherly set it to the words of 'Danny Boy'.

And so to Londonderry, a city steeped in Georgian architecture after it was largely rebuilt during the eighteenth century in the wake of the 1689 Siege of Derry, another ignominious reversal for the ousted Catholic James II during the Glorious Revolution. The 105-day siege saw the deaths of some 8,000 inhabitants, almost a quarter of the total population, but the city was held by Protestant loyalists until it was relieved by a Royal Navy fleet. The quick thinking of 13 apprentice boys, who managed to lock the city gates against an advancing 1,200-strong Scottish Catholic army, is still celebrated today in a march by the Apprentice Boys of Derry.

Bradshaw describes Londonderry's 'considerable commercial intercourse with America and the West Indies, it being favourably situated for commerce, and possesses an excellent secure harbour with a splendid line of quays'. In fact, by the time his *Descriptive Railway Handbook* was published this 'commerce' was largely of the human variety; during the 1860s around 100,000 emigrants per year left Ireland for America, and from 1876 to 1921 this was the destination for 84 per cent of Irish emigrants, compared with 7 per cent heading for Canada and 8 per cent to the British mainland. As Evelyn Waugh later observed, there were only two final realities for the Irish: Hell and the United States. Famine was the driving force behind emigration, and although Londonderry was by no means the largest embarkation port its rail link made it a popular choice.

The most famous of the city's shipping companies was the McCorkell Line and its services to New York, Philadelphia, New Orleans and Quebec were in huge demand during the famine years between 1845 and 1850. The *Mohongo*, a Canadian-built ship, completed more than 100 such crossings with no serious difficulty, while the *Minnehaha*, built in 1860, was able to cross the Atlantic quickly even during the winter months. She became the McCorkell Line's most celebrated vessel and passed into Irish-American folklore as the 'Green Yacht from Derry'.

For thousands of poverty-stricken emigrants the train ride to Londonderry would offer the last sights of home. It is a bitter irony that the railway which brought Ireland so much wealth and prosperity also delivered its people so efficiently into exile.

IT IS A BITTER IRONY THAT THE RAILWAY WHICH BROUGHT IRELAND SO MUCH WEALTH AND PROSPERITY ALSO DELIVERED ITS PEOPLE SO EFFICIENTLY INTO EXILE

INDEX

Entries in *italics* indicates photographs and images

PICTURE CREDITS